The Hidden Hand

The Hidden Hand

A Brief History of the CIA

Richard H. Immerman

WILEY Blackwell

This edition first published 2014
© 2014 John Wiley & Sons Inc.

Registered Office
John Wiley & Sons Ltd, The Atrium, Southern Gate, Chichester, West Sussex, PO19 8SQ, UK

Editorial Offices
350 Main Street, Malden, MA 02148-5020, USA
9600 Garsington Road, Oxford, OX4 2DQ, UK
The Atrium, Southern Gate, Chichester, West Sussex, PO19 8SQ, UK

For details of our global editorial offices, for customer services, and for information about how to apply for permission to reuse the copyright material in this book please see our website at www.wiley.com/wiley-blackwell.

The right of Richard H. Immerman to be identified as the author of this work has been asserted in accordance with the UK Copyright, Designs and Patents Act 1988.

Wiley also publishes its books in a variety of electronic formats. Some content that appears in print may not be available in electronic books.

Designations used by companies to distinguish their products are often claimed as trademarks. All brand names and product names used in this book are trade names, service marks, trademarks or registered trademarks of their respective owners. The publisher is not associated with any product or vendor mentioned in this book.

Limit of Liability/Disclaimer of Warranty: While the publisher and author have used their best efforts in preparing this book, they make no representations or warranties with respect to the accuracy or completeness of the contents of this book and specifically disclaim any implied warranties of merchantability or fitness for a particular purpose. It is sold on the understanding that the publisher is not engaged in rendering professional services and neither the publisher nor the author shall be liable for damages arising herefrom. If professional advice or other expert assistance is required, the services of a competent professional should be sought.

Library of Congress Cataloging-in-Publication Data is available for this title

ISBN 9781444351361 (hardback); ISBN 9781444351378 (paperback)

A catalogue record for this book is available from the British Library.

Cover image: Detail of *Kryptos* sculpture by Jim Sanborn in grounds of C.I.A. headquarters, Langley, Virginia. Photo from Carol M. Highsmith Archive, Library of Congress, Prints and Photographs Division.
Cover design by Simon Levy

Set in 10.5/13pt MinionPro by Laserwords Private Limited, Chennai, India
Printed in Malaysia by Ho Printing (M) Sdn Bhd

1   2014

To Anna, whom I hope will grow up in a world of greater transparency as well as security.

Contents

Preface and Acknowledgments

This is a short book with a long history. The number of debts I have accumulated along the way is therefore also long. The list begins with Walt LaFeber and Arnie Offner. Walt was almost solely responsible for shifting my interests from political science ("government" at Cornell) to history, specifically the history of US foreign relations. What is more, he provoked my curiosity about Latin America, particularly Central America. My decision to write my dissertation on the Central Intelligence Agency (CIA) intervention in Guatemala, accordingly, was a logical progression. The problem was that writing in the 1970s a history of a covert operation was highly illogical. There were no archives or, for that matter, documentation of any kind. As a graduate student, I received encouragement only from my faculty advisor, but he died. I then turned to Arnie Offner. Arnie, although at another university, believed in the project. More important, he believed in me. Under Arnie's guidance, I wrote my dissertation. It became a book, *The CIA in Guatemala*.

By the time of the book's publication, I had become a historian of intelligence, although I did not realize that I had. I continued to dabble in the subject over the subsequent years, but only dabble. Without fully appreciating the implications, during these same years I revived my interest in political science. Fred Greenstein and Bob Jervis are the reasons. Fred became the kind of mentor one never expects after completing the PhD. He introduced me to the literature on personality and politics, advising, and decision making. He also introduced me to Bob. Bob has no peer when it comes to applying theories of cognitive psychology to the study of international relations. He also has no peer as a scholar of intelligence. He inspired me in both spheres.

Athan Theoharis was the catalyst for my synthesizing these early influences and interests and finally admitting that I wanted to concentrate my writing on the CIA and the Intelligence Community. I knew Athan only by reputation. He of course is renowned for his scholarship on domestic surveillance, civil liberties, and the FBI. When he contacted me shortly after the 9/11 tragedy, however, it was to invite me to contribute to a collection of essays on the CIA. Athan wanted me to write a lengthy overview of the agency's history. All of the contributors would be co-editors.

I accepted Athan's invitation, and my "Brief History of the CIA" came out in 2006 as the first chapter of *The Central Intelligence Agency: Security under Scrutiny*. I took great pleasure in writing it, and it serves as the foundation of this book. The essay provided me with the opportunity to evaluate the CIA through a much broader lens than "operations." I examined its origins and evolution over time, its relations with other elements in the Intelligence Community, the problems produced by the tensions inherent in its roles and missions, and more. Still, the project was as frustrating as it was exciting. I very much enjoy the challenge of trying to capture vast swaths of history in relatively few words. But an 80-page history of the CIA was a bridge too far.

Enter Peter Coveney into my story. Peter is a terrific editor with Wiley-Blackwell, a long-time favorite of many of us who boast of our membership in the Society for Historians of American Foreign Relations. I have no idea how many people read my "Brief History." I would bet very few. But Peter was one, and he thought it had the makings of a book. We struck a deal, and I can't thank Peter enough for making it happen. *The Hidden Hand* not only was his idea, but I also benefited from his advice, editing, and attention from beginning to end. And I also benefited from those at Wiley-Blackwell whom Peter recruited to help me. Specifically, I must thank my copy editor, Jamila Niroop, and Annette Musker, who compiled the index, and Georgina Coleby, who managed the manuscript through production.

Peter was very patient with me. He had to be. That's because in 2007 the book, my career, and my life turned in a very unexpected direction. Thanks in large part to the late Nancy Bernkopf Tucker, a dear friend, distinguished scholar, and committed citizen, I was asked to come to Washington to serve as assistant deputy director of intelligence for analytic integrity and standards and analytic ombudsman for the Office of the Director of National Intelligence (ODNI). I was stunned. I had just returned to Temple from leave, I was finishing one book and had promised Peter I'd start on this one, and I had never, ever considered government work. But accepting was one of the smartest decisions I ever made. Leaving aside any assessments of my performance, I cannot exaggerate the new insights on the entire intelligence enterprise I gained during my eighteen-month tenure in the ODNI and the extent to which my appreciation for the dedication and capabilities of my coworkers grew. For this most rewarding and educational experience, I have my entire office to thank: Jim Marchio, Scott McCall, Karl Pieragostini, Kyle Rector, Steve Rieber, Glen Simpers, Jeff Stillman, Becky Strode, and Linda Whitehurst. I owe a special debt to my boss, Tom Fingar, the deputy director of national intelligence for analysis. As far as I am concerned, no one knows more than Tom about the finer points of intelligence. And no one is a better leader, or in my case, a better teacher.

I also must thank Tom and Bob Jervis, and Mel Leffler as well, for the advice and support they offered me in my ordeal with the requisite prepublication review of this book. I briefly describe this very difficult experience in a note immediately following these acknowledgments. Their assistance proved not only invaluable but also instrumental to reaching a resolution. I also express my gratitude to Jennifer Hudson. Her intervention months into the process was vital to reaching that resolution.

Whether I was struggling with my writing, readjusting to my comings and goings from Temple, or otherwise trying to find some semblance of balance in what became a very complicated life, I could not have asked for more support from my colleagues at Temple. The list is endless, but deserving special thanks are Petra Goode, Drew Isenberg, Jay Lockenour, Bryant Simon, Ralph Young, Vlad Zubok, and before they defected, Will Hitchcock and Liz Varon. For making me laugh as well as providing priceless assistance in so many ways, I also thank Vangie Campbell, Lafrance Howard, and, for always being there for me, Patricia Williams. My Temple students have always been a source of ideas as well as pleasure. Among the many that warrant thanks, Tim Sayle not only provided me with exceptional research help, but he also allowed himself to serve as my sounding board. I took full advantage. Matt Fay arrived at Temple as I was approaching the finish line, but not too late to provide essential assistance. Beth Bailey and David Farber warrant a category of their own, and not only for critiquing my text. For more than 25 years, whether or not at the same institution, they have been the closest of friends and the most gracious of colleagues and the closest of colleagues and the most gracious of friends. It's a distinction without a difference.

I have many friends and colleagues beyond Temple, and I have imposed on most of them over the years that it took to conceptualize and write this book. I can't name them all, but I must single out some. I asked Matthew Jones to read the entire manuscript. Matthew had been one of the principals in a British project on the CIA, "Landscapes of Secrecy." I could not have asked for a better critic. I did not ask Jeffrey Engel. He volunteered. I must apologize as well as thank Jeff. He was so thorough, and made so many good suggestions, that had I followed up on them all I would have doubled the manuscript's length. So I compromised. Because of Jeff, the book is only several thousand words better.

Others I must thank include Sid Milkis and Jeff Jenkins of the University of Virginia. Their invitation for me to present a paper at the Miller Center on the politics of intelligence reform raised a whole new set of questions for me to address. My many conversations with Frank Costigliola about not just intelligence but also the craft of history has made me a much improved scholar. But in this case, Frank went a step farther by arranging for me to present some of my formative ideas to the University of Connecticut's Foreign Policy Seminar. Klaus Larres was similarly helpful by providing me with the opportunity to contribute to his U.S. in World Affairs lecture series at the University of North Carolina, Chapel Hill. And I owe a debt to Ara Keys that I can never hope to repay. Ara encouraged me to apply for the Miegunyah Distinguished Visiting Fellowship at Australia's University of Melbourne. Once I applied, she shepherded through the paperwork, rewriting much of it. I am sure I would not have received the Miegunyah without her help. Winning this fellowship forced me to accelerate the pace of my completing the manuscript even as I refined my argument for the public lecture. I could also undertake the revisions in the most wondrous and hospitable of settings.

In all of my previous books, I've ended my acknowledgments by thanking my family—for their presence in my life and, frankly, for when necessary staying out of my way. This time, however, my debt to them is greater, and deeper. My wife Marion is my best friend and greatest booster. She has over the past thirty-something years regularly made sacrifices for me, but never more so than when she all but commanded me to accept the position with ODNI. I was prepared to turn down the offer. Marion insisted that I would always regret doing so. She was right. My daughters, Morgan and Tyler, sacrificed almost as much. Morgan had to be satisfied with seeing her father only on weekends and hitching rides with her friends to high school throughout her senior year. Tyler not only returned from college to a fatherless home, but she also took over my responsibility for caring for our dog in its dotage. I owe them for making my experience at ODNI richer, and that experience made this book much more rich. Finally, Marion, Tyler, and Morgan, added to whom now are my son-in-law Fred and darling granddaughter Anna Isabella, have made my life richer. How can anyone adequately express thanks for that?

Note on Redactions

Throughout this book you will encounter blacked-out text. These blackened passages were redacted by the CIA's prepublication reviewers. Let me explain.

On September 4, 2007, I Entered on Duty (EOD is the government acronym) as assistant deputy director of national intelligence for analytic integrity and standards and analytic ombudsman for the Office of the Director of National Intelligence (ODNI). This joint position was one of the few that was established with any specificity by the text of 2004 Intelligence Reform and Terrorism Prevention Act. Deputy director of national intelligence Thomas Fingar offered it to me without my applying. My mission, he explained to me, was to use the skills I had learned as a scholar to assist in the training of analysts throughout the Intelligence Community in order to improve the quality of their analysis. I was flattered. I also saw this offer as an opportunity to provide what I hoped would be valuable public service. I was honored to accept.

On that day, as required, I signed a nondisclosure or what is commonly called a secrecy agreement. Several years later, after I had left ODNI to return to my faculty position at Temple University, I accepted an invitation to serve on the Advisory Committee on Historical Diplomatic Documentation to the Department of State (HAC). A year or two after that, by which time I had been elected HAC chair, the CIA required all committee members to sign its secrecy agreement (we had access to classified CIA documents). Both agreements stipulated that I must submit manuscripts for prepublication review in order to ensure that I do not divulge the classified information to which I had access. The briefing I received in each instance emphasized that I could continue to publish scholarship which relied on sources produced by the research methods in which I was trained. Further, if the Prepublication Review Board (PRB) had an issue with any of my publications, it was mandated to provide me in writing with the reason. I had no reservations about signing, and I assured my colleagues on the HAC that they need not have any either.

I submitted the manuscript for *Hidden Hand* to the ODNI prepublication review staff on January 25, 2013. In the multiple previous cases when I had submitted a manuscript for prepublication review, I received a response promptly (the law requires a response within a month); invariably, the reviewers approved my manuscripts with few if any concerns. In this instance, however, ODNI sent the manuscript to the CIA because the agency had such a substantive stake (equity) in the history I had written. Despite my queries and eventual protestations, I did not receive a report until July 12, 2013, close to six months after my initial submission. What is more, the report I finally received insisted on scores of redactions without a single word of explanation.

I had not referred to, even indirectly, any classified document or conversation that I had seen or heard as a consequence of my service to either the Intelligence Community or the Department of State. As a trained historian, I systematically cited my sources, all of which came from the public record. Yet the Board insisted that I delete words, sentences, and entire passages. On occasion it required that I delete my citations of newspaper articles that I had come across in the course of my research. On other occasions, and more seriously, it redacted words that communicated the judgments and arguments that are fundamental to my conclusion. At the core of the discipline of history are the formulation, articulation, and support of judgments and arguments.

I appealed. Several weeks later, I received approval to publish a significant proportion of the "offending articles," to use the term used by a member of ODNI's pre-publication staff. Unable to discuss the redactions further over the phone or correspond by email because, officials explained to me, these modes of communication are insufficiently secure, some six month later I arranged to meet in person with two members of CIA's Prepublication Review Board. The meeting was cordial and frank. It resulted in authorization to publish more of the previously redacted material.

But as will be evident from the number of redactions remaining in this book, I did not receive authorization to remove all of them, or in my opinion, even enough of them. The CIA insists that any conduct which the U.S. government has not officially acknowledged is by definition classified, regardless of how widespread the press has reported on it or by other means it has "entered" the public sphere. Because of my privileged access to *some* classified material, I am prohibited from publishing *any* material deemed classified, including that to which I had no privileged access. My reminders that I served in ODNI only from September 2007 to January 2009, and that as a member of the HAC I have seen documentation with dates of issue no later than the early 1980s, were irrelevant.

Had I delayed publication another six months or more, I am confident I could have "won" the "release" of a bit more material here or there. But I am satisfied that as a result of my appeal and subsequent efforts, the integrity of the book remains intact. Nevertheless, I am highly dissatisfied with my experience. I valued my work at the ODNI very much, performed my duties to the best of my ability, and never expected a reward, Still, in return for my taking leave from my university position to perform public service, my rights were abridged and my scholarly career undermined. The appeal, which resulted in the PRB's backtracking on the majority of its initial demands, is evidence of the profound flaws that plague the prepublication process. It manifestly lacks an effective mechanism to police itself. Moreover, the remaining redactions, all of which hide material readily available in the public domain, reflect an obsession with secrecy in our government and a propensity for overclassification, which not only violates America's ideals and values but also undermines the national security.

1

Birth of an Enigma: 1945–1949

The Central Intelligence Agency (CIA) is America's most enigmatic institution. Its mission requires secrecy, and, as a consequence, it and its history are shrouded in mystery. The "Company," nevertheless, is among America's most well-known institutions, with its own YouTube site, Facebook page, and Twitter account. "CIA" is likewise among the world's most recognizable acronyms, and millions of people around the globe and within the United States consider the agency both a primary instrument of and an appropriate metaphor for US foreign policy.

The enigma of the CIA goes beyond its notoriety. Opinion poll after opinion poll in the United States reveal that it is among America's most unpopular, disrespected, and mistrusted institutions. "The agency's a funny place," reads a recent comment, by one of its own veterans no less. "It's like middle schoolers with clearances," he explained. Politicians and officials of both parties, from the president on down, are fine with this description and reputation. Attributing a policy disaster, security lapse, or even a war to an intelligence failure is easier for the American public to understand than would be a deep dive into the policymaking process, and of course the policymakers and legislators escape blame. Further, intelligence gaffes seem susceptible to quick fixes. The offending intelligence officers can readily be replaced, institutional reforms can be enacted, more spies can be sent into the field and better satellites built, and analysts can be more rigorously trained. For most Americans, writes another CIA veteran, the Company is a "combination of hope chest, voodoo doll, and the portrait of Dorian Gray."[1]

Still, despite, or in a perverse sense because of, the CIA's image and reputation, the Company is unequivocally a cultural icon. The year 2001 and the

The Hidden Hand: A Brief History of the CIA, First Edition. Richard Immerman.
© 2014 John Wiley & Sons, Ltd. Published 2014 by John Wiley & Sons, Ltd.

tragic attacks on the Pentagon and World Trade Center brought unprecedented and unwelcome attention to the agency for its failure to "connect the dots" and prevent al-Qaeda's long-gestating operation. It was also the year that three popular series focusing on the CIA debuted on network television: "Alias" on ABC; CBS's "The Agency," and Fox's "24". All featured an attractive cast of racially and ethnically diverse men and women who are committed, competent, and courageous. Coincidentally, yet in retrospect appropriately, each of the programs aired for the first time only weeks after the 9/11 tragedy. In fact, CBS changed the sequencing of "The Agency's" episodes because the framework for the pilot script, an al-Qaeda plot to attack the West (Harrods in London) that repeatedly refers to Osama bin Laden, would have struck a raw nerve. Shortly after the show proved a success, however, CBS ran the pilot.[2]

While coincidental (the writers and producers were of course unaware of al-Qaeda's plans), the plot lines and character of these programs are revealing and suggestive of how twenty-first century Americans have come to perceive and understand the CIA. The television shows prior to 2001 that revolved around the agency were very different. "Get Smart" (1965), for example, was a slapstick comedy. "I Spy" (1965), with Bill Cosby, the first African American to play a lead in a television drama, was a light-hearted vehicle for promoting civil rights. And "Mission Impossible" (1966), which featured a make-believe CIA and decades later was turned into a series of movies to show off Tom Cruise, was pure escapism. None made an attempt to portray the CIA seriously; none raised any one of the multiple ethical, let alone legal, questions inherent in its responsibilities and behavior. This is how the CIA wanted it. Indeed, the agency went so far to buy the movie rights to novels to ensure that they never became movies and to refuse to cooperate with those movies that actually illuminated the CIA.[3]

This changed with the films about the CIA made during and in the wake of the Vietnam War, Watergate, and the Congressional hearings held in the mid-1970s to investigate the agency's misconduct. These were big Hollywood productions that represented the agency as not only un- or anti-American, but also as institutionally evil. There was the deadly and paranoid CIA featured in the director Michael Winner's "Scorpio" (1973), the misanthropic CIA portrayed in Sydney Pollack's "Three Days of the Condor" (1975), and the reprobate and renegade CIA of Oliver Stone's imagination in his 1991 "JFK." The "Hunt for Red October" (1990), "Red Storm Rising" (1992), and "Patriot Games" (also 1992), all based on Tom Clancy novels, were the exceptions that proved the rule. Through the exploits of Harrison Ford's Jack Ryan, they sought to evoke what the historian Walter Hixson calls the Reagan-era "Cult of National Security." Because these films received Washington's cooperation, they signaled a transition in the CIA's filmography.[4]

With the end of the Cold War and as a result of the increased attention to domestic concerns paid by the White House, Congress, and the American public, the CIA leadership concluded that the agency was desperately in need of a public makeover. In the popular consciousness, James Bond was out, and Gordon Gecko was in. The CIA thus judged it vitally important to refurbish its image in order to bolster appropriations and to recruit America's best and brightest at a time when many Americans defined the Company as an unsavory relic of a bygone era. In 1996, therefore, the agency appointed Chase Brandon as its official liaison to Hollywood and permitted former employees to serve as consultants and even extras. For the purpose of projecting authenticity, "The Agency" was the first television program to receive official sanction to film inside the CIA's headquarters in Langley, Virginia. Although the three shows that came out in 2001, as illustrated most forcefully by "24's" Jack Bauer, uniformly concede the moral ambiguity that so pervades the CIA's culture and mission (that mission is all but exclusively identified with operations; intelligence analysts typically make only cameo appearances if they are present at all), they present agency personnel in virtually every instance as discovering that a career spent battling against the forces of evil is as rewarding as it is exciting.[5]

Blockbuster movies that came out during this same brief window of time after the 9/11 tragedy and before America's invasion of Iraq turned into a nightmare, such as "Spy Game" (2001) and "The Recruit" (2003), project the same dynamics as the trio of 2001 television series. They portray the CIA as a bastion of patriotism and a dream job. In the former, megastars Robert Redford and Brad Pitt engage in virtually criminal behavior, but the viewer cannot help but applaud their professionalism, courage, noble self-sacrifice, and sense of brotherhood. As an MIT-trained computer whiz in "The Recruit," Colin Farrell forfeits the certainty of earning great wealth, endures the rigors of training at the "farm" (the CIA's facility at Camp Peary in Virginia), and becomes a dazzling and dashing mole-hunter simply because, as Al Pacino explains, he "believes." The demographics of the recruits at the farm also showcase that the Old Boys network that once defined the CIA had become a mix of race, ethnicity, and gender. Indeed, the CIA in 2004 hired Jennifer Garner, the seductive Sydney Bristow who in "Alias" is as well educated (she is fluent in countless languages) as she is expert in martial arts, to introduce the recruitment video it showed at college job fairs as the agency sought to bolster its work force after years of erosion. "In the real world, the CIA serves as our country's first line of defense," Garner says. "Right now," she continues, "the CIA has important, exciting jobs for U.S. citizens."[6]

The silver and television screens have remained vehicles for communicating Garner's message. "Burn Notice," which debuted in 2007, and "Covert Affairs," first broadcast in 2010, have once again treated viewers to stylish and gorgeous agents who are highly principled and display almost superhuman skills and wisdom. They even reflect wholesome family values. Nevertheless, the contemporary environment's influence on popular representations of the CIA is palpable. Intense public criticism of the agency attended the congressional investigations of 9/11 and the production of the fatally flawed National Intelligence Estimate (NIE) in 2002. That estimate erroneously claimed that Iraq's tyrannical dictator Saddam Hussein had a hidden cache of weapons of mass destruction (WMD) which he was trying to supplement with a nuclear capability. The CIA was further pummeled as the death totals mounted in Iraq and it was branded as an agency that kidnapped, tortured, and assassinated. Adding insult to injury, Congress knocked it off its pedestal by enacting the 2004 reform legislation that established a director of national intelligence, effectively "demoting" the director of central intelligence (DCI) and, in principle, the agency itself.

Within this context, the darker images of the CIA resurfaced. In the 2004 summer miniseries "The Grid," which serendipitously premiered in a two-hour special the week that the report of the National Commission on Terrorist Attacks Upon the United States (9/11 Commission) became public, turf wars within the Intelligence Community marred the Global War on Terror that President George W. Bush declared soon after the 9/11 attacks. The chief culprit is the Tom Skerritt-played CIA director, who is only slightly less dastardly than the Middle Eastern terrorists. The next year, in "Syriana" George Clooney won an Oscar for portraying Bob Barnes, a CIA assassin whom the Company scapegoats, double-crosses, and ultimately kills when he unwittingly jeopardizes agency operations in the Middle East that almost unintelligibly blend geopolitics, oil, and arms sales. Matt Damon's Edward Wilson in "The Good Sheperd" (2006) is a composite of James Jesus Angleton and Richard Bissell: one a former chief of counterintelligence, the other a former deputy director of plans, both renowned, for different reasons and with various degrees of validity, as evil geniuses. Not only does a mole penetrate the highest corridors of the CIA and an agent fall victim to a seductress, but also the agents in this movie sanction an interrogation that ends up in suicide and are complicit in a woman's falling to her death from a plane. Although former agents consulted on these films and programs as well, they essentially "went rogue."[7]

The complexity of these depictions proved popular. Playing a very different kind of character, Damon turned the series of Bourne movies into a franchise; CIA assassins are out to get him because *he* was a CIA assassin. Leonardo DiCaprio and Russell Crowe, both "A-listers" like Damon, costar in "Body of Lies" (2008), a film based on a novel by the *Washington Post's* respected national security columnist David Ignatius. It portrays counterterrorism as the equivalent of just war, but the CIA's ends-justifies-the-means philosophy intentionally raises troubling questions for the viewer. "Salt" (2010), starring Angelina Jolie, whom one assumes the producers intended to supplant Jennifer Garner as the "face" of the CIA, is replete with so many double agents and so much double dealing that distinguishing the good from the bad becomes virtually impossible. "Fair Game" (2010) is faithful to the memoir by Valerie Plame Wilson about her "outing" as a covert CIA officer by the Bush administration. Allegedly, the White House cost Plame her career and potentially her safety in retribution for her husband, Joseph Wilson (Sean Penn was pointedly cast in the role), publishing an Op-Ed piece in the *New York Times*. Wilson maintained that the White House and Pentagon built the march to war in Iraq on a foundation of sand by challenging the claim that Saddam Hussein sought to purchase "yellowcake" uranium in Niger. As Plame, Naomi Watt is allied with angels; her CIA colleagues are not.

What is especially distinctive about "Fair Game" is that, absent from virtually all media portrayals of the CIA, analysts make a brief yet highly instructive appearance. Analysts are the bedrock of the CIA. For good reason, however, they do not fit the agency's conventional storyline. Nevertheless, as "Fair Game" intimates but does not make explicit, analysts were the lead actors in the mistaken Iraq War. Dramatically embodying the challenges posed by the need to estimate likelihoods based on weighing knowns against unknowns, what Richard Betts has famously labeled the "enemies of intelligence," Vice President Dick Cheney's chief of staff, I. Lewis "Scooter" Libby, berates a poor analyst both for not being able to eliminate uncertainty in his estimating and also for failing to appreciate the consequences of that failing. Insight and sophistication drive the dialogue. "I don't make the call, Sir," explains the young analyst. "Yes, you do Paul," retorts Libby. He then exposes the intelligence analyst as naive and, judging from each of their facial expressions, somewhere between useless and fraudulent. "Each time you interpret a piece of data. Each time you choose a 'maybe' over a 'perhaps,' you make a call. A decision. And right now you're making lots of little decisions adding up to a big decision and out there's a real world where millions of people depend upon you being right. But what if there's a one percent chance you're wrong. Can you say for sure you'll take that chance and state, as a fact, that this equipment is not intended for a nuclear weapons program?"[8]

"Fair Game" is evidence that in an era defined by insecurity and counterterrorism, popular representations of the CIA, while often critical, seek to complicate the agency's story by projecting its complexity. The agency envelops the good, the bad, and the ugly. Merely by casting Tom Hanks as Charles Wilson, the Texas Congressman whose memory would have been erased from the public consciousness had he not had such great success appropriating funds for the CIA's "covert" war in Afghanistan, the director (Mike Nichols) and screenwriter (Aaron Sorkin, made famous by his liberal rendering of the White House's "West Wing") of "Charlie Wilson's War" (2007) signaled that clandestine or not, and notwithstanding the leadership role of CIA Director William Casey, this was a "good war." Despite later developments associated with the formative experiences of Osama bin Laden and the rise of Taliban rule, in Afghanistan the United States in the 1980s was on the right side of history.

The same holds true for the more recent Ben Affleck-directed "Argo" (2012), which won the "Best Picture" Academy Award and in which the celebrated actor also starred. The film's introduction does refer to the CIA's 1953 operation to restore the Shah to Iran's Peacock Throne, a catalyst for the movie's subject: the 1979 Hostage Crisis. Further, reminding CIA agent Tony Mendez (Affleck) how the agency dismissed Iran's potential for revolution, a foreign colleague implies that the agency contributed to the crisis in the first place. Nevertheless, the effort to rescue the six "houseguests" of the Canadian embassy is as daring and imaginative (the movie takes much literary license with the true story) as it is successful. This triumph is that much more impressive because the agency is content knowing that the operation must remain classified, and thus it will not receive any credit for its creativity and heroism.[9]

More complicated, and more controversial, is another 2012 film, "Zero Dark Thirty," which tells the story of the successful hunt for bin Laden. Like "Argo," it packs star power. The director Kathryn Bigelow and writer Mark Boal are both Academy Award winners. And like "Argo," "Zero Dark Thirty" was a box office draw that received critical acclaim (it was also nominated for the Best Picture Oscar nomination). In this case, however, not only did the CIA and other government agencies cooperate extensively but also Boal, a former embedded journalist in Iraq, conducted his own research and interviews. One consequence is that the CIA's workforce, the everyday analyst and operative with a GS 13 or 14 pay grade, emerge as protagonists. Another consequence is that the film, which debuted to allegations by conservatives that its intent was to bolster Barack Obama's presidential campaign, ultimately received withering criticism from liberals that may have cost it the Best Picture Oscar. They charged that "Zero Dark Thirty" implies that torture, especially waterboarding, the graphic depiction of which introduces the story, yielded crucial information. Yet, lost on most critics is that the storyline suggests that mundane data mining yielded even more crucial information. What distinguished the movie from practically all others distinctive about the movie is its juxtaposition of Ian Fleming and Malcolm Gladwell. It credits hard work and professionalism more than adventurism and risk taking. "Bin Laden wasn't killed by superheroes," Boals commented in explaining the narrative. "These are people doing their job, and in a sense that's extraordinary, and in a sense it's not."[10]

Like these films, Americans' image and opinion of the CIA is complicated and even dissonant. The television program that won the Emmy in 2012, and certainly the most acclaimed show about the CIA ever on TV, perhaps reflects the complex and, indeed, alien universe that most Americans associate with the Company even more effectively than does "Zero Dark Thirty." "Homeland" is riddled with ambiguities of every kind. The values and commitment of CIA agent Claire Danes' Carrie Mathison are unimpeachable. Her mental health is not, however, and especially when off her medication, neither is her judgment. She is in love — or not — with Nicholas Brody, a Marine captured in Iraq who returns to the United States years later as either a hero — or terrorist. In the second season, Brody is unmasked as the latter and a tearful Carrie realizes, post-electric shock treatment, that, in contrast to the prelude to 9/11, about which she is obsessed with making amends, she got it right. The ambiguities, nevertheless, remain (congruent with the show's framing, what turned Brody against the United States was a drone strike that killed the son of the terrorist Abu Nazir, Carrie's Moby Dick). The second season ends with Quinn, who represents the blackest of the CIA's special operations (SO), refusing to assassinate a repentant Brody. He only shoots "bad guys," he explains. But after a bomb kills 200 attendees of the vice president's funeral service, including the official who ordered the assassination, the viewer is left wondering whether Brody is a "bad guy" after all. Only Carrie seems certain he is not. There are no superheroes in the "Homeland's" CIA. Both state and society are unremittingly vulnerable, and the boundaries between friend and foe are blurred and fluid.[11]

One need not exhaust the catalog of films and television shows (that catalog is massive) to demonstrate that, whether represented as virtuous or villainous, the CIA is as central to America's popular culture as it is to its national security. (In 2011, Valerie Plame signed a deal with Penguin to write a series of novels that, she hopes, will transform "how female C.I.A. officers are portrayed in popular culture.").[12] This is significant. Even as a fictional and very often caricatured CIA became ubiquitous (and the number of novels far surpasses that of movies and TV series), the history of the "real" CIA has remained carefully guarded. Most Americans, and even more non-Americans, know much of what they know about the CIA from their imagined representations in film and television. As attested to by the intense controversy during the 2012 presidential election over the confused intelligence reporting concerning the killing of the US ambassador to Libya in Benghazi, what Americans know is, accordingly, limited and frequently misguided.[13]

This is not to claim that there are not very solid studies of the CIA by historians, political scientists, and other scholars, and journalists have written even more. The spate of memoirs by former CIA agents and officials, moreover, sometimes seems endless. But they uniformly suffer from some shortcoming: limited access to documents, a focus that is either too narrow or too broad, an axe to grind, or a score to settle. Further, capturing the CIA as an institution presents a unique set of problems. It is a distinct entity that is also shorthand for the entire intelligence community. In addition to the Federal Bureau of Investigation (FBI) and the National Security Agency (NSA), that community is composed of more than a dozen other elements, about which most Americans are ignorant. Most observers and even experts perceive the CIA as a nest of spies and clandestine operators. Yet it was established for the express purpose of intelligence analysis and dissemination, a mission that has been sacrificed to a misguided emphasis on covert and paramilitary projects that its designers did not intend for it to undertake. Put another way, examining the CIA requires not only addressing questions about what it does and has done. Equally important are questions about what it is, and as I argue in this book, what it should be. The central goal of this history is to provide answers to these questions.

Geneology

What makes resolving the issue of the CIA's identity more difficult is the place intelligence occupies in American political (as opposed to popular) culture. Only with memories of the devastation wrought by the Japanese at Pearl Harbor still vivid, and when confronted with what many Americans, public officials, and private citizens perceived as a life or death struggle against an evil greater than Nazi Germany, the Godless Soviet Empire, did the United States establish a CIA. Before the middle of the twentieth century, the very concept of a permanent civilian intelligence agency seemed anathema to American ideals and values. Americans did, of course, recognize, and frequently celebrate, the contributions of espionage to their history. Although he did not succeed in providing George Washington with any useful intelligence, and although prior to hanging in 1776 he probably never said, "I regret that I have but one life to lose for my country," Nathan Hale, the nation's first spy, remains among the pantheon of martyred American heroes. Yet, he is peripheral to, if not, an outlier in the American narrative.[14]

As is the case with so much associated with the history of intelligence in the United States, the story of Nathan Hale blends myth with history. What is indisputable, nevertheless, is that espionage was crucial to America's growth and safeguarding its security. The Revolutionary War produced the Culper Ring, the United States' initial spy network organized in New York City in 1778, and the Civil War gave rise to most notably, but not exclusively, the Pinkertons. In 1889, as the United States began its ascent to global power, the Navy Department established the Office of Naval Intelligence (ONI), and shortly thereafter the War Department followed suit with the Division of Military Information (soon renamed the Military Intelligence Division, MID, and organized under the General Staff as G-2). The State Department, moreover, had long relied on its Foreign Service officers for vital intelligence.[15]

Successive US administrations made no attempt to coordinate intelligence collection and analysis, however, let alone establish a centralized institution for these purposes. During the First World War, for example, the War Department created an effective signals intelligence (codebreaking or cryptanalytic) unit known, instructively, as the Black Chamber. In the war's aftermath, this unit continued under the leadership of Herbert Yardley and the joint direction and funding of the War and State Departments.

Allegedly uttering the infamous sentence "Gentlemen do not read each other's mail," Secretary of State Henry Stimson shut the Black Chamber down in 1929, just as the Versailles system began to unravel. Suffice it to say, for more than a century Americans had been reading each other's mail. Yet, to Stimson and the nation's elite, sanctioning such behavior as an institutionalized feature of the state would undermine US values, its ideals, its exceptionalism.[16]

The shock of Pearl Harbor and US entry into World War II substantially ameliorated America's antipathy toward spying. And Stimson's definition of an American "gentleman" led the way. Convinced that the reports on the situation in Europe he received in the late 1930s from his ambassador to Great Britain, Joseph Kennedy, were unreliable, President Franklin D. Roosevelt sent William "Wild Bill" Donovan to England to provide him with a second opinion. Roosevelt appreciated that Donovan, a prominent Republican millionaire attorney who had once run for governor of New York, a Congressional Medal of Honor recipient, and an intimate of Secretary of the Navy Frank Knox would insulate the administration from the criticism of anti-New Deal partisans and isolationists, which many at the time considered inseparable. Donovan assessed the British chances against the Germans, particularly with US assistance, more positively than did Kennedy. He also developed a relationship with William Stephenson, London's intelligence liaison to Washington, and became a fan of the British Secret Intelligence Service (SIS or, as more commonly known, MI6). The World War I hero recommended that the United States set up a comparable institution; Roosevelt was sympathetic to the idea. In July 1941, while the United States was still at peace, by executive order the president established the Office of the Coordinator of Intelligence (COI), appointing Donovan as its chief. Some six month after Pearl Harbor, Roosevelt abolished the Office of the COI and replaced it with the Office of Strategic Services (OSS). In doing so, the president followed Donovan's advice that it would be less bureaucratically divisive if the intelligence organization reported to the military. "Wild Bill," resuming his World War I rank of colonel, remained in charge."[17]

Four future directors of the CIA (DCIs) served in the OSS: Allen W. Dulles, Richard Helms, William Colby, and William Casey. Other OSS veterans included Ray Cline and Frank Wisner, who later became CIA deputy directors, and subsequent government officials and public intellectuals such as Arthur M. Schlesinger, Jr., David Bruce, Walt Rostow, Carl Kaysen, and Douglas Cater. Its ranks included an inordinate number of the Ivy

Leagues' "Best and the Brightest," the majority of whom held positions in the OSS's Research and Analysis (R&A) Branch. Represented by such later CIA legends as Sherman Kent and Walter Pforzheimer, more than forty members of the Yale class of 1943 worked in World War II intelligence.[18]

The continuation of a centralized US intelligence agency once the war ended was anything but inevitable; the evolution from the OSS to the CIA, anything but inexorable. There is some truth to the claim by Donovan's most recent biographer that "his OSS was the Petri dish for the spies who later ran the CIA."[19] But the story of the CIA's lineage is much more complex, and much less linear. Despite the dramatic expansion of the OSS between 1941 and 1945 and its panoply of activities, which ranged from sabotage, "black propaganda," and even secret negotiations to espionage, code-breaking, and analysis, from the start Donovan's efforts to ensure the office's permanency and make it equal to other military services generated heated opposition. The Army's G-2, the Navy's ONI, and the Department of State resisted what all construed as Donovan's infringements on their autonomy. No less resolutely, J. Edgar Hoover of the FBI (the FBI had a branch for Latin American intelligence, the Special Intelligence Service), fiercely defended his turf. In a context that one political scientist suggests proves true the adage that politics make for strange bedfellows, they joined forces against Donovan.[20]

Defining precisely what kind of wartime agency Donovan ran presented him and his advocates with additional difficulties. Comprising the OSS were three different branches: Research and Analysis, Secret Intelligence (SI), and Special Operations. While the William Langers, Arthur Schlesingers, Walt Rostows, Sherman Kents, and other scholars and intellectuals tended to populate the R&A, Donovan favored the SI and SO divisions, which generated the most publicity and produced many of the CIA's future leaders. The branches, in an omen of what would become a principal characteristic of the agency, had little use for one another. This was correctly perceived in postwar Washington as a potential problem in terms of mission and structure. Further, the question of whether a powerful, permanent spy agency could be reconciled with the democratic ideals for which the United States fought troubled a broad spectrum of Americans, as it had their ancestors since the nation's founding.[21]

Donovan's best hope to defeat the powerful forces arrayed against his plans was the burgeoning Executive Office of the President (EOP), and more specifically, Franklin Roosevelt. "Wild Bill" proposed to outflank the military and make the OSS accountable directly to the president. Roosevelt's propensity to experiment with the unconventional, to innovate, and to centralize made him a likely supporter and perhaps even a champion of Donovan and a permanent postwar intelligence agency. On April 12, 1945, however, Roosevelt died. His successor, Harry S. Truman, was a novice in matters of international relations let alone foreign intelligence. To wade into such unfamiliar and turbulent waters would require doing battle with those military and government experts on whom he would desperately need to rely. Truman was also concerned that Donovan, politically ambitious and an ardent Republican to boot, was constitutionally incapable of respecting the boundary between a liberal democracy and a police state. To put him in charge of a den of superspies, or a "Gestapo" (the label Truman used repeatedly to express his anxiety over creating a CIA), was unimaginable for the new president.[22]

Accordingly, on September 20, 1945, Truman ordered the abolition of the OSS, to take effect in less than two weeks. Yet, recognizing that the fluidity of the global environment and the deterioration of relations with the Soviet Union demanded that America maintain its guard and keep abreast of developments overseas, he assigned responsibility for counterintelligence and gathering foreign intelligence to the Strategic Services Unit (SSU), which he placed under the War Department, and responsibility for assessing this intelligence to the State Department's Interim Research and Intelligence Service. By these measures, he explained to Donovan, the existing "framework of the Government" could accommodate "a coordinated system of foreign intelligence" without violating America's principles. The president made no effort to accommodate the OSS's paramilitary (the use of violence or support for others who do) capability.[23]

Still, Truman recognized the need for a mechanism to oversee this coordinated system. A battle royal erupted over its form—"tougher than I'd seen before; as tough as anything I saw afterwards," commented a participant. Truman cared only that the entity would be weak. The involved offices cared about their bureaucratic interests. The Departments of War and Navy, in conjunction with the service chiefs, proposed establishing a "National Intelligence Authority" (NIA). Composed of a representative of the Joint Chiefs of Staff and the Secretaries of War, Navy, and State, this authority, which would be funded by the participating departments, would assume responsibility for overall intelligence planning and development. Its instrument for doing so would be a "Central Intelligence Agency," directed by either a military officer with appropriate experience or a "specially qualified civilian." The president would appoint this director, who would be advised by an "Intelligence Advisory Board" (IAB).[24]

State, supported by the Bureau of the Budget and ultimately the Department of Justice (home to the FBI), vigorously objected to the proposal. Already concerned that the influx of OSS personnel would overwhelm its Foreign Service officers, Foggy Bottom balked at the premise that the military services "should have a voice reaching the President as unmistakable as that of the State Department." It held that the secretary of state should "control America's intelligence effort" by "determin[ing] the character of the intelligence furnished the President." Establishing a National Intelligence Authority was a sound proposal, but the secretary of state, the chief architect of US foreign policy, should chair it.[25]

State relied on Alfred McCormack, special assistant to Secretary of State James Byrnes, to stake the department's claim to primacy in matters of intelligence. In terms of bureaucratic skill, stature, and conviction, McCormack was no match for Secretary of the Navy James Forrestal. Forrestal was ahead of the national curve in judging the threat posed by the Soviet Union to the United States and its allies as horrifically severe. He was also in the vanguard of government officials convinced that the United States required a substantially improved national security machinery to assess and address that threat. Forrestal commissioned his friend Ferdinand Eberstadt, a prominent investment banker, to recommend measures to reorganize America's defense establishment and promote more coherent policymaking.[26]

Eberstadt concluded that the effectiveness of any national security structure required an intelligence agency that could provide "authoritative information on conditions and developments in the outside world." To draft the section of his report outlining the organization and character of that agency, Eberstadt turned to Rear Admiral Sidney W. Souers, a reserve naval officer who served under Forrestal during World War II. At the time the deputy chief of naval intelligence, Souers's contribution to the Eberstadt report reflected the perspective of the Departments of War and Navy, and above all, Forrestal. McCormick's advocacy of a CIA that institutionalized the predominance of the Department of State fell by the wayside.[27]

Driven largely by the Eberstadt report, Truman's initial effort at forging a compromise tilted significantly toward the military's preference. In January 1946 the president did create a National Intelligence Authority. In fact, his memorandum announcing the NIA's establishment repeated verbatim much of the wording of a memorandum produced by the Joint Chiefs of Staff six months earlier. Rather than a JCS representative joining with the secretaries of war, navy, and state on it, however, a personal representative of the president would. The NIA would supervise a Central Intelligence Group

(CIG). This CIG would take responsibility for performing the functions necessary to provide the White House and managers of the nation's security with "authoritative information on conditions and developments in the outside world." But each department's intelligence service would retain its personnel and "continue to collect, evaluate, correlate, and disseminate departmental intelligence." Truman's memorandum prohibited the NIA and CIG from engaging in domestic intelligence gathering or surveillance, and in retrospect of great significance, granted neither the authority to conduct covert operations. The CIG director, to be called the director of central intelligence (DCI), would be the president's representative to the NIA. For this position, President Truman chose Souers; Forrestal was delighted.[28]

Officially activated on February 8, 1946, and housed in a building with vacant offices and prefabricated huts along the reflecting pool directly to the east of the Lincoln Memorial in Washington, the Central Intelligence Group manifested confusion about its mission from the start. Its primary components were a Central Planning Staff, charged with coordinating intelligence activities, and the Central Reports Staff, which was responsible for producing "national policy intelligence." At issue was a question that more than a half-century later remains unresolved: What defines national policy (or strategic) intelligence, and through what channels should it flow? Truman wanted "current intelligence," daily summaries that would obviate his need to read lengthy reports or the volumes of intelligence data that the CIG received. Moreover, while strategic intelligence seeks to imagine the future with the goal of estimating likely developments and identifying opportunities to shape those developments, current intelligence focuses on the present. It especially highlights immediate threats. For most presidents, the immediate threat is the top priority because the administration's top priority is to avoid a disaster. That was certainly the case with Truman in 1946. Souers obliged him by directing the Central Reports Staff to produce succinct briefs that excluded all material that the president did not need to know at that particular moment. Truman normally read these summaries each evening and drew on them for discussions with his personal military advisor and the presiding officer of the Joint Chiefs of Staff, Admiral William D. Leahy.[29]

While Truman's wish was Souers's command, the memorandum establishing the Central Intelligence Group assigned it the task of correlating and evaluating "intelligence relating to the national security, and the appropriate dissemination within the government of the resulting strategic and national policy intelligence." Directed to concentrate on producing "current intelligence," however, the Central Reports Staff lacked the resources to fulfill this assignment, too. In addition, Secretary of State Byrnes claimed that the responsibility for furnishing the president with "current intelligence" belonged to his department. Souers designed a compromise. The Central Reports Staff would produce national intelligence, but current intelligence would be its "first priority." Splitting this difference did not satisfy the State Department at all. Further, the Central Reports Staff did not receive the additional resources required to produce both; hence, preparing current intelligence for the president's use came to dominate its "culture." As a CIA historian wrote, "National estimative intelligence was reduced to also-ran status."[30]

Souers agreed to serve as DCI only on an interim basis, and his brief tenure was hardly successful. During the three months prior to his stepping down in July 1946, the NIA met but three times. With Forrestal's star rising in the administration and Byrnes's poised to fall, the likelihood of Truman's selecting someone from outside the military to succeed Souers was remote. The odds fell further after Souers recommended Lt. General Hoyt Vandenberg. The chief of the Army's G-2, its intelligence staff, Vandenberg had the necessary experience — and the connections. He was the nephew of Michigan's Arthur Vandenberg, the ranking Republican on the Senate Foreign Relations Committee and pivotal to whatever bipartisan support for his internationalist agenda Truman could hope to engender on Capitol Hill. The combination of General Vandenberg's ambitions and Senator Vandenberg's political skill and influence augured well for the CIG's future development. For Truman, appointing Vandenberg DCI was an easy decision.[31]

Vandenberg hesitated to accept, however. He was concerned that occupying the position would interfere with his career trajectory in the military. But in the end, the general agreed to take charge of the fledgling agency in order to bolster his credentials as a leader and empire builder. Not afraid to step on the service chiefs' toes, Vandenberg was eager to challenge the status quo of the military establishment; his ultimate goal was to be named the first chief of staff of an independent Air Force. Hence, while Souers premised his stewardship of the Central Intelligence Group on the primacy of the services' (and to a lesser extent the State's) intelligence assets, Vandenberg sympathized with Donovan's proposal for a centralized intelligence agency that exceeded the sum of its parts. From his point of view, the DCI should exercise preponderant control of all foreign intelligence and counterintelligence operations. In the words of a history of the CIA written by a staff member of Frank Church's Senate Committee that investigated the CIA in the mid-1970s, "The appointment of Lieutenant General Hoyt Vandenberg as DCI on June 10, 1946 marked the beginning of CIG's gradual development as an independent intelligence producer."[32]

Vandenberg at first took baby steps, albeit well-designed ones. As the executive agent of the NIA, the Central Intelligence Group could not request appropriations directly from Congress. It depended on the Departments of War, Navy, and State for its funding. But none of these departments had dedicated lines in their budgets for the CIG. Vandenberg's remedy was to persuade Truman to instruct each department to earmark appropriations explicitly for the CIG and empower him, as director of central intelligence, to disperse them. Although direct congressional appropriations would have been better, through this method the CIG received sufficient funds through vouchers (to ensure that the precise amount of department funds targeted for the CIG remained secret) to purchase supplies and hire its own personnel. Acquiring the independent resources to hire personnel was especially important to Vandenberg. He sought ultimately to wrest control of strategic intelligence from all three of his "patrons." Improving America's capacity to assess and disseminate intelligence on the Soviet Union was the raison d'être for the Central Intelligence Group's establishment in the first place. Moreover, doing so would guarantee it a seat at the national security policymaking table.[33]

Vandenberg displayed intent, ambition, and bureaucratic mettle. He phased out the Strategic Services Unit, the OSS's foreign intelligence component that Truman had assigned to the Department of War, and folded its responsibilities into an Office of Special Operations (OSO), which would operate under the Central Intelligence Group as he directed. OSO's mission was to conduct "all organized Federal espionage and counterespionage operations outside of the US and its possessions for the collection of foreign intelligence information required for national security." Vandenberg then won approval from the National Intelligence Authority to cede to the CIG responsibility for collecting intelligence pertaining to the field of atomic energy and to award it the Foreign Broadcast Intelligence Service. (Later renamed the more innocuous Foreign Broadcast Information Service, FBIS monitored and translated open source material from abroad).[34]

But Vandenberg's next move was the most significant. He predicted that institutionalizing the CIG's authority for evaluating and disseminating intelligence would prove more critical for its future legitimacy and clout than its mandate to procure it, because that capacity would make it indispensable to the formulation of national policy. So in July 1946 he reconstituted the Central Reports Staff as the Office of Research and Evaluation (ORE), which he could now staff with personnel that he did not need to borrow from other departments but could hire independently. When State complained that it was in charge of research and evaluation, Vandenberg renamed his bureau the Office of Reports and Estimates.[35]

What the Central Intelligence Group and State contested, of course, was not the name but what kind of reports and estimates ORE would produce. This debate reflected the continuing confusion between "current" and "national" intelligence. And who consumed the intelligence was contingent on the kind of intelligence. The conflict was not resolved until a National Intelligence Authority meeting in February 1947. There the representatives from State, War, and Navy agreed to the definition of strategic intelligence that Vandenberg proposed. This definition assured that the reports and judgments produced by the CIG's Office of Research and Estimates would be a linchpin of the national security policymaking process. The approved wording read, "Strategic and national policy intelligence is that composite intelligence, *interdepartmental in character*, which is required by the President and other high officers and staffs to assist them in determining policies with respect to national planning and security in peace and war and for the advancement of broad national policy." Because this intelligence addressed a "political-economic-military area of concern to more than one agency," its production "*must transcend the exclusive competence of any one department*."[36]

Notwithstanding Vandenberg's significant achievements, the Central Intelligence Group remained, as described by Lawrence Houston, the CIG's general counsel who was the principal author of the legislation that established the CIA, "a step-child of three separate departments."[37] Houston's vantage point enabled him not only to speak with authority but also to appreciate fully the implications of the predicament. As general counsel to the CIG, Houston scrutinized the paper trail that led to its establishment. He concluded that its problem, stripped down to the core, was that it lacked any "authority to act on its own responsibility in other than an advisory and directing capacity." Houston also learned from his study that the CIG likewise lacked its own statutory basis. And because it lacked a statute that provided it independent standing, federal guidelines precluded it from continuing to function legally in any capacity for more than a year. For Vandenberg, Houston's discovery was a blessing. By necessity, the general counsel was forced to draft enabling legislation that would allow the Central Intelligence Group to survive. As a foundation, he drew on the 1944 memorandum written by William Donovan.[38]

Houston actually began the drafting process while Souers was still DCI. The general counsel dredged up the memorandum that Donovan had written to Roosevelt because it proposed establishing an autonomous entity situated within the Executive Office of the President. Transforming the Central Intelligence Group from a "stepchild" of three departments into an independent organ responsible directly to the president would provide the framework necessary to place it on a sound legal footing. By the time Houston had prepared his initial recommendations, moreover, pivotal members of his "audience" had become more receptive to an independent and empowered CIG. Houston submitted his report three days after Souers had retired, on June 13, 1946. Because of this circumstance, the recipient of Houston's draft was the far more aggrandizing and independent-minded Hoyt Vandenberg.

Probably more important in terms of Houston's ultimate success, by June 1946 the US government and its informed public were substantially more disposed toward a powerful spy agency and other pillars of a national security state. George Kennan's February "Long Telegram" from Moscow and Winston Churchill's Iron Curtain speech in March of that year were the talk of Washington, the Soviets had behaved badly in Iran, the Council of Foreign Ministers meeting in Paris was degenerating into acrimony, and the hope of reaching an understanding between the Soviets and Americans to control atomic weapons was about to be dashed in the United Nations. Dramatic institutional initiatives were becoming integral to the Truman administration's nascent Cold War arsenal.

Houston's enabling legislation for the Central Intelligence Group, nevertheless, ran up against the expected bureaucratic interests and the problem of providing it with a confidential budget. It also became caught in the quagmire over the proposed reorganization of the armed services to produce a single Department of Defense (initially called the National Military Establishment), establish a Joint Chiefs of Staff, and institutionalize other reorganization measures. Then, on top of everything else, Vandenberg resigned. The legislation to establish an autonomous, "enabled" CIA had been incorporated into a broader National Security Act that focused primarily on the reorganization of the defense establishment, including the creation of an Air Force independent of and equal to the other military services. The prospect of breaking the Air Force off from the Army had caused Vandenberg to hesitate before accepting the appointment of the DCI. This was his dream.

With the Air Force's establishment in the offing, Vandenberg resigned so that he could receive his fourth star and become available to become its chief of staff.

Truman submitted the National Security Act to Congress on February 26, 1947. The single section dealing with a CIA was remarkably brief, even cryptic. It included virtually none of Houston's initial recommendations, and, for that reason, owed little directly to Donovan's vision. In addition to creating the Department of Defense, the Joint Chiefs of Staff, and an independent Air Force, the Act called for the establishment of a National Security Council (NSC) composed of the president, vice president, the secretary of state, and the secretary of defense as statutory members. Designed to coordinate among its pillars the increasingly complex national security architecture, the NSC would be situated in the Executive office of the President. Subordinate to it, and accordingly also within the EOP, was the Central Intelligence Agency, the renamed Central Intelligence Group. The president would still appoint the director, but the appointee would now require Senate confirmation. If an active military officer, the DCI could retain his commission and rank. The National Intelligence Authority was abolished.

Covert and Paramilitary Operations

Although the National Security Act specified that the CIA would inherit all the responsibilities of the Central Intelligence Group, it enumerated only in the most general terms what those responsibilities were to be. The Act did, however, incorporate into the section establishing the CIA an elastic clause stipulating that the agency's duties included performing "such additional services of common concern as the National Security Council determines can be more efficiently accomplished centrally." That clause would serve as something of a blank check for the future, justifying the CIA's involvement in a remarkable range of clandestine and paramilitary operations few at the time could imagine. But the evidence suggests that Congress did not appreciate this potential. It passed the National Security Act overwhelmingly, and the president signed it into law on July 26, 1947.[39]

Truman appointed Admiral Roscoe H. Hillenkoetter, who had taken over the directorship of the CIG from Vandenberg while Congress considered the legislation, as the first director of the central intelligence (as opposed to the director of "just" the CIA; as would his successors through the start of the twenty-first century, Hillenkoetter was dual-hatted as both DCI and DCIA). If there was a bureaucratic "winner" (other than Vandenberg), it was

Forrestal. Whatever influence he may have lost over intelligence by the creation of the CIA was more than compensated for by his appointment as the first secretary of defense. What is more, Truman also appointed Forrestal's ally, Sidney Souers, executive secretary of the National Security Council.

In the fear-ridden Cold War environment of 1947, Congress and the president established the CIA as a component of the largest reorganization in US history of America's national security machinery—at least until the creation of the Department of Homeland Security in 2002. The significance of this effort both to integrate and cross lines of authority cannot be exaggerated. Although a consensus had developed even before the end of the World War II on the US need for a single agency to coordinate the intelligence services, officials in Washington conceived the CIA as an instrument to fight the Cold War. In addition, the juxtaposition of the CIA's birth with that of the Office of the Secretary of Defense (OSD), the JCS, and the NSC all but assured that the confusion and discord that had afflicted its predecessor, the Central Intelligence Group, would abate but not cease.

The underlying source of that confusion and discord could not have been more basic. In question was what the CIA should do, and by extension, what the CIA really was. With the National Security Act providing little guidance as to the new agency's mission, Congress logically identified the Central Intelligence Group as its direct antecedent. In contrast to the multitasked OSS, therefore, Truman's security managers proceeded from the premise that the CIA's responsibilities were confined to producing, coordinating, and disseminating intelligence analysis; counterintelligence; and collecting foreign intelligence. Its capacity for collecting foreign intelligence was limited, moreover, because the legislation did not vest in the CIA a mandate for covert operations, often a prerequisite for intelligence collection. Nor did the legislation authorize the agency to undertake paramilitary activities. General Counsel Houston was emphatic when writing for the record: in 1947 that there was not "any thought in the minds of Congress that the CIA under this authority would take positive action for subversion and sabotage," he made explicit. But there was a loophole: The National Security Act's elastic clause.[40]

Truman's close advisor Clark Clifford claims in his memoir that both Congress and the president understood that the elastic (what Clifford calls the "catchall") clause granted the CIA license for covert and paramilitary actions. Extant evidence does not support Clifford's claim, which in contrast to Houston's he made forty years after the fact.[41] Historical circumstances, organizational interests, and bureaucratic politics, not institutional planners or risk-taking adventurers, drove the CIA's transformation from an agency established to collect, analyze, and disseminate intelligence to an instrument for engaging in covert, frequently paramilitary operations.

The catalyst for this transformation was the intensifying Cold War and America's sense of vulnerability in 1947. While the year wore on, the salience of the ongoing Civil War in Greece to the formulation of US grand strategy receded as Communist propaganda threatened to score victories in such vital countries as Italy and France. It was in 1947 that the Kremlin resurrected the disbanded Communist International (Comintern) and reincarnated it as the Cominform (Communist Information Bureau). Top officials in the Truman administration gravitated toward a reliance on psychological warfare as an effective, perhaps the most effective, means of defense. Lacking this capability demanded the "immediate development of an organization, within the framework of the NSC, to implement both white and black psychological warfare designed to the attainment of U.S. national objectives." Forrestal and George Marshall, the retired five-star general and secretary of state as of January 1947, agreed that America's military "should not have a part in these activities." Its mission was defense and armed combat, and its personnel should train accordingly.[42]

Virtually by default, then, the administration added psychological warfare to the CIA's portfolio as an "additional service of common concern." In December the president approved NSC-4, which instructed the "the Director of Central Intelligence to initiate and conduct, within the limit of available funds, covert psychological operations designed to counteract Soviet and Soviet-inspired activities which constitute a threat to world peace and security or are designed to discredit and defeat the United States in its endeavors to promote world peace and security." Two months later, a Moscow-directed coup in Czechoslovakia purged the non-Communists from the Prague government, leading to the death of the pro-Western foreign minister Jan Masaryk and the hyperbolic "War Scare" of March 1948. In March, Hillenkoetter established the "Special Operations Group" within the Office of Special Operations for the purpose of planning and implementing "all measures of information and persuasion short of physical in which the originating role of the United States Government will always be kept concealed."[43]

Proceeding on a concurrent yet distinct track, George Kennan, the director of the State Department's Policy Planning Staff, aggressively promoted political warfare as a seminal Cold War tool. The "logical application of Clausewitz's doctrine in time of peace," Kennan wrote, political warfare encompassed "the employment of all the means at a nation's command, short of war, to achieve its national objectives." While overt operations

constituted the "traditional policy activities of any foreign office," he continued, covert ones included white and black propaganda but also spanned
economic assistance programs, political alliances, influencing by funding
and supplementary means government officials, labor leaders, intellectuals,
and other opinion makers, and even assistance to resistance movements
and insurgents. As his definition of political warfare signals, Kennan did
not identify the United States as at war. But in his judgment, neither was it
at peace. Unlike Europeans, Americans were paralyzed by this ambiguous
state of "semiwar," to use Forrestal's term. "We have been handicapped"
Kennan lamented, "by a popular attachment to the concept of a basic difference between peace and war, by a tendency to view war as a sort of sporting
context [sic] outside of all political context." The Soviets' exploitation of
this advantage would threaten America's most vital interests.[44]

As redress, Kennan drafted a directive to designate an official to oversee
the conduct of covert operations. He gave the position the title of director
of special studies, situated it in the NSC, and assigned the secretary of state
the authority to submit the nomination to the president. Kennan had two
reasons for devising this organizational chart. First, he feared that the CIA
would fall under the influence of former OSS personnel, and he did not
trust them. During World War II a ranking British intelligence officer complained about the "hankering" of OSS operative for "playing cowboys and
red Indians." Kennan agreed fully with this criticism. He recalled that OSS
"eager beavers" had developed tactical plans which, if implemented, would
have severely impaired the achievement of allied strategic objectives.[45]

Secondly, and inseparable from the first reason, Kennan's expansive definition of covert operations required their careful integration into and coordination with the spectrum of US foreign policy initiatives. Kennan defined
covert operations as essentially any operation that did not precipitate an
armed conflict involving "recognized" military force, more precisely recognized US military force, "designed to influence the thought, morale, and
behavior of a people in such a manner as to further the accomplishment of
national aims." This required their rigorous alignment with the fundamental foreign policy objectives identified by the Department of State.[46]

CIA Director Roscoe Hillenkoetter objected to locating the position
in the NSC. Doing so would conflict with the CIA's Special Operations
Group's responsibility for psychological operations. The best resolution,
Hillenkoetter proposed, was to place the director of special studies under
the CIA's umbrella. Over the previous months the agency had made
"great strides" in improving its covert capabilities, it had "obligated itself

to a considerable expenditure of funds for equipment, transportation, and experienced personnel," and it had made "firm commitments for clandestine psychological operations outside the United States for a long period of time," read a memorandum he sent to Souers, the NSC's executive secretary. Further, seeming to endorse on the one hand but on the other turn on its head Kennan's argument about the eroding boundary between war and peace, Hillenkoetter asserted that "War-time activities in that field [psychological warfare] should be a natural growth and expansion of peace-time activities." He judged Kennan's design as severely misguided.[47]

For support, Hillenkoetter could point to the CIA's recent operation in Italy. By channeling money to the pro-Western Christian Democrats, orchestrating a letter writing campaign, and taking other such measures, it helped to engineer the defeat of the pro-Soviet Popular Alliance in the April 1948 elections. Kennan, however, saw things differently. This time turning Hillenkoetter's claim on its head, he countered that the CIA's success magnified the very concerns he had expressed. In Kennan's judgment, the "full might" of the Soviets had now engaged the United States in a "Cold War," but its effort in Italy was but half-hearted. Americans and their allies could not expect to be so fortunate next time. "The United States cannot afford in the future, in perhaps more serious political crises, to reply [sic] upon improvised covert operations as was done at the time of the Italian elections," he warned when drafting a report for use as an NSC statement of policy.[48]

Reversing Hillenkoetter's diagnosis and prescription, Kennan's remedy was to strip the CIA of its psychological warfare mission and transfer these responsibilities and the attendant budget to a newly created office with a broader mandate and more dedicated capabilities. The administration would design this entity "to strengthen and extend current covert operations in the interest of our national security and to provide for plans and preparations for the conduct, in time of war, of covert operations and the overt phases of psychological warfare." Kennan recommended adding paramilitary activities to this portfolio. They included "preventive direct action, including sabotage, anti-sabotage, demolition and evacuation measures; subversion against hostile states, including assistance to underground resistance movements, guerrillas and refugee liberation groups; and support of indigenous anti-communist elements in threatened countries of the free world."[49]

Kennan's proposal spawned NSC 10/2, the seminal document in establishing the CIA's covert capability and modern identity, and the grist for today's popular culture mill. Yet, because Kennan opposed developing that capability within the CIA, the lineage zigged and zagged. This evolution explains the unorthodox structure and the convoluted history of the organization established to "plan and conduct convert operations." NSC 10/2 stipulated that the director of what it initially called the Office of Special Projects (OSP) but later renamed the Office of Policy Coordination (OPC) would be "acceptable" and report to the DCI. But it would be nominated by the secretary of state and approved by the NSC. The DCI would, in principle, have no more influence over its behavior than the secretaries of state and defense, and the NSC would arbitrate all disputes. Although the Office of Special Projects would operate largely independently of the CIA, it would receive its funds through the agency's budget (which, until 1949, was still channeled though State and Defense). Several layers removed from the president and responsible, in a sense, to everyone and therefore no one, the OSP was the foundational stone in erecting the edifice of "plausible deniability."[50]

Notwithstanding this Rube Goldberg-type structure and, to generously describe the DCI's authority, his shared responsibility for the Office of Special Project's operations, the CIA became home to the OSP. That it did facilitated the agency's incremental acquisition of and progressively less contested control over covert operations. This outcome, once again, was not foreordained. One contributing factor was the mundane operation of government. The consensus within the administration was that the United States needed a covert capability, and it needed one immediately. The only viable alternative to the CIA was the military. But confronted with the perceived increase in the risk of a war in Europe, especially after the Czech coup, and seeking to husband resources in order to exploit its capabilities most effectively, the military leadership balked. A "military organization cannot deal with the political subtleties of this activity," wrote Forrestal when explaining his reluctance to take on the burden of political and psychological warfare, which Kennan had firmly tied to paramilitary activities. Secretary of the Army Kenneth Royall was more explicit, and more forceful. He did not "want any Army representative to have anything to do with this activity." That left only the CIA, and little time to devise a work-around. Congress was set to adjourn. If "we are to get into operation in this field before the end of the summer," Kennan wrote to Marshall and Undersecretary of State Robert Lovett in late spring, the Executive Branch had to act soon or "the possibility of getting secret funds out of Congress for covert operations will be lost."[51]

But more than the military's forfeiture and the congressional calendar were responsible for the CIA's "mission creep." Around the time of the CIA's first anniversary, Hillenkoetter and NSC officials created a commission to evaluate its performance, its efficiency, and its relations with other governmental agencies. Selected as chair was Allen Dulles, whose OSS career had already established him as something of a legend in intelligence circles, and whose brother, John Foster, had become a linchpin in the administration's effort to reach across the political aisle. Filling out the committee were William Jackson, a veteran of General Omar Bradley's World War II intelligence staff, and Mathias Correa, the former aide to James Forestall when he was still secretary of the navy. Although this "Intelligence Survey Group" did not complete its now-well-known study until January 1949, it submitted a much less familiar interim report on May 13, 1948, a day after Kennan finished drafting his proposal to quarantine the CIA from covert operations.[52]

Dulles, Jackson, and Correa entitled their interim report "Relations between Secret Operations and Secret Intelligence" and proceeded from the premise that covert operations would be "directed particularly towards affording encouragement to the freedom-loving elements in those countries which have been over-run by Communism and toward combating by covert means the spread of Communist influence." The report was emphatic that because of their complexity and dangers, these operations must not be "farmed out" to various agencies lest doing so lead to "duplication of effort, crossing of wires," and "serious risk for the chains and agents." For that reason, covert operations should be centralized in one government agency, and the agency designated for that purpose "would have an important bearing on the future of intelligence operations of CIA." By positing the symbiosis between covert operations and secret intelligence, moreover, the Intelligence Survey Group left no doubt that the centralizing agency should be the CIA. "Allied experience in carrying out secret operations and secret intelligence during the last war has pointed up the close relationship of the two activities," the report read. Secret operations, it explained "provide one of the most important sources of SI, and the information gained from secret intelligence must immediately be put to use in guiding and directing secret operations."[53]

NSC staffers found the report persuasive. Their next draft of the directive on covert operations vested authority for their design and execution in an office (which, certainly not by coincidence, it called the Office of Special Services, or OSS) housed in the CIA and directed by a DCI-nominee. Representatives of State and Defense served only in an advisory capacity. Kennan's objections intensified, leading to him and Hillenkoetter engaging in a game of chicken over who would retreat first. Kennan made the initial move. In early June he drew a line in the sand by recommending that the NSC shut the process down and start all over. Establishing the Office of Special Projects had been the idea of his Policy Planning Staff, he reminded Undersecretary Lovett. The intent was to "devise some means by which this Government could conduct political warfare as an integral part of its foreign policy." Setting up this new office in the CIA and consigning the State Department to an advisory role not only "does not appear to meet this need" but, without careful guidance and close supervision, also could easily "cause embarrassment to this Government." Thus, all projects of the office "must be done under the intimate direction and control of this department," he exclaimed. Unless this condition was met, and despite the severe cost, above all to policy in Europe, "I think it would be better to withdraw this paper entirely and to give up at this time the idea of attempting to conduct political warfare."[54]

A frustrated Hillenkoetter seemed prepared to surrender, thereby excising covert operations from the CIA's mission, perhaps forever. "I should suggest," he wrote to the NSC, "that since State evidently will not go along with CIA operating this political warfare thing in any sane or sound manner, we go back to the original concept that State proposed. Let State run it and let it have no connection at all with us." Not finished, Hillenkoetter sought to project himself as the mature statesman whose concern for the greater good compelled him to placate the childish and churlish Kennan, suggesting that he was not prepared to surrender after all. Rather than "try to keep a makeshift in running order, subject to countless restrictions which can only lead to continued bickering and argument, I think maybe the best idea is to go back and make OSP work for State alone," his broadside concluded, probably disingenuously.[55]

As the battle of memoranda raged, the NSC drafters developed second thoughts. There was merit to the arguments on both sides, and hanging over everything was the question of whether the fledgling CIA could manage this responsibility, especially if a war broke out. This uncertainty combined with bureaucratic politics and the rapidly closing window of opportunity to produce the compromise that framed the directive's final form. The next draft restored the name of the organization to Kennan's Office of Special Projects and the authority of the secretary of state to nominate the director. No less significantly, the new directive distinguished between conducting covert operations in peacetime and war. The draft added a sentence to the directive that read, "Covert operations, in time of war or emergency when the president directs, shall be conducted under appropriate arrangements to be recommended by the OSPs in collaboration with the Joint Chiefs of Staff and approved by the National Security Council." But to Kennan's chagrin, the OSP's home was to be the CIA, not the NSC.[56]

Truman signed the directive as NSC 10/2 on June 18, 1948. Kennan's reservations were eased when Marshall selected him as the State Department's representative to the Office of Special Projects, which officially became active on September 1. This apparent connection between the OSP and the Policy Planning Staff augured well for coordinating covert operations with national strategy. In addition, after his first choice, Allen Dulles, turned him down, Kennan recommended that Marshall nominate Frank Wisner as OSP director; the secretary of state predictably accepted the recommendation.[57]

In this case, Kennan bet on the wrong horse. Unfamiliar with Wisner personally, he had based his recommendation on his experience and credentials. Although Kennan had not misread Wisner's record, he should have done more homework. An OSS veteran and disciple of Donovan who was well connected in his own right, Wisner had earned a reputation during World War II only slightly less lustrous than that of Allen Dulles. He was capable, hard-charging, and ambitious. He was also predisposed to resist "interference" from either the diplomats or the generals. And as the East–West divide hardened, Wisner, a staunch anti-communist, reconfigured the Office of Special Projects (which, within months, he renamed the Office of Policy Coordination to better mask its mission) in order to increase its influence over covert operations and autonomy from State. The military abetted his effort. By appearing to bring the United States close to a direct confrontation with the Soviets, the Berlin Crisis of June 1948 through May 1949 underscored the gaps in American intelligence, gaps that could only be addressed through the collection of secret intelligence. In an effort to furnish it, the military turned increasingly to the one institution responsible for "all-source intelligence": the CIA. For the CIA, these sources included not just those from within the Soviet bloc, defectors, for example, but also resistance movements, refugee groups, indigenous anti-communists, and parallel organizations and clusters that neither Hillenkoetter nor anyone else could place firmly on one side of the war/peace divide. It was precisely because of these elements' potential as sources of intelligence that Allen Dulles' Intelligence Survey Group cautioned against separating secret intelligence from covert operations.[58]

Wisner, whose official title was assistant director for policy coordination, redesigned his organizational chart to make more transparent his commitment to satisfying the military's as well as the policymakers' needs. His chart divided the Office of Policy Coordination into "functional groups." On one end of the spectrum was "Psychological Warfare," the CIA's initial charge, which in large part merged with and became indistinguishable from political warfare. Situated under this umbrella was the OPC's (i.e., CIA's) first front organization, the National Committee for Free Europe founded in 1949. The progenitor of Radio Free Europe, this "longest running … covert action campaign," on whose board served Dwight D. Eisenhower, Henry Luce, Lucius Clay, and Cecil B. de Mille, aimed to rally dissidents, primarily in Eastern Europe, to challenge communist domination. Within a few short years, the OPC's political warfare programs had become so diverse and so imaginative that Wisner referred to the effort as a Mighty Wurlitzer, the giant organ thought to approximate a one-person orchestra because it could masquerade as so many different instruments.[59]

At the other end of spectrum of Wisner's organizational chart for the Office of Policy Coordination were activities, including paramilitary operations, that Kennan considered appropriate for the military—but not the CIA. These were "Support of Guerrillas," "Sabotage," and "Demolition." To carry out them out, Wisner heavily recruited his former colleagues, many of whom "found in their wartime experiences a sense of drama and meaning that could not be matched back at their law firms or lecture halls in peacetime." Developing an *esprit to corps* that OSS veteran, charter OPC member, and future CIA director William Colby described as resembling "an order of the Knights Templar," they became the backbone of "The Company." Facilitated as well as sanctioned by Congress' June 1949 enactment of the CIA Act, which allowed the CIA to operate under a greater cloak of secrecy by exempting it from the need to disclose publicly its activities, budget, and personnel, covert and paramilitary operations came to define what the CIA was.[60]

Wisner was accountable to virtually no one. As the CIA's director, Hillenkoetter technically managed his operations. But in practice, it was Kennan, as the director of State's Policy Planning Staff and the department's representative to the OPC who had the responsibility for ensuring that those operations were congruent with US policies and programs. Yet, Kennan's influence within both State in particular and the administration in general declined in almost direct proportion to rollback's challenge to containment and the militarization—and "paramilitarization"—of America's Cold War strategy. In 1949, Robert Joyce, who had served in the OSS during World War II and sympathized with an active covert operations agenda, succeeded Kennan as State's representative to the office. As a result, under Wisner's guidance, to quote the history of the CIA written for the Church Committee, the "OPC achieved an institutional independence that was unimaginable at the time of its inception."[61]

The consequences proved irreversible. In a dramatic departure from the intent of the CIA's designers, the growth of covert operations in frequency and complexity diverted both resources and commitment from the agency's core mission of collecting, analyzing, and distributing intelligence. As for Kennan, he came to consider his role in establishing the OPC (albeit not his advocacy of political warfare, in which he continued to engage after leaving the Policy Planning Staff) "probably the worst mistake I ever made in government." It would take decades, nevertheless, for the full cost of that mistake to become manifest.[62]

Notes

1   Paul R. Pillar, *Intelligence and U.S. Foreign Policy: Iraq, 9/11, and Misguided Reform* (NY: Columbia University Press, 2011), 3, 179–81; Greg Miller, "In 'Zero Dark Thirty,' She's the Hero; in Real Life, CIA Agent's Career is More Complicated," *Washington Post*, December 11, 2012.

2   David Grove, "Everything Old is New Again," *PopMatters*, n.d., accessed on November 7, 2012, at http://www.popmatters.com/tv/reviews/a/agency.html.

3   Erik Lundegaard, "You're Not Reading This: The CIA in Hollywood Movies: From '3 Days of the Condor' to 'Good Shepherd'," December 21, 2006, *msnbc.com*, accessed on June 11, 2012, at http://today.msnbc.msn.com/id /16270828/ns/today-entertainment/.

4   Walter Hixson, "Red Storm Rising: Tom Clancy Novels and the Cult of National Security," *Diplomatic History* 17 (October 1993): 599–613.

5   Todd S. Purdum, "Hollywood Rallied Round the Homeland," *New York Times*, February 2, 2003; Tricia Jenkins, "Get Smart: A Look at the Current Relationship between Hollywood and the CIA," *Historical Journal of Film, Radio and Television* 29 (June 2009): 229–43.

6   "New Recruitment Video on the Central Intelligence Agency Careers Web Site Features Jennifer Garner," CIA Press Release, March 8, 2004, accessed on June 11, 2004, at https://www.cia.gov/news-information/press-releases -statements/press-release-archive-2004/pr03082004.html; "Jennifer Garner Makes CIA Video," *Democratic Underground.com*, accessed on June 11, 2012, at http://www.democraticunderground.com/discuss/duboard.php?az=view _all&address=105x876646.

7   Tricia Jenkins, *The CIA in Hollywood: How the Agency Shapes Films and Television* (Austin: University of Texas Press, 2012).

8   Richard K. Betts, *Enemies of Intelligence: Knowledge & Power in American National Security* (New York: Columbia University Press, 2007); *Fair Game* Script, written by Jez Butterworth and John-Henry Butterworth, *The Internet Movie Script Database*, accessed on 14 January 2012 at http://www .imsdb.com/scripts/Fair-Game.html.

9   Alessandra Stanley, "Cold War-Style Spying is Back (How Quaint)," *New York Times*, July 13, 2010; Gail Russell Chaddock, " 'Charlie Wilson's War' Would be Harder to Fight These Days," *Christian Science Monitor*, February 11, 2010, accessed on November 7, 2012, at http://www.csmonitor.com/USA/Politics /2010/0211/Charlie-Wilson-s-War-would-be-harder-to-fight-these-days; Matthew L. Wald, "Halting a Slow Fade to History," *New York Times*, October 17, 2012; See also Antonio Mendez and Matt Baglio, *Argo: How the CIA and Hollywood Pulled Off the Most Audacious Rescue in History* (NY: Viking, 2012).

10   Ann Hornaday, " 'Zero Dark Thirty' and the New Reality of Reported Filmmaking," *Washington Post*, December 15, 2012; Manohla Dargis, "Jessica Chastain in 'Zero Dark Thirty,' " *New York Times*, December 18, 2012.

11   Allesandra Stanley, "Homeland's Season Finale, With a Twist," *New York Times*, December 18, 2012.

12   Julie Bosman, "In Novels, Ex-Spy Returns to the Fold," *New York Times*, March 19, 2011.

13   David Ignatius, "CIA Documents Supported Susan Rice's Description of Benghazi Attacks," *Washington Post*, October 19, 2012.

14   Robin W. Winks, *Cloak and Gown: Scholars in the Secret War, 1939–1961* (New Haven, CT: Yale University Press, 2nd ed., 1996), 15–18.

15   David Rudgers, *Creating the Secret State: The Origins of the Central Intelligence Agency, 1943–1947* (Lawrence: University of Kansas Press, 2000), 5.

16   Henry Stimson and McGeorge Bundy, *On Active Duty in Peace and War* (NY: Harper & Brothers, 1947), 18; William E. Odom, *Fixing Intelligence: For a More Secure America* (New Haven, CT: Yale University Press, 2003); H. O. Yardley, *The American Black Chamber* (NY: Ballantine, 1981); David Kahn, *The Reader of Gentlemen's Mail: Herbert O. Yardley and the Birth of American Codebreaking* (New Haven, CT: Yale University Press, 2004).

17   Thomas F. Troy, *Donovan and the CIA* (Frederick, MD: University Publications of America, 1981), 23–70; John Ranelagh, *The Agency: The Rise and Decline of the CIA* (NY: Simon & Schuster, 1986), 37–61.

18   Winks, *Cloak and Gown*, 35–42; Tim Weiner, "W. L. Pforzheimer, 88, Dies: Helped to Shape the C.I.A.," *New York Times*, February 16, 2003; See also Burton Hersh, *The Old Boys: American Elite and the Origins of the CIA* (NY: Charles Scribner's Sons, 1992).

19   Douglas Waller, *Wild Bill Donovan: The Spymaster Who Created the OSS and Modern American Espionage* (NY: Free Press, 2011), 389.

20   Amy B. Zegart, *Flawed by Design: The Evolution of the CIA, JCS, and NSC* (Stanford, CA: Stanford University Press, 1999), 175.

21   Rudgers, *Creating the Secret State*, 15–32;

22   Rhodri Jeffreys-Jones, *The CIA and American Democracy* (New Haven, CT: Yale University Press, 1989), 29–30.

23 William D. Leahy, Memorandum for the Secretary of War and Secretary of Navy, "Establishment of a central intelligence service upon liquidation of OSS," with enclosed Memorandum for the President by the Joint Chiefs of Staff and Appendix, 19 September 1945, in *The CIA under Harry Truman*, ed. Michael Warner (Washington, DC: Center for the Study of Intelligence, 1994), 5–10; Truman to Major General William J. Donovan, September 20, 1945, in Warner, *The CIA under Truman*, 15.

24 Rudgers, *Creating the Secret State*, 63–64; Leahy, Memorandum for the Secretary of War and Secretary of Navy, with enclosed memorandum and Appendix, 19 September 1945.

25 Sydney W. Souers Memorandum for Commander [Clark] Clifford, 27 December 1945, in Warner, *The CIA under Truman*, 17–19.

26 Rudgers, *Creating the Secret State*, 90–97; Michael J. Hogan, *Cross of Iron: Harry S. Truman and the Origins of the National Security State* (NY: Cambridge University Press, 1998), 23–68.

27 Anne Karalekas, "History of the Central Intelligence Agency," in *The Central Intelligence Agency: History and Documents*, ed. William M. Leary (University: University of Alabama Press, 1984), 20–21.

28 Harry S. Truman to the Secretaries of State, War, and Navy, January 22, 1946, in Leary, *The Central Intelligence Agency*, 126–27.

29 Preface to *Assessing the Soviet Threat: The Early Cold War Years*, ed. Woodrow Kuhns (Washington, DC: Center for the Study of Intelligence, 1997), 1–9; Ludwell Montague, Memorandum for the Assistant Director, Research and Evaluation, 26 February 1946, in Warner, *CIA under Truman*, 123–24; Sydney Souers, "Progress Report on the Central Intelligence Group," 7 June 1946, in Warner, *CIA under Truman*, 41–51; For an accessible introduction to strategic intelligence, see Richard L. Russell, *Sharpening Strategic Intelligence: Why the CIA Gets It Wrong and What Needs to be Done to Get It Right* (NY: Cambridge University Press, 2007).

30 Preface to Kuhns, *Assessing the Soviet Threat*, 1–9.

31 Rudgers, *Creating the Secret State*, 113–15; Ranelagh, *The Agency*, 104.

32 Karelekas, "History of the Central Intelligence Agency," 22.

33 Karelekas, "History of the Central Intelligence Agency," 22–23; Donald P. Steury, "Origins of CIA's Analysis of the Soviet Union," in *Watching the Bear: Essays on the CIA's Analysis of the Soviet Union*, ed. Gerald K. Hanes and Robert E. Leggett (Washington, DC: Government Printing Office, 2003), 6.

34 Rudgers, *Creating the Secret State*, 117–25; Vandenberg memorandum for the Assistant Director for Special Operations [David Galloway], "Functions of the Office of Special Operations," 25 October 1946, in Warner, *CIA under Truman*, 87; Preface to *Selected Estimates of the Soviet Union, 1950–1959*, ed. Scott S. Koch (Washington, DC: Center for the Study of Intelligence, 1993), XIn5.

35 Karelekas, "History of the Central Intelligence Agency," 25–26.

36   Minutes of the Meeting of the National Intelligence Authority, 12 February 1947, in Warner, *CIA under Truman*, 113–21. Author's emphasis.

37   George M. Elsey, Memorandum for the record, 17 July 1946, in Warner, *CIA under Truman*, 53–54.

38   Ranelagh, *The Agency*, 106.

39   Public Law 253, Section 102, The National Security Act of 1947 (80th Cong., 1st Sess.), accessed on June 16, 2013, at http://www.oup.com/us/companion. websites/9780195385168/resources/chapter10/nsa/nsa.pdf.

40   Memorandum by CIA General Counsel Lawrence Houston to the DCI, September 25, 1947, *Foreign Relations of the United States, 1945–1950: Emergence of the Intelligence Establishment* (Washington, DC: Government Printing Office, 1996): 622–3 (hereafter cited as *FRUS, Intelligence*).

41   Clark Clifford with Richard Holbrooke, *Counsel to the President: A Memoir* (NY: Random House, 1991), 169–70. In "Drastic Actions Short of War: The Origins and Application of CIA's Paramilitary Function in the Early Cold War," *Journal of Military History* 77 (July 2012): 775–808, CIA Historian Nicholas Dujmovic accepts Clifford's claim without providing corroborating evidence.

42   Memorandum from the Executive Secretary of the NSC (Souers) to Forrestal, October 24, 1947, *FRUS, Intelligence*, 627–28; Memorandum from Deputy Director (Edwin Wright) to Director CIA, November 4, 1947, *FRUS, Intelligence*, 630–32; Memorandum of Discussion at NSC meeting, November 14, 1947, *FRUS, Intelligence*, 637–38.

43   Memorandum from Souers to the Members of the National Security Council, NSC 4-A, "Psychological Operations," December 9, 1947, *FRUS, Intelligence*, 643–44; NSC 4, "Report by the National Security Council on Coordination of Foreign Information Measures," December 16, 1947, *FRUS, Intelligence*, 640–42; Roscoe H. Hillenkoetter memorandum for Assistant Director for Special Operations (Galloway) and enclosure, 22 March 1948, in Warner, *CIA under Truman*, 191–95.

44   Scott Lucas and Kaeten Mistry, "Illusions of Coherence: George F. Kennan, U.S. Strategy, and Political Warfare in the Early Cold War, 1946–1950," *Diplomatic History* 33 (January 2009): 39–66; Andrew J. Bacevich, *Washington Rules: America's Path to Permanent War* (NY: Henry Holt, 2010), 27–28; Policy Planning Staff Memorandum, May 4, 1948, *FRUS, Intelligence*, 668–72.

45   Mark Mazzetti, *The Way of the Knife: The CIA, a Secret Army, and a War at the Ends of the Earth* (NY: Penguin, 2013), 7; Kennan quoted in Richard Harris Smith, *OSS: The Secret History of America's First Central Intelligence Agency* (Berkeley: University of California Press, 1972), 80.

46   Draft Proposed NSC Directive, May 5, 1948, *FRUS, Intelligence*, 672–73.

47   Memorandum from Hillenkoetter to Souers, May 6, 1948, *FRUS, Intelligence*, 675–76.

48 James E. Miller, "Taking Off the Gloves: The United States and the Italian Elections of 1948," *Diplomatic History* 7 (Winter 1983): 35–56; Kaeten Mistry, "Approaches to Understanding the Inaugural CIA Covert Operation in Italy: Exploding Useful Myths," *Intelligence and National Security* 26 (April 2011): 246–68; Draft Report by the National Security Council, NSC 10, Director of Special Studies, May 12, 1948, *FRUS, Intelligence*, 677–81.

49 NSC 10.

50 NSC 10/2, NSC Directive on Office of Special Projects, June 18, 1948, *FRUS, Intelligence*, 713–15.

51 Memorandum of Discussion at the NSC meeting, June 3, 1948, *FRUS, Intelligence*, 694–98; Memorandum from Kennan to Lovett, May 19, 1948, *FRUS, Intelligence*, 684–85; Memorandum from Kennan to Lovett, May 28, 1948, *FRUS, Intelligence*, 690.

52 Karelekas, "History of the Central Intelligence Agency," 29n9–n10.

53 Memorandum from the Intelligence Survey Group to the Executive Secretary of the National Security Council, May 13, 1948, *FRUS, Intelligence*, 681–83.

54 Memorandum from Kennan to Lovett, June 8, 1948, *FRUS, Intelligence*, 702–03.

55 Letter from Hillenkoetter to Lay, June 9, 1948, *FRUS, Intelligence*, 703–04.

56 NSC Memorandum, June 4, 1948, *FRUS, Intelligence*, 699; Memorandum from Lay to Hillenkotter, and attachment, Proposed NSC Directive, June 7, 1948, *FRUS, Intelligence*, 699–702; Note by Souers and enclosure, NSC 10/1, Proposed NSC Directive, June 15, 1946, *FRUS, Intelligence*, 706–08.

57 Hugh Wilford, *The Mighty Wurlitzer: How the CIA Played America* (Cambridge, MA: Harvard University Press, 2008), 10.

58 Gregory Mitrovich, *Undermining the Kremlin: America's Strategy to Subvert the Soviet Bloc, 1947–1956* (Ithaca, NY: Cornell University Press, 2000), 20–22.

59 "The National Committee for Free Europe," 1949, CIA Featured Story Archive, accessed on July 25, 2012, at https://www.cia.gov/news-information/featured-story-archive/2007-featured-story-archive/a-look-back.html; Wilford, *Mighty Wurlitzer*, 7.

60 Memorandum from Wisner to Hillenkoetter, October 29, 1948, *FRUS, Intelligence*, 730–31; Evan Thomas, *The Very Best Men: Four Who Dared: The Early Years of the CIA* (NY: Simon & Schuster, 1996), 11; William Colby and Peter Forbath, *Honorable Men: My Life in the CIA* (NY: Simon & Schuster, 1978), 73; Central Intelligence Act of 1949, June 20, 1949, in Warner, *CIA under Truman*, 287–94; Frank Wisner, Memorandum for the Director of Central Intelligence, "Observations upon the report of the Dulles-Jackson-Correa report to the National Security Council," February 14, 1949, in Warner, *CIA under Truman*, 247–50.

61 Stephen J. K. Long, "Strategic Disorder, the Office of Policy Coordination, and the Inauguration of US Political Warfare Against the Soviet Bloc, 1949–1950," *Intelligence and National Security* 27 (August 2012): 459–87; Karelekas, "History of the Central Intelligence Agency," 43.

62 Kennan quoted in John Lewis Gaddis, *George F. Kennan: An American Life* (NY: Penguin, 2011), 318.

2

Halcyon Days and Growing Pains: 1950–1961

Frank Wisner received such license to expand and redesign the Office of Policy Coordination, in part because in an era when the CIA had few technological assets, collection of secret intelligence was wholly dependent on covert operations. And analysis, while not wholly dependent on secret intelligence, did of course benefit from its collection.[1] Therein lay the fundamental problem. Increasingly over time, the CIA's analytic branch played second fiddle to operations, which exacerbated the former's deficiencies. Those deficiencies were manifold. Topping the list was the still-unresolved ambiguity over priorities and the problematic skill and expertise of the analysts. Despite all the politicking and infighting that attended the CIA's establishment, there was a consensus that the threat posed by the Soviet Union demanded a CIA that could draw on all the sources available throughout the community, whether civilian or military, to produce its assessments.

It was therefore highly appropriate that assessing Moscow's intentions was the subject of the first intelligence estimate produced by the Central Intelligence Group's Office of Reports and Estimates (ORE) in 1946. But the estimate was hardly the product of "all-source intelligence." In fact, ORE-1, "Soviet Foreign and Military Policy," largely reflected the influence of one individual—George Kennan. Appointed a consultant to the Central Intelligent Group by Souers because of his expertise on the Soviet Union, Kennan, while counselor to the embassy in Moscow, had earlier that year dispatched his "Long Telegram" to Washington. ORE-1 closely paralleled Kennan's analyses of and predictions for the Kremlin's beliefs and behavior. Although the estimate expected the Kremlin leadership to postpone "overt conflict for an indefinite period," it stressed that "the Soviet Union

The Hidden Hand: A Brief History of the CIA, First Edition. Richard Immerman.
© 2014 John Wiley & Sons, Ltd. Published 2014 by John Wiley & Sons, Ltd.

anticipates an inevitable conflict with the capitalist world." ORE-1 judged Moscow's "ultimate objective" as a qualified "may be world domination."[2]

The thrust of subsequent estimates by the Office of Reports and Estimates was similarly imprecise. Consequently, as "actionable intelligence" these products were of no greater value to Truman and his national security managers than the reports and evaluations produced by the less centralized intelligence agencies. The same held true for ORE estimates on other areas and topics because, bluntly put, its resources were no better, and sometimes worse, than elsewhere in the community. "[O]ur information relating to this subject is meager," began ORE 3/1, an estimate written in 1946 on "Soviet Capabilities for the Development and Production of Certain Types of Weapons and Equipment." It forecast that "the capability of the USSR to develop weapons based on atomic energy will be limited to the possible development of an atomic bomb to the stage of production at some time between 1950 and 1953." As late as 1948, after the CIA's creation and the intensification of the Cold War, only thirty-eight analysts worked in ORE's Soviet and East European branch. Of these, but nine had lived there, twelve spoke any Russian, and one had a PhD. Six had no college degree at all.[3]

Undertrained and under stress because the office was understaffed, ORE analysts were normatively risk averse. Not confident they could "get it right" (intelligence estimates are just that, estimates, and very difficult in the best of circumstances), their priority was to avoid a major misstep. They were particularly gun shy because they did not want to precipitate a confrontation with Secretary of Defense Forrestal, whose alarmist personal assessments of Soviet intentions as well as capabilities often received support from the military's intelligence services. The ORE therefore preferred to focus on bounded, current intelligence reporting. While the rare national estimate began with a set of conclusions (now called key judgments) followed by detailed analysis, the daily and, for that matter, weekly summaries were by and large limited to descriptions of events and developments. These summaries, antiseptically noncontroversial, were less likely to generate pushback, let alone a backlash. Truman read them, but many of his key advisors had their own sources and did not. As a result, intelligence reports and estimates produced by the Office of Reports and Estimates contributed little to policy formulation.[4]

This dynamic persisted and even intensified after 1947, when the Central Intelligence Group evolved into the Central Intelligence Agency. Hillenkoetter divided the ORE into geographically-based branches, staffing each with appropriate experts to the extent they were available.

The most effective way for an analyst to gain recognition and hence career advancement was to author an ORE publication. The narrow daily and weekly summaries provided many more opportunities than a long-term estimate, which also posed greater risks. The slightly more ambitious digests entitled "Review of the World Situation as it Relates to the Security of the United States" were somewhat more analytic and farsighted, but not much. The Church Committee's history of the CIA lamented the consequence: "[I]ndividuals in ORE perpetuated and contributed to the current intelligence stranglehold."[5]

Hillenkoetter, to his credit, sought to encourage the analytic workforce to produce more national intelligence. But he had little success. Despite the 1947 legislation, the director of central intelligence's authority was limited largely to the CIA. He therefore could ask for but rarely receive from the other intelligence services that comprised the "community." They answered to the more powerful and more respected George Marshall and James Forrestal, with their independent budgets. The Dulles–Jackson–Correa report, which played a pivotal role in the CIA's acquiring a capacity for covert action, did not mince its words when criticizing the agency's analytic products. The CIA's responsibility to coordinate intelligence activities was "not being adequately exercised," read the January 1949 evaluation of the CIA's performance. The Office of Research and Estimates, the report continued, had "been concerned with a wide variety of activities and with the production of miscellaneous reports and summaries that by no stretch of the imagination could be considered national estimates." Rather than fulfill the mission for which it was established by producing "all-source intelligence," the CIA was "just one more intelligence agency producing intelligence in competition with older established agencies of the Government departments." Against the State and Defense Departments, it was hardly competitive.[6]

This inability to forge collaboration and integration would plague the intelligence community throughout the Cold War—and beyond it. The Dulles committee suggested a quick fix, however: change the leadership. "[O]rganizational charts can never replace individual initiative and ability," and the CIA's shortcomings are "necessarily a reflection of inadequacies of direction," read its report.[7] Truman required little persuasion from the committee or anyone else. The CIA had failed to predict the Czech coup, in February 1948, the much publicized *Bogotázo*, the riots that broke out during the Inter-American Foreign Ministers Meeting that inaugurated the Organization of American States in Bogotá, Colombia, the following month, or the Berlin Blockade in June. In 1949 things went from bad to worse for the CIA, and US foreign policy, with the successful (and surprise) Soviet test of an atomic devise and the communist victory in the Chinese civil war.

The year 1949 was also the beginning of the disastrous joint operation between the Office of Policy Coordination and Britain's Secret Intelligence Service (called Operation BGFIEND in Washington; VALUABLE in London) to overthrow the Communist government of Enver Hoxha in Albania by surreptitiously offloading or airdropping agents into the country. The project, which laid the foundation for the CIA's collaboration with British intelligence (termed an intelligence liaison) that would become a linchpin of US foreign policy and an integral dimension of the Anglo-American "Special Relationship," finally ended four years later with the death or capture of virtually every one of the operatives, and many indigenous Albanians. Poor training contributed to failure, but so did worse counterintelligence. Not until too late did either the Americans or British detect that H.A.R. "Kim" Philby, MI6's key liaison to the CIA, was a double agent. Then, in June 1950, the North Korean invasion of South Korea once again caught the United States off guard.[8]

The outbreak of the Korean War was a turning point, whether US global strategy or CIA history serves as the baseline. In fact, from this time on they were inseparable. It took the Communist North's decision to invade the South for a hesitant President Truman to approve in September 1950 NSC 68, the new statement of national security policy that, assessing the Soviet Union as a greater threat than Nazi Germany, required the United States to respond aggressively, no matter the location or the expense. NSC 68's principal author, Paul Nitze, read the CIA's estimate of the Soviet Union's intentions now that it had an atomic capability. Although ORE 91-49 assessed that sometime between mid-1954 and 1955 the Soviets "will probably have a stockpile of 200 bombs," it judged it unlikely that "the USSR presently intends deliberately to use military force to attain a Communist world or further to expand Soviet territory if this involves war with a potentially stronger US." Rejecting this judgment as too benign, Nitze decided to rely instead on a report of the Joint Chiefs of Staff's Joint Intelligence Committee. It was the JIC, not the CIA, that conflated capabilities and intentions by forecasting an impending "year of maximum danger" (initially 1954, but subsequently 1953) because Washington now confronted the serious risk of a surprise Soviet attack on the continental United States. As a result, the CIA's contribution to the administration's most important policy statement was once again minimal. Truman did not pay attention to such bureaucratic matters. He was acutely aware, nevertheless, that the Korean War was an international game changer. Therefore he, and America's national security, would need a capable CIA more than ever.[9]

Even before the outbreak of the Korean War, Truman had decided to appoint Walter Bedell Smith his new director of central intelligence. Beetle, the name used by Smith's friends, was in many ways everything that Hillenkoetter was not. A four-star general who had served as Dwight D. Eisenhower's chief of staff during World War II and as ambassador to the Soviet Union from 1946 to 1948, Smith had the prestige and clout to compete with any military officer or cabinet secretary. He likewise had the appropriate personality. Strong-willed and frequently irascible, attributes exacerbated by severe stomach ulcers, Smith could be fearsome as well as intimidating. An ardent cold warrior with vast administrative experience, he was ideally suited to lead the CIA into a new era. Ray Cline, an OSS veteran who was present at the agency's creation and rose through its ranks to become deputy director, reveled in Smith's appointment: "For the first time since Donovan, central intelligence was in the hands of a man with vision and drive, a man with the prestige persuasive to military commanders, ambassadors, and Congressman, and, finally, a man with the full support of the President."[10]

Americans "expect you to be on a communing level with God and Joe Stalin, and I'm not sure they are so much interested in God," Smith reportedly said when commenting on the unrealistic expectations the US public had about intelligence.[11] Nevertheless, it is doubtful that Smith fully appreciated the challenges he confronted at the time he accepted Truman's appointment. The day after his confirmation by the US Senate, the CIA's new director received from general counsel Lawrence Houston a lengthy memorandum spelling out those challenges. Houston's bottom line was that the CIA had marked time since Vandenberg headed the Central Intelligence Group. He stressed particularly that the agency had been unable to establish its authority over the government's other intelligence services, especially those in the military. As a result, their analysts, some of whom were under qualified regardless, rarely received the raw intelligence they needed to produce comprehensive and useful estimates. The hybrid character of the Office of Policy Coordination, moreover, rendered it unworkable. It had to be under the direct control of the DCI, fully incorporated into the CIA, and tied tightly to especially the collection but also the analysis components.[12]

Smith did not need to be told twice; his recognition of the inherent limits notwithstanding, he had developed a great appreciation for the value of intelligence during World War II. Having headed the US embassy in Moscow at the birth of the Cold War, he was determined to make it equally valuable to contemporary and future crises. The take-no-prisoners Smith wasted no time making the adjustments he considered essential. Appointing as his deputies two-thirds of the Intelligence Survey Group, first William Jackson and then Allen Dulles, he overhauled the CIA's bureaucratic structure. After creating a directorate of administration to manage the agency's personnel, financial, and other support functions, the new DCI divided ORE into three different offices: the Office of National Estimates (ONE), the Office of Research and Reports (ORR), and the Office of Current Intelligence (OCI). ONE would be responsible for producing National Intelligence Estimates (NIEs), which by their very nature required contributions from sources collected by intelligence officers beyond the CIA. Smith judged NIEs as the most important analytic product. Hillenkoetter had confronted too many obstacles to produce them; Smith would overcome those obstacles.

Smith took to heart the Dulles Committee's admonition that individuals matter more than organization charts. To head up the Office of National Estimates, he named former OSS chief of Research and Analysis and Harvard professor William Langer. As Langer's deputy and expected successor, Smith appointed another history professor, Yale University's Sherman Kent, another veteran of the OSS. Kent, who in 1949 published the acclaimed *Strategic Intelligence for American and World Policy*, succeeded Langer in 1952. Over the subsequent decades he would achieve legendary status. Smith chose another professor, Max Millikan from MIT's Economics Department, to direct the Office of Research and Reports. Millikan, a close colleague and collaborator of Walt Rostow, wrote the guidelines for this office's priority on providing economic analyses of present and future threats. The Office of Current Intelligence housed the individual country analysts and focused on political intelligence.[13]

Overseeing ONE, ORR, and OCI was another Smith innovation, the Board of National Estimates (BNE). Composed of leading military and civilian intelligence experts, the BNE's charge was to review all estimates, especially the National Intelligence Estimates produced by ONE's staff, and ensure that they incorporated "all-source intelligence" and highlighted differences in their judgments. Of the initial eight members of the "College of Cardinals," the Board of National Estimates' popular name, five held doctorates in history, one, a doctorate in economics, another was a prominent attorney, and the final member was a four-star general. Lest the college's academic composition undermine its utility, first Jackson and then Dulles began a tradition of regularly convening meetings of the Princeton Consultants, former officials like Kennan who could apply their experience to evaluating the estimates. In 1952 Smith finished the redesign by placing all the new organs within a Directorate of Intelligence (DI). Loftus Becker, a lawyer who had served as an advisor at the Nuremberg trials, became the CIA's first deputy director of intelligence (DDI). A year later, Robert Amory, another OSS veteran and Harvard professor, succeeded Becker as the CIA's DDI.[14]

Smith's reorganization signaled his conviction that the CIA needed to refocus its resources and commitments on its core mission: collection and analysis. He accepted covert actions as necessary means to acquire otherwise unobtainable source material. That responsibility, which Truman vested in the Central Intelligence Group before CIA was stood up, lay with the Office of Special Operations (OSO). But in the words of one of the CIA's most recently declassified internal histories, Smith "was perplexed if not dumbfounded by the wide-ranging responsibilities of OPC."[15] He judged the political warfare and paramilitary activities that Wisner was pursuing detrimental to American security as well as the agency's development. They produced few benefits compared to the costs, and if policymakers considered a particular operation vitally important, the military should undertake it. Further, as Kennan had feared, Wisner's success in distancing the Office of Policy Coordination from the State Department produced disconnects between its activities and the administration's strategic priorities and specific foreign policies and programs. As things stood when Smith took over from Hillenkoetter, Wisner's OPC was out of control.[16]

Smith lacked the authority either to divorce covert operations from the CIA or to abolish the OPC. So he sought to bring both tightly under his command. Less than a week into his tenure, the new DCI, empowered by the 1949 Central Intelligence Act, announced that he was assuming administrative control of the Office of Policy Coordination; State and Defense would now submit their guidance, such as it was, to him, not Wisner. Because Smith was Smith, not Hillenkoetter, the departments agreed. A year later, the NSC confirmed the DCI's authority over covert operations by replacing NSC 10/2 with NSC 10/5. After ordering a review of all ongoing or planned OPC operations, Smith then canceled one-third of them.[17]

Smith's other major institutional initiative for the purpose of reigning in Wisner was not completed until 1952: he merged the Office of Policy Coordination with the Office of Special Operations. This merger resulted in the improved integration of covert action and clandestine collection. In addition, Smith expected that because Wisner's autonomy was now undercut, the staff members of the OSO were normatively more experienced and "professional" than those in OPC. Further, their loyalty was entirely to CIA and not divided between State, Defense, and the Office of Policy Coordination, and their priority on collection would override OPC's predisposition toward operations. Smith was wrong. In fact, his reforms actually achieved the opposite of what he intended.[18]

Two phenomena conspired against Smith's achieving his goal, only one of which he could control. That was his choice of personnel. When Smith merged the Office of Policy Coordination and the Office of Special Operations, he appointed Allen Dulles to head the new entity—called the Directorate of Plans. But shortly thereafter, he promoted Dulles, naming him to succeed William Jackson as his deputy director of central intelligence (DDCI). Frank Wisner was the logical replacement to lead the Directorate of Plans. But as Wisner's deputy, Smith appointed Richard Helms. Helms was another OSS veteran, but he came out of the Office of Special Operations. In principle, Smith therefore assumed that Helms would serve as a check and balance. But miscalculating, Smith insufficiently took into account the influence of Allen Dulles. Dulles was as predisposed toward operations as Wisner, and his selection as DDCI tipped the scales in that direction.

Operations Eclipse Analysis

Even had Smith not appointed Dulles the agency's deputy director, the climate of the time all but assured the supremacy of operations. Both NSC 10/5 and NSC 68 called for a stepped-up campaign of covert economic, political, and psychological warfare against the Soviet Union, its clients, and its potential targets. Initially the Office of Policy Coordination concentrated on Europe, setting up "stay behind" networks to prepare for sabotage and related activities in the event of a Soviet invasion, establishing relations with labor unions and among Soviet and East European emigrés in Germany and Vienna, and seeking to promote resistance organizations in Eastern Europe, such as Poland's Freedom and Independence Movement (known by its Polish initials, WIN). It also funded "liberationist" broadcasts through Radio Free Europe and Radio Liberty.

The volume of this activity then spiked with the outbreak of the Korean War. Within a short time, and with the encouragement of the Joint Chiefs of Staff, the CIA's Office of Policy Coordination was engaged in paramilitary activities, normally in support of conventional military operations, throughout the Far East, most prominently in Indochina (Vietnam and Laos, in particular). In the Philippines, directed by Edward Lansdale, an

OSS veteran and Army colonel who would soon gain notoriety because of his activities in Vietnam and Cuba, the CIA played a vital role in the defeat of the Huk (Hukbong Mapaspalaya ng Bayan or Hukbalahap) rebellion and the elevation of Raymond Magsaysay to the presidency.[19] By 1952, when the Office of Policy Coordination was officially folded into the Directorate of Plans, its reach had extended to Latin America, where the aborted 1952 Project FORTUNE intended to oust the perceived communist-influenced government of Jacobo Arbenz Guzmán in Guatemala The scope of these activities required a much expanded covert capacity. So OPC grew, and Smith's organizational revisions institutionalized that growth.[20]

Indeed, compared to the Office of Policy Coordination prior to the outbreak of the Korean War and its merger with the Office of Special Operations, the Directorate of Plans in 1952 was almost unrecognizable. The metrics tell an astounding story. OPC personnel totaled 302 in 1949. By 1952 it had mushroomed to 2812, excluding 3142 overseas contractors. The OPC had 7 overseas bases 1949; in 1952 it had forty-seven. During that same time, the budget rose from $4,700,000 to $82,000,000. Combining all it components, by 1952 clandestine collection accounted for more than half (60%) of the CIA's personnel strength and almost three-quarters (74%) of the total budget allocation. Significantly, when measured by either of these indices, operations by 1952 eclipsed collection and counterintelligence. This scale and structure would remain essentially unchanged until after the Vietnam War.[21]

Smith was anxious about the implications of this imbalance of resources and focus on the CIA's future. He feared, it turns out justifiably, the continual expansion of the CIA's clandestine, indeed paramilitary operations and, concomitantly, the continual erosion of its core mission: collection and analysis. The CIA's growing capacity for covert operations, he warned the NSC, "will inevitably militate against the performance" of the agency's "primary intelligence functions."[22]

But bureaucratic momentum is difficult to reverse regardless of the circumstances, and Smith confronted a zeitgeist that all but guaranteed that he would not have the opportunity to exercise the influence necessary to engineer a reversal. President Dwight D. Eisenhower entered office committed to improving America's intelligence capabilities and integrating the CIA more seamlessly into a better coordinated and more coherent process for the formulation and implementation of national security policy and strategy. He designated Smith, his former chief of staff in whom he had supreme confidence, as a pivotal figure. Eisenhower appointed John Foster Dulles secretary of state, and as director of central intelligence, he promoted the current deputy director of central intelligence and Foster's brother, Allen. Smith would serve as Foster Dulles's undersecretary of state (a lateral move in those days). In this capacity, the president expected that his long-time aide could not only assist the two Dulleses but he also could keep a watchful eye on both on behalf of Eisenhower, who knew neither of the brothers well.

Thus began the heyday of the CIA. As undersecretary of state, Smith chaired the Operations Coordinating Board (OCB), established by Eisenhower in 1953 to monitor implementation of international programs, overt and covert, and evaluate their effectiveness. The OCB never functioned well, and in October 1954 a frustrated as well as ill Walter Bedell Smith left the administration. As a result, the administration lost the most powerful voice in restraining the expansion of the CIA's covert capabilities and the Directorate of Plans' virtual colonization of the agency. The official probably most responsible for and certainly most identified with this expansion and colonization was Smith's successor as DCI, Allen Dulles. Dulles spent the bulk of World War II running the OSS office in Bern, Switzerland, the center of an array of operations directed against both the Germans and the Italians. In the most famous of these, Operation Sunrise, Dulles caused a stir within the Grand Alliance by coming within a hair of arranging the secret surrender of the German forces in Italy.[23]

Having emerged from the war with the reputation as America's greatest spymaster, and after that playing a seminal role in the CIA's evolution, first as the head of Interim Survey Group and subsequently as the initial deputy director of plans and then as deputy director of central intelligence DCI, and then taking over the agency from Smith at the same time that his brother took charge of the State Department, Allen Dulles's appointment as director assured the CIA's elevation to the constellation of government organs' top echelon. Eisenhower, whose enthusiasm for intelligence, including covert operations, also dated to World War II, selected Dulles as DCI largely because he knew he would boost the agency's profile. Dulles did not disappoint him. Many of the CIA's top officers, individuals like Wisner; Richard Helms; Tracy Barnes, Wisner's chief deputy; and Richard Bissell, who would succeed Wisner as deputy director for plans, shared Dulles's background and values and welcomed his leadership. Outgoing and gregarious, the secretary of state's younger brother moved comfortably through the halls of Congress and counted among his friends movers and shakers from the worlds of business, law, and, perhaps most important, journalism. Dulles became the highly regarded public face of the CIA, protecting its personnel from the witch hunts associated with Joseph McCarthy. No DCI ever had such intimate ties to Foggy Bottom, the Pentagon, and the White House. Dulles's leadership, stature, and bureaucratic acumen were vital to the CIA's transformation from the NSC's stepchild to its vital instrument.[24]

Even more important than its new director to the evolution of the CIA's stature, nevertheless, were the president's priorities. Eisenhower had campaigned on a platform calling for the aggressive "liberation" of "captive peoples." His rhetoric can in no small part be attributed to partisan posturing. Still, Eisenhower firmly believed that shadow warfare provided a low-risk means to achieve highly desirable Cold War gains, whether defined as reversing perceived communist successes, especially in the developing world, or forcing the Soviets to defend their own backyard. The growth in the size and power of the atomic and then nuclear arsenals of both Washington and Moscow under Eisenhower's watch heightened the appeal of covert projects. Any conventional war held the potential for spiraling out of control and across the nuclear threshold, producing intolerable costs to both sides. As a military strategist and long-range planner, moreover, Eisenhower believed that policies and programs must be informed by most reliable intelligence reports and estimates.[25]

Accordingly, Eisenhower's initiatives went well beyond his appointment of Allen Dulles. In his first term, he approved NSC 5412/2, establishing a "Special Group" of representatives from State and Defense who would meet with DCI Dulles and the White House special assistant for national security affairs, initially Robert Cutler, for the purpose of reviewing plans for covert projects and providing better cover for the president to "plausibly deny" authorizing them. (Often called the 5412 committee, it was renamed the 303 Committee during the administration of Lyndon B. Johnson, after the room in which it met in White House Annex, and under Nixon it became the 40 Committee, following the number of the president's new directive, National Security Decision Memorandum (NSDM) 40, issued on February 17, 1970.) Eisenhower also created the President's Board of Consultants on Foreign Intelligence Activities (PBCFIA), composed of retired military officials, distinguished educators, business leaders, and comparable others, to provide him with "fresh eyes" advice.

Perhaps even more revealing of Eisenhower's perspective and predisposition, he assembled an ad hoc committee under the chairmanship of General James Doolittle, the World War II Air Force ace and Medal of Honor recipient, to "make any recommendations calculated to improve the conduct of these [covert] operations." The Doolittle Committee reported that America's security demanded that it possess a "covert psychological, political, and paramilitary organization more effective, more unique, and if necessary, more ruthless than that employed by the enemy." This organization must "subvert, sabotage and destroy our enemies by more clever, more sophisticated and more effective methods than those used against us." It must reconsider "long-standing American concepts of 'fair play.'"[26] The Doolittle Commission did not need to remind its readers that this concept of "fair play" had historically deterred the development of US intelligence capabilities.

The Special Group met infrequently and, much like the Operations Coordinating Board, never arrived at sufficiently precise criteria by which to evaluate CIA projects. That left the initiative with the agency itself, which is what DCI Allen Dulles and Deputy Director for Plans Frank Wisner preferred. Intrinsically drawn to covert actions and recognizing that the greater their number the more integral to security strategy the CIA would become, and the larger its budget would grow, Dulles encouraged Wisner and his staff to develop the most imaginative plans. "[N]o matter how important [intelligence] collection is," Richard Helms quoted Dulles as explaining in 1953, "in the short and even the long run, it just doesn't *cost* very much." While comparatively inexpensive, covert operations did cost, and that was the name of Washington's bureaucratic game. "If there's no real money involved," Helms reported that Dulles continued, neither those in Congress nor in the administration itself would "pay much attention to us."[27]

The 1949 Central Intelligence Act exempted Dulles from the need to report or justify how he spent his funds. In addition, because Congress had little interest in exercising oversight, for the CIA's first quarter-century that oversight was, in the words of one of agency's foremost early scholars, "sporadic, unsystematic, incomplete." Legislators across the aisle agreed that that the CIA represented "a first line defense against Communism," and Dulles cultivated outstanding relations with the members who counted most, regardless of party affiliation. The select senators and representatives who chaired understaffed subcommittees of the Armed Services and Appropriations Committees of each House closely guarded the agency's secrets, setting a precedent which met with their colleagues' enthusiastic approval. Ignorance was an excellent strategy for avoiding accountability. When the CIA's director appeared before the committees, recalled Massachusetts Republican Leverett Saltonstall, a ranking member of both the Senate Armed Forces and Appropriations Committees, "members would ask few questions which dealt with internal Agency matters or with specific operations." Saltonstall freely admitted that personally he preferred to know as little as possible. Occasional proposals intended to strengthen legislative oversight produced some reforms, but their cumulative effect was inconsequential. The leaders of each chamber established CIA subcommittees in their respective Armed Services and the Appropriations Committees. The legislators who comprised these committees, however, were the same who had previously been privy to Dulles's classified briefings, most notably Senator Richard Russell, Representative Carl Vinson, and Representative Clarence Cannon. A total of about a dozen congressmen monitored CIA operations, and even among this small number some knew much more than others. The Eisenhower years were the centerpiece of an era of "Congressional undersight."[28]

Thus, although President Eisenhower approved every covert action undertaken during his administration, the CIA operated under few formal controls in the 1950s. Under Wisner's direction, the Directorate of Plans developed responses to a broad array of contingencies. DCI Dulles would often bounce the ideas off his brother when the two regularly lunched on Sundays at the home of sister Eleanor Lansing Dulles, who also worked for State.[29] For approval he would meet informally with the president and his chief advisors, which included, of course, the secretary of state. Only after Foster Dulles's death in 1959 did the 5412 Committee play an active role in the process. In fact, the committee had not yet been created when the administration launched its first, and some argue to this day its most successful, operations.

The CIA directed its initial covert operation during the Eisenhower administration in 1953 against the government of Dr. Mohammad Mossadegh in Iran—Project TPAJAX. Mossadegh had locked horns with the British-dominated Anglo-Iranian Oil Company (AIOC) when he nationalized the company months after becoming Iran's prime minister in 1951 following the assassination of his predecessor. The CIA's intelligence capabilities in Iran were at the time negligible. The country was long situated within Britain's sphere of influence, and as a consequence the CIA had developed few assets of its own. Focused as they were on the Soviet threat, the agency, therefore, had no reason to challenge the judgment of the Clement Attlee government's Secret Intelligence Service (MI6). It concluded that Mossadegh's nationalization of the AIOC was more than an attack on British economic interests; it was evidence of the pervasive influence of the communist Tudeh party. Truman's security advisers agreed, but when MI6 proposed to collaborate with the CIA on a plan by which the Iranian shah, Muhammad Reza Pahlevi, would remove Mossadegh from power, Smith resisted. This was precisely the kind of operation he wanted the agency to avoid. Secretary of State Dean Acheson, moreover, fretted that an unsuccessful action against Mossadegh could produce a serious disruption of the global oil supply even as it provided grist for the communists' propaganda mill. The Soviets might even be able to use the opportunity to regain the influence in Iran that it lost in 1946.[30]

The Eisenhower administration found MI6's proposal more appealing. This was to a degree because, soon after their electoral promise aggressively to pursue liberation, Eisenhower and Secretary of State Dulles saw the ouster of Mossadegh as a low-risk and low-cost means to set the tone for the presidency. Yet a complementary factor was the transition from Smith to Allen Dulles as director of central intelligence. Much more than his predecessor, Dulles wanted the agency actively engaged in the business of covertly engineering regime change. Kermit ("Kim") Roosevelt, Teddy Roosevelt's grandson and the chief of the CIA's Near East and Africa Division, tweaked the MI6-generated plan to ensure that the agency was the leading partner and that British financial interests would not benefit at the expense of justifiable Iranian ones. Those desiderata achieved, on July 1, 1953, Prime Minister Winston Churchill, Foreign Secretary Anthony Eden, and MI6 chief John Alexander Sinclair approved for the United Kingdom. Ten days later, Eisenhower and both Dulles brothers did the same for the United States. TPAJAX began in August. Despite some initial missteps that caused the shah to panic and flee to Rome, through strategically placed bribes, staged demonstrations supported by the Iranian Army, and Kim Roosevelt's imaginative improvisation, the operation succeeded. By the close of August 19, Mossadegh was in prison and General Fazlollah Zahedi was Iran's premier. Shortly thereafter the shah was welcomed back and restored to the Peacock Throne. The CIA had come of age.[31]

TPAJAX was a prelude to a larger, more complex, and also, according to Washington's criteria at the time, triumphal operation. PBSUCCESS, which the CIA launched only a year after it successfully restored the shah to power in Iran, registered what the Eisenhower administration considered its greatest covert coup—ousting the regime of Jacobo Arbenz Guzmán in Guatemala. As was the case with Iran, Eisenhower inherited a situation in Guatemala in which communists appeared poised to gain predominant power, if they had not already done so. Indeed, the administration assessed the threat in Guatemala as more imminent and more severe than that in Iran. A 1944 revolution had overthrown the long-time *caudillo* (strong-man) Jorge Ubico Castañeda, leading to the election of Juan José Arévalo, a "spiritual socialist." When the Arévalo government began to implement its agenda of social and economic reform by instituting programs such as rent control and a labor code, the United Fruit Company, Guatemala's largest landholder and most powerful economic force, sounded the alarm that communists had penetrated Arévalo's regime.

Initially the State Department discounted these warnings. The CIA, however, which relied on contacts cultivated by the FBI during the time when Latin America came under its aegis, corroborated United Fruit's assessment. When, in the last year of Truman's tenure, Guatemala's National Assembly enacted legislation proposed by Arévalo's successor, Arbenz, to nationalize massive swaths of United Fruit's property, United Fruit's charge that communism had come to Guatemala became the accepted wisdom. Nevertheless, Truman aborted a plan hatched by Nicaragua's *caudillo* Anastasio Somoza to orchestrate a collective effort by Guatemala's Central American neighbors to oust Arbenz. Smith characteristically expressed reservations, and again Acheson supported him.[32]

But as had been the case with Iran, Allen Dulles was eager and confident, and his brother and President Eisenhower were sympathetic. Buoyed by the success of TPAJAX, in the latter months of 1953 the CIA planned PBSUCCESS. In Iran, the CIA strategy was to buttress bribery with psychological warfare. In Guatemala, the CIA reversed the equation, and added assassination as a variable to hold in reserve.[33] By early 1954 it had financed the creation in Nicaragua of an "Army of Liberation," composed largely of mercenaries and headed by Colonel Carlos Castillo Armas. It concurrently established a "Voice of Liberation" radio station, which broadcast inflated accounts of the size and quality of the Army of Liberation. On June 18, 1954, the Voice of Liberation announced that the invasion had begun, although the military operations were literally for show. The invasion was not intended "in any sense [as] a conventional military operation," explained a CIA official. Rather, what mattered was the "psychological impact."[34] The CIA designed PBSUCCESS to convince the Army, or more specifically its leadership, that it could not avoid choosing between continuing to support Arbenz or defecting to the counterrevolutionary forces. Because the United States stood behind the latter, the Army's very survival depended on its making the "right" choice. If the Army continued to collaborate with Arbenz, as an institution it would suffer "a terrible fate."[35]

PBSUCCESS was a $3,000,000 gamble that succeeded. Still, there were complications that required more direct and heavy-handed involvement than Eisenhower would have preferred. Britain and France threatened to support a Guatemalan-sponsored resolution to the Security Council, calling for a United Nations investigation of Washington's role. But both relented after some arm-twisting from the administration. Moreover, when Arbenz resigned on July 27 before fleeing the country, he turned over power to General Enrique Díaz, the chief of his armed forces. Castillo Armas remained distant from Guatemala City. Consequently, it took the not-at-all-subtle engagement of US Ambassador John Peurifoy to arrange for Castillo Armas to march unopposed into the city and wrest control of the government from other aspirants. While DCI Allen Dulles savored the victory in silence, brother Foster proclaimed to the world "the biggest success in the last five years against Communism." Of course, he credited the Guatemalan people, not the CIA.[36]

The operations in Iran and Guatemala served as cornerstones for a legend of invincibility that came to define the CIA by the end of Eisenhower's two terms in office. Yet that legend, which over the subsequent decades would lead to a reckless number of covert and paramilitary operations on the one hand and unrealistic expectations on the other, was built on quicksand. While Allen Dulles, Frank Wisner, and their colleagues, with the support of the White House and Foggy Bottom, poured their hearts and the CIA's funds into the Directorate of Plans, they neglected a basic requirement for effectiveness: training. It warrants acknowledgment that a number of CIA officials and operatives were veterans of the OSS, and covert and paramilitary operations were central to the OSS's mission. That said, the OSS lacked anything resembling a doctrine, what training its operatives had was almost entirely experiential learning, and Donovan's very mixed record in World War II service was a poor reason to assess those experiences as sufficient. When paramilitary operations became integral to the CIA's portfolio with the establishment of the Office of Policy Coordination, the agency tried to recruit more military personnel. Achieving only limited success, it expanded its own training programs. For this purpose at first it borrowed space from the Army at Fort Benning, Georgia, but by the time Eisenhower took office, the CIA had built its own facility ██████████████████, known popularly as the Farm, to train its officers. Although the site is no longer a secret, the curriculum still is.[37]

The few snippets about paramilitary training at the "the Farm," which have appeared in memoirs of former CIA personnel, have undergone rigorous pre-publication review. Hence, while Valerie Plame, for example, refers in *Fair Game* to "three months of hard training," the many redacted sentences, paragraphs, and entire pages leave the reader guessing as to the specifics of the training. Perhaps because she was less of a lightning rod, the CIA's pre-publication reviewers allowed Lindsay Moran to provide more details in her memoir. She identifies a range of challenging exercises that she undertook, and makes clear that she found them exhilarating and beneficial. In the end, nevertheless, she concludes that "The farm ... was all part of an elaborate game for men who'd never really grown up," a "kind of intense adult summer camp experience." Because the reliability of such memoirs is questionable, confident assessments of CIA case officers' paramilitary training must await the release of more evidence. That granted, while this training improved over the years, it remains less intensive, extensive, or comprehensive that that received by military personnel. From the formative years of the Office of Policy Coordination on, CIA expected its covert and paramilitary operatives, reads the recently declassified internal history, "to learn by doing."[38]

They did, but the lessons were often painful. Even during the halcyon days under Eisenhower, Iran and Guatemala were the exceptions that proved the rule that covert, paramilitary operations more often than not ended in failure. For three years beginning in 1953, the CIA expended vast amounts of dollars and man hours to build a tunnel into East Berlin for the purpose of tapping into Eastern bloc military communications. The Soviets knew about the project from the start. They allowed the CIA to build the tunnel so that they could conceal the identity of their mole and then "discover" the tunnel. Propaganda from sources such as Radio Free Europe, covertly funded by the CIA, encouraged if not caused uprisings in East Germany in 1953 and Hungary in 1956. In neither case did the CIA have the capacity to take significant action to support the insurrectionists, and Eisenhower did not authorize it to take any. In the latter instance, the paralysis of the CIA even after Soviet tanks rolled through the streets of Budapest contributed to Frank Wisner's mental breakdown and eventual suicide. Subsequent CIA projects, most notoriously its efforts to oust Sukarno in Indonesia and Patrice Lumumba in Congo (which contributed to Lumumba's execution by government forces with whom the United States conspired) but also less familiar operations in Syria, the Congo, the Dominican Republic, Tibet, British Guiana, Southeast Asia, and elsewhere ended up either as abject failures, achieved little of consequence, or (and sometimes) would come back to haunt the United States for years. Yet the legend of invincibility endured.[39]

The CIA career of Richard Bissell and the agency's most public failure, the Bay of Pigs operation, underscore this dynamic. Prior to joining the agency, Bissell lacked experience with intelligence. His education at Groton, Yale, and the London School of Economics had led him to Ivy

League professorships and then the Commerce Department during World War II, where he coordinated allied shipping. In the war's aftermath he played a vital role in launching the Marshall (European Recovery) Plan, after which he followed Paul Hoffman, his former boss at the Economic Cooperation Administration, to the Ford Foundation. But Bissell was as restless as he was brilliant. By 1954 he was ready for a change in careers, and his close relationships with such CIA stalwarts as Wisner and Tracy Barnes, coupled with the Ford Foundation's intimate connection with the agency, pointed him in the direction of the CIA. Allen Dulles welcomed him enthusiastically and immediately placed him high up in the chain of command of PBSUCCESS as his personal assistant.[40]

Following Wisner's breakdown in 1958, Dulles appointed Bissell deputy director for plans. After only four years in the agency, and having received no training other than what he learned "by doing," he was put in charge of all covert and paramilitary operations. Almost immediately his skill level was put to the test. On the first day of January 1959, Fidel Castro and the 26th of July Movement forced long-time dictator Fulgencio Batista into exile and declared the start of a new Cuba. Bissell's first assignment for the CIA had been to assist Dulles in orchestrating the overthrow of the Arbenz regime in Guatemala. As deputy director for plans, he was assigned to plot the overthrow of the Castro regime in Cuba.

Although the Eisenhower administration had quickly granted recognition to the Castro government, each passing month brought seemingly more robust evidence of communist influence and sympathies. Castro instituted an agrarian reform that, as had Arbenz's a half-dozen years earlier, primarily targeted US interests. It expropriated some $1 billion of US property. Castro then took a page out of Stalinist books by holding public trials that led to the execution of Batista's henchmen. More generally, the bearded revolutionary railed against the Yanqui imperialists from the north. More substantively, he demanded that the United States relinquish its naval base on Guantánamo Bay and, convinced that US spies abounded, reduce the size of its Embassy in Havana. Eisenhower responded by embargoing Cuban exports to the United States. Castro responded by concluding a treaty with the Soviet Union by which Cuba exchanged its sugar for arms, machinery, and advisors.[41]

In fall 1959 Eisenhower approved a State Department proposal that the CIA formulate a plan to rid the Cuban people of its communist leader. Bissell, not surprisingly, drew on PBSUCCESS for his model. He established a task force directed by Jacob Esterline within J. C. King's Western Hemisphere Division to devise the strategy, which began with training exiles in preparation for an invasion of Cuba. Initially, the camps were located in the United States and the Panama Canal Zone, but by spring 1960 they had moved to Guatemala. Soon thereafter, David Atlee Philips reprised a role he had auditioned in Guatemala, establishing an anti-Castro "black" radio station on Swan Island off the coast of Honduras. Philips was even able to use some of the equipment that he had left on the island in 1954. In March, Eisenhower gave the CIA the go-ahead to continue preparations for "A Program of Covert Action Against the Castro Regime." Radio Swan began to broadcast two months later.[42]

Bissell appreciated the difficulties and the risks. CIA planners recognized that an amphibious invasion of Cuba presented considerably more problems than did the Army of Liberation's entry into Guatemala from neighboring Honduras. So, too, would pursuing combat operations from unprotected beachheads. Hence Bissell and the CIA modified the original plan. TRINIDAD (originally code-named PLUTO) called for a significantly larger force of better-trained and equipped exiles, supported by unidentifiable planes based in Nicaragua, to land on Cuba's southern coast. The premise was that the combination of the invasion, air strikes, and black propaganda would incite disenchanted Cubans to revolt and/or cause Castro's military to defect and his government to disintegrate. The worst scenario Bissell envisioned was that a stalemate between Castro and the invading force would ensue. In that circumstance, the deputy director for plans predicted, the Organization of American States would intervene. US control of the OAS ensured a satisfactory outcome in Cuba, one that excluded Castro from power.[43]

Eisenhower never approved TRINIDAD's execution. Encouraging the CIA to continue to be "bold and imaginative" in its planning, however, he bequeathed the operation to his successor, John F. Kennedy. TRINIDAD's appeal to Kennedy was all but irresistible. By disarming the "dagger" aimed at America's heart, as JFK described Castro's Cuba during the 1960 campaign, the successful operation would solidify the image of himself that the young president sought to cultivate: the daring, dashing, and vigorous representative of a new generation of American leaders. Kennedy also had confidence in Bissell, whom he identified as Allen Dulles's successor as director of central intelligence.[44]

Both civilian and military advisors to Kennedy expressed doubts whether the invading force, even when buttressed by propaganda and supported by air strikes, was sufficient to achieve Castro's ouster. But the president intrinsically preferred the CIA's creativity to State's conservatism, and the military did not rule out success. Further, Bissell continued to argue that on the one hand the plan would work and, on the other hand, to abort the project now would anger and alienate the trained Cuban exile force. He could not guarantee the CIA could control them. Kennedy agreed that planning should continue, with the proviso that the planners scale back the invasion to decrease the likelihood of allegations of US culpability. The CIA dutifully reformulated TRINIDAD as Operation ZAPATA (ZAPATA was the Pentagon's code name; in the CIA it was JMARC). Supported by fewer dramatic air strikes both on D-Day and two days before, the brigade of Cuban exiles (the 2506 Brigade) would establish a quieter beachhead (actually three beachheads) at the more remote Bay of Pigs. These revisions convinced many of Bissell's chief lieutenants that the plan was doomed. Bissell remained a believer, however, and Kennedy believed in Bissell. On April 14, 1961, the president greenlighted the operation. In his view, if the initial invasion proved unsuccessful, the brigade of exiles would turn into a guerilla force and continue the fight from the mountains and countryside. Bissell assumed a different plan B: if secured beachheads did not produce a stalemate conducive to OAS resolution, Kennedy would approve direct US intervention.[45]

Both Bissell and Kennedy were mistaken, and the result was a "Perfect Failure." At the last minute, the president, jittery over the prospect of America's exposure, reduced the number of B-26 air strikes scheduled on D-Day minus two, April 15, from sixteen to eight. Then, on the advice of Secretary of State Dean Rusk, the president canceled the D-Day strike altogether. There was no popular uprising, the exiles could not escape from the beaches, and Kennedy never had any intention of committing US forces. The conclusion of the post mortem inquiry conducted by a committee headed by General Maxwell Taylor and including Attorney General Robert Kennedy, Chief of Naval Operations Arleigh Burke, and DCI Dulles, was that this cancelation of the airstrikes was the chief cause of the debacle. Success depended on neutralizing Castro's T-33 fighter planes, and the failure to do so exposed the invaders to capture, imprisonment, or death. The Taylor Committee missed the most fundamental cause, however. Bissell and his allies in the CIA fully appreciated the risks, and they fully appreciated that the odds of success diminished as both Eisenhower and Kennedy modified the plan. Yet flushed with the pride and arrogance produced by the successes in Iran and Guatemala, the deputy director for plans and his allies perceived no reason why they could not beat those odds once again. The CIA's invincibility may have been a myth, but they believed that myth. They also believed in

Kennedy's campaign rhetoric and his exhortation that Americans pay any price and bear any burden.[46]

They paid the price. Allen Dulles's participation on the Taylor Committee was his final substantive act as director of central intelligence. During the summer of 1961 Dulles did restore some of his credibility with Kennedy. By briefing the President on vital intelligence, the CIA (in collaboration with the Britain's MI6) had gained through the defection of Colonel Oleg Penkovsky, the deputy head of the foreign section of the Soviet military's Office of Scientific Research, he helped Kennedy successfully manage the Berlin Crisis. Kennedy then arranged for Dulles to retire on a high note, shortly after he had dedicated the CIA's new headquarters on 125 acres in Langley, Virginia. Bissell, his promotion to DCI now out of the question, retired the following February. Among his last acts as deputy director for plans was to reactivate Operation Mongoose, a sweeping covert program aimed at bringing down Cuba's Communist regime by psychological warfare, sabotage, disrupting the economy, arming dissidents, and assassinating key leaders, including Castro.[47]

Spies in the Sky

The pivotal role Richard Bissell played in the Bay of Pigs fiasco ended his CIA career and forever tarnished his name. That it did is both ironic and appropriate. It is ironic because, while the CIA's paramilitary operation in Guatemala and Cuba bookended his CIA career, he was far outside his element in managing such undertakings. It was Bissell's contributions to collection and, by extension, analysis that drove his meteoric rise in rank and reputation. Thus, the fallout from his identification with the Bay of Pigs is appropriate, because the history of the CIA is a history of competition between covert, particularly paramilitary operations, and its core mission of collection and analysis. As a consequence of this competition, the latter has consistently suffered.

For Bissell, the past really was prologue. As soon as he completed his assignment on PBSUCCESS, Dulles assigned him to the CIA's most pressing task: developing a greater capacity for acquiring intelligence on Soviet capabilities. For political as well as strategic reasons, no collection effort was more vital to Eisenhower. And for the still-fledgling agency, no challenge was more difficult. In his capacity as DCI, Allen Dulles began each meeting of Eisenhower's National Security Council with a briefing. With regard to the Soviet Union, he conceded early in the administration, US intelligence manifested "shortcomings of a serious nature." Richard Helms later referred to the absence of American knowledge about military and technological advances in the Soviet Union, especially the missile program, as "extraordinary;" Lawrence Houston called it "appalling." Underscoring this deficiency was the surprise by which the death of Joseph Stalin caught the administration in March 1953, and the agency's struggle to provide confident estimates of the consequences and implications of the successor regime.[48]

The series of "CAESAR" reports, produced by a small group of "Kremlinologists" established within the CIA's Office of Current Intelligence to focus exclusively on Soviet internal developments, showed little improvement. The problem, it became evident, was the lack the human assets (HUMINT) capable of piercing the Soviet Union's veil of secrecy. Pyotr Popov was the rare exception. A Soviet military intelligence officer whom the CIA did not need to turn because he approached the agency in 1953, Popov provided valuable information on the strength of Moscow's ground forces and technological advances. But he was arrested in 1959 and executed in 1960. Of greater historical significance, for the CIA's first fifteen years, Popov was unique. To compensate, on the recommendation of Smith, in October 1952 (the year before Popov surfaced) by secret executive order Truman established the National Security Agency (NSA) to collect Signals Intelligence and Electronic Intelligence (SIGINT and ELINT, respectively). But the agency's technological assets were immature, and with the secretary of defense serving as its executive agent (and controlling the budget), the NSA reported directly to the National Security Council. What intelligence it collected often did not find its way to the CIA. The Soviet Union was the Company's most impenetrable "hard target."[49]

As early as 1946, the United States began to consider aerial surveillance as a potentially valuable instrument for monitoring scientific and technical (S&T) developments in the "denied areas" within the Soviet Union especially, but also in the People's Republic of China and the Eastern bloc. Truman officials fully appreciated, however, that the Kremlin would perceive such overflights as hostile. In addition, US public opinion, with recollections of World War II's "Grand Alliance" still fresh and also still suspicious of any peacetime spying, could not be expected complacently to accept such provocative and devious acts. Hence, even ardent advocates of overflights stressed that it "is extraordinarily important that a means of long-range aerial reconnaissance be devised which cannot be detected."[50]

Washington devised the means. By 1948, scientists and engineers had developed a 100-inch focal length camera capable of taking photographs from F-13 aircraft that could detect Soviet military installations the previous "oblique photography" would miss. Two years later, following the successful Soviet test of an atomic device and outbreak of the Korean War, the need to collect intelligence on possible Soviet intentions to launch an attack, especially a surprise attack, drove Truman to authorize overflights of Soviet and Chinese "denied territory." RB-45C air-refuelable reconnaissance bombers and modified B-47B jet bombers flew out of Britain's Sculthorpe Royal Air Force Base and Yokota Air Base, west of Tokyo. When Eisenhower took office in 1953, he expanded aerial surveillance by authorizing the use of additional bases in Alaska and Greenland. Yet the potential for producing an international incident was a continuing concern. If these "secret" flights extended sufficiently deep into the Soviet Union to photograph the most remote and presumably valuable installations, the likelihood of the Soviets shooting one down was considerable.[51]

There matters stood through the first eighteen months of the Eisenhower administration. Using reconfigured jet bombers (such as the RB-57A-1, nicknamed the "Heart Throb"), the Air Force conducted overflights of Eastern Europe and Asia in order to acquire intelligence. The targets were somewhat hit or miss, and no attempts were made to overfly the Soviet Union's hardest targets. Air Force coordination with the CIA was at best unsystematic, moreover, in large part because Allen Dulles was reluctant to assume significant responsibility. At the start of his tenure, DCI Smith had established a Scientific Intelligence Committee to manage the CIA's S&T efforts, but the agency had not developed much of a capacity. Dulles was content to leave the inadequacy unaddressed. By ceding aerial surveillance to the Air Force, the CIA could concentrate on activities for which he considered it best suited: stealing secrets, recruiting assets, and conducting paramilitary operations. Richard Helms, Wisner's deputy in the Directorate of Plans at the time, put into words Dulles's attitude. "I am persuaded that this Agency should stick to its knitting and not permit itself to be pushed into an area of activity which would inevitably overstrain its resources," he wrote.[52]

Regardless of what Dulles, Helms, and others defined as "knitting," intelligence collection was integral to the CIA's mission and vital to American security policy. So the Eisenhower administration pushed, and Dulles made incremental concessions. The CIA would collaborate with the Air Force on overflights, but its primary mission would be to drop, supply, and retrieve agents, distribute leaflets, and engage in complementary activities related to political and psychological warfare and even paramilitary operations. Only as a "secondary" mission would the agency assist in aerial surveillance, and even then "no methods will be used which will in any way militate against the success or security of the primary mission." The CIA insisted as well that the Department of Defense assume financial responsibility for Research and Development and share with the CIA the cost for purchasing, installing, and maintaining equipment.[53]

But the Soviet successful test of a thermonuclear device in August 1953 and the administration's adoption of a New Look strategy at the end of that year that relied heavily on a retaliatory capability as a deterrent turned out to be a game changer for the CIA. Eisenhower's national security planners had "a critical need for intelligence information on Soviet capabilities for the delivery of mass destruction warheads, particularly against the continental United States," DCI Dulles wrote Air Force Chief of Staff Nathan Twining in May 1954. "Clandestine penetration efforts have not been sufficiently rewarding, and the [NSA's] electronic intercept approach is slow and the data is inherently difficult to analyze and interpret," he added. The United States therefore had to develop rapidly the specialized aircraft and operational capabilities necessary to undertake more effective air photographic and electronic reconnaissance.[54]

Although Dulles would have preferred that the Air Force take the lead in developing the aircraft and capabilities, Eisenhower assigned the task to the CIA. Dulles turned the assignment over to Bissell, who reached out to the resources he had available. Edwin H. Land, the Polaroid camera's inventor, headed the intelligence subcommittee of the Technological Capabilities Panel ("Surprise Attack Panel") that Eisenhower established in July 1954. Also on the subcommittee was Edward Purcell, a Nobel Prize-winning physicist from Harvard. Both appreciated that advancements in the quality of cameras, film, and lenses made possible very high-altitude photography. The key was to design an appropriate aircraft. Clarence "Kelly" Johnson of Lockheed had actually submitted such a design, the CL-282, but the Air Force had rejected it. It preferred to stick with its commitment to a proposed twin-engine spy plane, the X-16, and to experiment with balloons that could overfly the Soviet Union and then splash down in the Pacific.[55]

Land became a proponent of Kelly's CL-282 and, using Bissell as his point of contact, lobbied to have the CIA take over the overflight program. Despite the Air Force's protests, a still-reluctant Allen Dulles accepted the "offer." After a meeting on Wednesday, November 24, 1954, with DCI Dulles, Secretary of State Dulles, Secretary of Defense Charles Wilson, and Air Force Chief of Staff Twining, Eisenhower authorized the CIA to oversee and finance (through its secret contingency reserve fund) Lockheed's development of Kelly Johnson's design. Dulles put Bissell in charge of Project AQUATONE the day after Thanksgiving. While Lockheed went to work on constructing what came to be called the U[tility]-2 at its "Skunk Works" hangar in Burbank, California, Bissell set up a small office in downtown Washington, DC. Virtually unencumbered by any constraints because of the freewheeling style of management that became Bissell's trademark, by mid-1955, after only about a half-year of development, Lockheed informed him that the first plane, "Kelly's Angel," was ready to test. As insisted upon by Eisenhower, pilots could be recruited from the Strategic Air Command, but, given the sanctity of the doctrine of plausible deniability, they would fly as private citizens under contract to the CIA.[56]

The U-2's rapid development influenced Eisenhower's decision to electrify and thereby redefine the July 1955 Geneva summit by proposing his dramatic "Open Skies" initiative. Nikita Khrushchev, just then emerging from the pack of contenders as Stalin's successor, dismissed Open Skies as a ruse to allow the United States to spy on the Soviets. Not for the last time, Khrushchev miscalculated. By rejecting Eisenhower's perhaps disingenuous but more likely sincere offer for intelligence reciprocity, the Soviet Communist Party's first secretary allowed the United States to spy unilaterally.[57] Tests of the U-2 began in July 1955 and were completed by early 1956. Bissell, rebuffing with Eisenhower's support the Air Force efforts to wrest control of the project back from the CIA, arranged with Chancellor Konrad Adenauer to use the West German base at Wiesbaden. In May and June came the first missions. They targeted the Mediterranean and the Middle East. (A U-2 mission months later serendipitously photographed the movements of British, French, and Israeli forces in the lead-up to the October 1956 Suez crisis.) Bissell tasked the CIA's Photo-Intelligence Division (PID), under the direction of Arthur Lundahl, with interpreting the expected large volume of photographic intelligence.[58]

The initial overflight of the Soviet Union occurred, as fate would have it, on July 4, 1956. Eisenhower imposed a regimented system of control to lessen the risk. A proposal for a flight could originate in the military, the State Department, or the CIA. The initiator would send the proposal to Lt. General John K. Gerhart, the Air Force deputy chief of staff for plans and programs. Once he approved it, he would send it on to the Air Force chief of staff, who would forward it to the chair of the Joint Chiefs of Staff (initially Admiral Arthur Radford, then Twining), to the director of central intelligence, to the secretary of state, and finally the White House. Normally

Eisenhower's staff secretary, Colonel (later Brigadier General and ultimately General) Andrew Goodpaster, would hand-deliver the "proposal" to Eisenhower. Occasionally Bissell, usually accompanied by both Dulles brothers, would discuss a proposal with the president directly. Eisenhower reviewed every mission personally, and more than once revised the flight plan before signing off on it. Less than a handful in Congress ever learned officially that the United States overflew the Soviet Union.[59]

Most of the U-2 flights probed radar defenses and took photographs of military installations on the periphery of the Soviet Union. About twenty of them directly overflew Soviet territory in an effort to uncover military preparations for a possible surprise attack. Although coverage was imperfect because of the U-2s limited coverage of the massive Soviet land mass, intelligence collected from such flights provided Eisenhower with the confidence he needed to ward off allegations of US strategic inferiority and vulnerability. Often politically and bureaucratically motivated (Democrats and the Air Force were the worst offenders) and based on estimates of Soviet capabilities that did not include aerial photograph, these allegations were manifested most publicly in claims of first a "bomber gap" and then a "missile gap." To confirm that these gaps were illusory, Eisenhower, albeit with decreased frequency and great trepidation, continued to approve the flights. The president had reason to worry. The Soviets tracked the flights from the start. But they refrained from protesting publicly lest they concede that the Soviet military could not protect its own air space.[60]

The Soviet downing of Francis Gary Powers flight on May 1, 1960, realized Eisenhower's recurrent nightmare. Khrushchev's scuttled the Paris summit at which the president hoped to reach an arms control agreement. Eisenhower put an end to U-2 overflights of the Soviet Union.[61] The effect on America's strategic intelligence, nevertheless, and for that matter the CIA, was minimal. In part, this was because Eisenhower remained confident that America retained a strategic retaliatory capacity sufficient to deter a Soviet strike. In larger part, it was because the CIA was on the verge of becoming less dependent on the U-2. By 1960, the agency, which under Eisenhower progressively became the equal of the military services in estimating Soviet military power, had been at work for several years to produce a sleek supersonic jet successor to the U-2: the A-12.[62]

More significant still, for aerial surveillance the CIA intended to rely primarily on satellite photography, which had the potential to cover effectively the great expanse of Soviet territory more effectively and at far less risk. Dulles put the indefatigable Richard Bissell in charge of developing this project, too. As a spin-off from Air Force-directed satellite-development programs and in response to the Soviets' Sputnik successes, the CIA in 1958 launched Project CORONA. Massive technological obstacles and another, and more serious, turf battle between the agency and the Air Force plagued its early years. Compounding the problem was Bissell's need to balance his supervision of CORONA with his continuing responsibilities overseeing the U-2 and, after his appointment by Dulles as deputy director for plans, his new responsibilities for covert operations. To his disappointment and the frustration of Eisenhower, who hoped to replace the vulnerable U-2 with CORONA satellites, tests of the booster (first THOR and then ATLAS), the satellite with camera and film (AGENA), and the recovery system failed repeatedly. Had the CORONA system come on line by May 1, 1960, Eisenhower would not have felt compelled to approve one last U-2 flight to prepare for arms control talks with Khrushchev at Geneva.[63]

A successful CORONA launch and "catch" finally took place on August 18/19, 1960, the very day that the Soviets sentenced Francis Gary Powers to ten years in prison (In 1962, the Soviets agreed to exchange Powers for Rudolf Abel, the KGB's master spy whom the FBI had arrested in 1957). Before returning its payload, Discoverer XIV had completed seven passes over Soviet Union, thereby providing "more photographic coverage of the Soviet Union than all previous U-2 missions." For more than a decade afterward the satellite program, overseen by the CIA's Committee on Overhead Reconnaissance (COMOR) but run by the 1960-created National Reconnaissance Office (NRO), produced an increasing volume of progressively higher quality pictures of the Soviet Union — and elsewhere.[64]

Not even the most sophisticated advances in technology could keep precise track of the buildup of Soviet strategic forces, especially once the scope and pace accelerated in the mid-1960s. Nevertheless, the intelligence CORONA and its successor satellite programs provided about Soviet missile capabilities, the development of a nuclear program in the People's Republic of China, damage incurred during the 1967 Middle East War, and much more was unparalleled and invaluable. This intelligence provided the foundation for National Intelligence Estimates. These estimates, notwithstanding the frequent dissent of the military services, the Air Force, above all, bolstered successive administrations' confidence in the efficacy of the US nuclear deterrent. CORONA remained officially a secret until President Bill Clinton ordered its declassification in 1995; it remains one of the America's greatest intelligence successes.[65]

Notes

1   Open source intelligence—newspapers and other print publications, radio broadcasts, etc.—is of course very useful to analysts. But both producers and consumers of intelligence have historically, albeit often misguidedly, valued secret intelligence more.

2   Central Intelligent Group, Office of Research and Evaluation, ORE 1, "Soviet Foreign and Military Policy," with enclosures on "Soviet Foreign Policy" and "Soviet Military Policy," July 23, 1946, in *The CIA under Harry Truman*, ed. Michael Warner (Washington, DC: Center for the Study of Intelligence, 1994), 65–76.

3   ORE 1/1, "Revised Soviet Tactics in International Affairs," January 6, 1947, in Warner, *The CIA under Harry Truman*, 99–104; ORE 3/1, "Soviet Capabilities for the Development and Production of Certain Types of Weapons and Equipment," October, 31 1946, in *Assessing the Soviet Threat: The Early Cold War Years*, ed. Woodrow Kuhns, (Washington, DC: Center for the Study of Intelligence, 1997), 87; Preface, in Kuhns, *Assessing the Soviet Threat*, 13.

4   Douglas F. Garthoff, "Analyzing Soviet Politics and Foreign Policy," in *Watching the Bear: Essays on the CIA's Analysis of the Soviet Union*, ed. Gerald K. Hanes and Robert E. Leggett (Washington, DC: Government Printing Office, 2003), 57–60. For representative examples of daily and weekly summaries and national estimates, see Kuhns, *Assessing the Soviet Threat*.

5   Anne Karalekas, "History of the Central Intelligence Agency," in *The Central Intelligence Agency: History and Documents*, ed. William M. Leary (University: University of Alabama Press, 1984), 23–28.

6   "The Dulles-Jackson-Correa Report to the National Security Council on the Central Intelligence Agency and National Organization for Intelligence [summary]," in Leary, *The Central Intelligence Agency*, 134–42.

7   Dulles-Jackson-Correa Report, 134–42.

8   Sarah-Jane Corke, *US Covert Operations and Cold War Strategy: Truman, Secret Warfare and the CIA* (London: Routledge, 2008), 82–100; Peter Grose, *Operation Rollback: America's Secret War Behind the Iron Curtain* (NY: Houghton Mifflin, 2000), 45–52.

9   ORE 91-49, "Estimate of the Effects of the Soviet Possession of the Atomic Bomb on the United States and upon the Probabilities of Direct Soviet Military Action," April 6, 1950, with Appendices A (State), B (Army), C (ONI), D (Air Force), accessed on December 31, 2012, at http://www.foia.cia.gov/docs/DOC_0000258849/DOC_0000258849.pdf (emphasis in the original); Gregory Mitrovich, *Undermining the Kremlin: America's Strategy to Subvert the Soviet Bloc, 1947–1956* (Ithaca, NY: Cornell University Press,

2000), 50–53; NSC 68: United States Objectives and Programs for National Security (April 14, 1950): A Report to the President Pursuant to the President's Directive of January 31, 1950, in *American Cold War Strategy: Interpreting NSC 68*, ed. Ernest R. May (Boston, MA: Bedford/St. Martin's Press, 1993), 26–27, 33–34, 39.

10 Ludwell L. Montague, *General Walter Bedell Smith as Director of Central Intelligence, October 1950–February 1953* (University Park: Pennsylvania State University Press, 1992).

Ray S. Cline, *Secrets, Spies, and Soldiers: Blueprint for the Essential CIA* (Washington, DC: Acropolis Books, 1976), 108–09.

11 Quoted in Paul R. Pillar, *Intelligence and U.S. Foreign Policy: Iraq, 9/11, and Misguided Reform* (NY: Columbia University Press, 2011), 9.

12 Lawrence Houston memorandum to Walter Bedell Smith, August 29, 1950, in Warner, *CIA under Truman*, 341–45.

13 James Norent, "CIA's Analysis of the Soviet Economy," in Hanes and Legett, *Watching the Bear*, 17–56.

14 Appendix to *Selected Estimates of the Soviet Union, 1950–1959*, ed. Scott S. Koch (Washington, DC: Center for the Study of Intelligence, 1993), 297.

15 "Office of Policy Coordination," 1948–1952, p. 22, accessed on June 22, 2012, at http://www.foia.cia.gov/docs/DOC_0000104823/DOC_0000104823.pdf.

16 Minutes of Staff Conference, 22 October 1951, in Warner, *CIA under Truman*, 435–36; Stephen J. K. Long, "Strategic Disorder, the Office of Policy Coordination, and the Inauguration of US Political Warfare against the Soviet Union, 1948–1950," *Intelligence and National Security* 27 (August 2012): 459–87.

17 NSC 10/5, Scope and Pace of Covert Operations, 23 October 1951, in Warner, *CIA under Truman*, 437–39; Nicholas Dujmovic, "Drastic Actions Short of War: The Origins and Application of CIA's Paramilitary Function in the Early Cold War," *Journal of American Military History* 77 (July 2012): 793.

18 Walter Bedell Smith memorandum to Deputy Directors, "Organization of CIA Clandestine Services," July 15, 1952, in Warner, *CIA under Truman*, 465–67.

19 Andrew E. Lembke, *Landsdale, Magsaysay, America, and the Philippines: A Case Study of Limited Insurgency* (Fort Leavenworth, KA: Combat Institute Studies Press, 2001).

20 William Colby, *Honorable Men: My Life in the CIA* (NY: Simon & Schuster, 1978), 81–105; Harry Rositzke, *The CIA's Secret Operations*, (NY: Reader's Digest Press, 1977), 169–71; Karalekas, "History of the Central Intelligence Agency," 43–50.

21 Karalekas, "History of the Central Intelligence Agency," 43–44; 50–53; Loch Johnson, "Covert Action and Accountability: Decision-Making for America's Secret Foreign Policy," *International Studies Quarterly* 33 (March 1989): 87.

22 Memorandum for the NSC, "Report by the Director of Central Intelligence," April 23, 1952, in Warner, *CIA under Truman*, 457–64.

23 Bradley F. Smith and Elena Agarossi, *Operation Sunrise: The Secret Surrender* (NY: Basic Books, 1979).

24 Peter Grose, *Gentleman Spy: The Life of Allen Dulles* (Boston: Houghton Mifflin, 1994).

25 Robert R. Bowie and Richard H. Immerman, *Waging Peace: How Eisenhower Shaped an Enduring National Security Strategy* (NY: Oxford University Press, 1998), 41–54.

26 Report of the Special Study Group [Doolittle Committee] on Covert Activities of the Central Intelligence Agency, September 30, 1954 [excerpts], in Leary, *The Central Intelligence Agency*, 143–45.

27 Helms quoted in Zachary Karabell, "Two Agents, Two Paths: How the CIA Became a Vital Operation," *Foreign Affairs* 82 (July/August 2003): 184.

28 Harry Howe Ransom, "Congress and the Intelligence Agencies," in *Congress Against the President*, ed. Harvey C. Mansfield (NY: Praeger Press, 1975), 159; Walter L. Pforzheimer, "Memorandum for the Record, CIA Appropriations," October 25, 1951, reproduced in Warner, *CIA under Harry Truman*, 441–43; Saltonstall quoted in Karalekas, "History of the Central Intelligence Agency," 65–6; David M. Barrett, *The CIA and Congress: The Untold Story from Truman to Kennedy* (Lawrence: University of Kansas Press, 2005), 99–100, 447–59; Amy B. Zegart, *Flawed by Design: The Evolution of the CIA, JCS, and NSC* (Stanford, CA: Stanford University Press, 1999), 193.

29 Author's interview with Eleanor Lansing Dulles, October 9, 1979 (transcript in author's possession).

30 Stephen Kinzer, *All the Shah's Men: An American Coup and the Roots of Middle East Terror*; (NY: John Wiley & Sons, 2003); Evrand Abrahamian, *The Coup: 1953, the CIA, and the Roots of Modern U.S.-Iranain Relations* (NY: New Press, 2013).

31 In addition to the sources cited in the previous note, see CIA Clandestine Service History, "Overthrow of Premier Mossadeq of Iran, November 1952–August 1953," March 1954, by Dr. Donald Wilber, and another undated internal CIA history by an unidentified author, *The Battle for Iran*, both accessed through the National Security Archive Electronic Briefing Book No. 435 on August 19, 2013, at http://www2.gwu.edu/~nsarchiv/NSAEBB/NSAEBB435/; Kermit Roosevelt, *Countercoup: the Struggle for the Control of Iran* (NY: McGraw Hill, 1970); Mark J. Gasiorowski, "The 1953 Coup D'etat in Iran," *International Journal of Middle East Studies* 19 (August 1987): 261–86.

32 Richard H. Immerman, *The CIA in Guatemala: The Foreign Policy of Intervention* (Austin: University of Texas Press, 1982); Steven Schlesinger and Steven Kinzer, *Bitter Fruit: The Untold Story of the American Coup in Guatemala*

(Garden City, NY: Doubleday, 1982); Piero Gleijeses, *Shattered Hope: The Guatemalan Revolution and the United States, 1944–1954* (Princeton, NJ: Princeton University Press, 1991); Nick Cullather, *Secret History: The CIA's Classified Account of its Operations in Guatemala, 1952–1954* (Stanford, CA: Stanford University Press, 1999).

33 Appendix C, "A Study of Assassination," in Cullather, *Secret History*, 137–42.

34 Quoted in Immerman, *CIA in Guatemala*, 161.

35 Quoted in Cullather, *Secret History*, 68.

36 CIA Memorandum, "CIA's Role in the Overthrow of Arbenz," May 12, 1975, accessed on June 27, 2012, at http://www.foia.cia.gov/docs/DOC_0000919933 /DOC_0000919933.pdf; Dulles quoted in Immerman, *CIA in Guatemala*, 179. Almost a half-century after PBSUCESS, the State Department finally published the official documentary history: *Foreign Relations of the United States, 1952–1954: Guatemala* (Washington: Government Printing Office, 2003). CIA documents in addition to the May 12, 1975 are accessible through the CIA's Freedom of Information Act Reading Room at http://www.foia.cia.gov/.

37 Dujmovic, "Drastic Actions Short of War," 799–803; ██████████████

██

██.

38 Valerie Plame, *Fair Game: How a Top CIA Agent Was Betrayed by Her Own Government* (NY: Simon & Schuster, 2007), 1–27 (quote on p.2); Lindsay Moran, *Blowing My Cover: My Life as a CIA Spy* (NY: Berkley Books, 2005; 59–113 (quotes on pp. 73–80); "Office of Policy Coordination, 1948–52," 10.

39 For a catalog of operations, see William Blum, *The CIA: A Forgotten History* (London: Zed Books, 1986).

40 Richard M. Bissell, Jr., with Jonathan E. Lewis and Frances T. Pudlo, *Reflections of a Cold Warrior: From Yalta to the Bay of Pigs* (New Haven, CT: Yale University Press, 1996), 30–80; Evan Thomas, *The Very Best Men: Four Who Dared: The Early Years of the CIA* (NY: Simon & Schuster, 1995), 87–127; author's interview with Richard Bissell, November 1, 1977 (transcript in author's possession). On the Ford Foundation's CIA projects see Frances Stonor Saunders, *The Cultural Cold War: The CIA and the World of Arts and Letters* (NY: The New Press, 1999), 129–35.

41 Thomas G. Paterson, *Contesting Castro: The United States and the Triumph of the Cuban Revolution* (NY: Oxford University Press, 1994).

42 For the Bay of Pigs planning see Peter Wyden, *Bay of Pigs: The Untold Story* (NY: Simon & Schuster, 1979) Trumbull Higgins, *The Perfect Failure: Kennedy, Eisenhower, and the CIA at the Bay of Pigs* (NY: Norton, 1987); Howard Jones, *The Bay of Pigs* (NY: Oxford University Press, 2008); and *Operation ZAPATA: The "Ultrasensitive" Report and Testimony of the Board of Inquiry on the Bay*

of Pigs, introduction by Luis Aguilar (Frederick, MD: University Publications of America, 1981). The latter volume contains much of the memoranda and testimony produced by the Taylor Committee that President John Kennedy established to examine the failure of the Bay of Pigs Operation. Additional Taylor Committee memoranda are available in a National Security Archive Electronic Briefing Book, *The ULTRASENSITIVE Bay of Pigs: Newly Released Portions of Taylor Commission Report Provide Critical New Details on Operation Zapata*, ed., Peter Kornbluh, accessed on May 3, 2006, at http://www.gwu .edu/~nsarchiv/NSAEBB/NSAEBB29/index.html. In 2011 the National Security Archive also made available at http://www.gwu.edu/~nsarchiv/NSAEBB /NSAEBB355/index.htm the first four volumes of the *Official History of the Bay of Pigs Operation*, written between 1974 and 1984 by CIA historian Jack Pfeiffer. The fifth volume, in which Pfeiffer challenges the judgments of the 1961 report by Lyman Kirkpatrick, the CIA's Inspector General, remains classified. For Kirkpatrick's report, see *Bay of Pigs Declassified: The Secret CIA Report on the Invasion of Cuba*, ed. Peter Kornbluh (NY: New Press, 1998).

43   Memorandum No.1, "Narrative of the Anti-Castro Cuban operation, Zapata, June 13, 1961," in *Operation ZAPATA*, 3–6; Bissell interview with author, November 1, 1977.

44   Thomas F. Paterson, "Fixation with Cuba: The Bay of Pigs, Missile Crisis, and Covert War Against Fidel Castro," in *Kennedy's Quest for Victory: American Foreign Policy, 1961–1953*, ed. Thomas G. Paterson (NY: Oxford University Press, 1989), 123–37.

45   Piero Gleijeses, "Ships in the Night: The CIA, the White House, and the Bay of Pigs," *Journal of Latin American History* 27 (February 1995): 1–42. See also the National Security Archives' Chronology and its supporting documentation and oral history transcripts at http://www.gwu.edu/~nsarchiv /bayofpigs/chron.html.

46   Higgins, *Perfect Failure*; Aguilar, *Operation ZAPATA*.

47   Grose, *Gentleman Spy*, 529–66; Bissell, Jr., *Reflections of a Cold Warrior*, 191–204; Thomas, *The Very Best Men*, 268–72; Don Bohning, *The Castro Obsession: U.S. Covert Operations Against Cuba, 1959–1965* (Washington, DC: Potomac Books, 2006).

48   Memorandum of discussion of a Special Meeting of the National Security Council, March 31, 1953, *Foreign Relations of the United States, 1952–54: National Security Affairs* (Washington, DC: Government Printing Office, 1984), II: 268; Philip Taubman, *Secret Empire: Eisenhower, the CIA, and the Hidden Story of America's Space Espionage* (NY: Simon & Schuster, 2003), 24–5; Bowie and Immerman, *Waging Peace*, 109–10.

49   Douglas Garthoff, "Analyzing Soviet Politics and Foreign Policy," 65–67; "A Look Back ... CIA Asset Pyotr Popov Arrested," CIA Featured Story Archive, accessed on July 31, 2012, at https://www.cia.gov/news-information/featured -story-archive/2011-featured-story-archive/pyotr-popov.html; James Bamford, *The Puzzle Palace: Inside the National Security Agency, America's Most Secret Intelligence Organization* (NY: Penguin Group, 1982), 15–19.

50   Richard S. Leghorn, "Objectives for Research and Development in Military Aerial Reconnaissance," Excerpt from a Paper presented before a Symposium at the Optical Research Laboratories, Boston University, December 13, 1946, in *Early Cold War Overflights: Symposium Proceedings*, ed. R. Cargill Hall and Clayton D. Laurie (Washington, D.C.: Government Printing Office, 2003), II: 407–08.

51   R. Cargill Hall, "Early Cold War Overflight Programs: An Introduction," in Hall and Lourie, *Early Cold War Overflights*, I: 2–4.

52   Gerald A. Cooke, "Heart Throb Pilot: Overflights in the European Theater," in Hall and Lourie, *Early Cold War Overflights*, I: 184; Cecil H. Rigsby, Project Slick Chick Overflights in Europe, 1944–56," in Hall and Lourie, *Early Cold War Overflights*, I: 165; Richard Helms, Chief of Operations, Directorate of Plans, Central Intelligence Agency, to Deputy Director for Plans, "Denied Area Overflights, August 27, 1953," in Hall and Lourie, *Early Cold War Overflights*, II: 495.

53   Eric W. Timm, Chief, Foreign Intelligence, Central Intelligence Agency, to Deputy Director of Central Intelligence, "Denied Area Overflights for the Collection of Strategic Intelligence," August 26, 1953, in Hall an Lourie, *Early Cold War Overflights*, II: 491–94.

54   Allen W. Dulles, Director, Central Intelligence Agency, to General Nathan F. Twining, Chief of Staff, US Air Force, May 29, 1954, in Hall and Lourie, *Early Cold War Overflights*, II: 533–34; Twining to Dulles, July 6, 1954, in Hall and Lourie, *Early Cold War Overflights*, II: 535.

55   Taubman, *Secret Empire*, 77–83.

56   Taubman, *Secret Empire*, 99–140; Gregory W. Pedlow and Donald E. Welzenbach, *The Central Intelligence Agency and Overhead Reconnaissance: The U-2 and OXCART Programs, 1954–1974* (Washington, DC: History Staff of the Central Intelligence Agency, 1992), accessed on August 16, 2013, at http://www.gwu.edu/sites/www.gwu.edu/files/downloads/U2%20%20history %20complete.pdf.

57   Richard H. Immerman, " 'Trust in the Lord but Keep Your Powder Dry': American Policy Aims at Geneva," in *Cold War Respite: The Geneva Summit of 1955*, eds. Günter Bischof and Saki Dockrill (Baton Rouge: Louisiana State University

Press, 2000), 35–54; John Prados, "Open Skies and Closed Minds," in Bischof and Dockrill, *Cold War Respite*, 215–33; Raymond L. Garthoff, *Assessing the Adversary: Estimates by the Eisenhower Administration of Soviet Intentions and Capabilities*, (Washington, DC: Brookings Institution Press, 1991).

58   In 1958 the CIA's Photo-Intelligence Division was renamed the Photographic Intelligence Center (PIC). The PIC produced Photographic Intelligence Reports (PIRs) and Photographic Evaluation Reports (PERs). In 1961, with the advent of satellite photography, DCI Dulles assigned all photographic interpretation to the National Photographic Interpretation Center (NPIC). *CORONA: America's First Satellite Program*, ed. Kevin C. Ruffner, (Washington: Center for the Study of Intelligence, 1995), 99.

59   Foster Lee Smith, "Overflight Operations: Another View," in Hall and Laurie, *Early Cold War Overflights*, I:35; Taubman, *Secret Empire*, 281–82.

60   Roger K. Rhodarmer, "Recollections of an Overflight 'Legman,'" in Hall and Laurie, *Early Cold War Overflights*, I: 22–23; Donald E. Hillman with R. Cargill Hall, "A Daytime Overflight of Soviet Siberia," in Hall and Laurie, *Early Cold War Overflights*, I: 245; Taubman, *Secret Empire*, 177–89. On the criticism that Eisenhower received for allegedly allowing the United States to fall behind the United States in the nuclear race, see Desmond J. Ball, *Politics and Force Levels: The Strategic Missile Program of the Kennedy Administration* (Berkeley: University of California Press, 1981); John Prados, *The Soviet Estimate: U.S. Intelligence and Soviet Strategic Forces* (Princeton, NJ: Princeton University Press, 1986), 38–126; Robert A. Divine, *The Sputnik Challenge: Eisenhower's Response to the Soviet Satellite*, (NY: Oxford University Press, 1993); David L. Snead, *The Gaither Committee, Eisenhower, and the Cold War* (Columbus: Ohio State University Press, 1999); Christopher Preble, *John F. Kennedy and the Missile Gap* (DeKalb: Northern Illinois University Press, 2004).

61   The most comprehensive study of the Soviets' downing of Powers' U-2 flight remains Michael R. Beschloss, MAYDAY: *Eisenhower, Khrushchev and the U-2 Affair* (NY: Harper & Row, 1986).

62   In contrast to less than eighteen months for the U-2, the A-12, later called the XF-12 and then the SR-71, took ten years to develop. Smith, "CIA's Analysis of Soviet Science and Technology," 120–21.

63   Taubman, *Secret Empire*, 212–355.

64   Ruffner, ed., *Corona*, xiii–xiv; Kenneth E. Green, "Corona," *Corona*, 3; James Q. Rebert, "List of Highest Priority Targets, USSR," August 18, 1960, in Ruffner, *Corona*, 49.

65   National Intelligence Estimate, 11-8/1-61, "Strength and Deployment of Soviet Long Range Ballistic Missile Forces," September 21, 1961, in Ruffner. *Corona*, 127–55; Special National Intelligence Estimate 13-4-64, "The Chances of

an Imminent Communist Chinese Nuclear Explosion," August 26, 1964, in Ruffner, *Corona*, 237–44; CIA/NPIC, Photographic Interpretation Report, IH-4 Mission 1042-1, June 17–22, 1967, Middle East Edition, in Ruffner, *Corona*, 289–305; Raymond Garthoff, "Estimating Soviet Military Intentions and Capabilities," 144–47. For a survey of successive NIEs and SNIEs and an assessment of their accuracy, see Prados, *The Soviet Estimate*, 151–99.

3

The CIA and its Discontents:
1961–1976

Richard Bissell had been forced into retirement from the CIA long before
CORONA would prove its value. He had also retired before October 1962.
That is when the tension between the CIA's emphasis on paramilitary
operations and its core mission of collection and analysis, a tension that he
personified and that plagued the agency throughout its history, took the
United States to the brink of nuclear war. Bissell doubtless regretted that he
was on the sidelines throughout the Cuban Missile Crisis. In a fundamental
sense, these most famous Thirteen Days of October represented the final
days of glory for the U-2 spy plane, which was Bissell's greatest accomplishment. The crisis also provided the CIA with an opportunity to redeem itself
after Bissell's greatest failure, the fiasco at the Bay of Pigs. In this regard,
it was somewhat successful. But the agency's performance during what
many consider the high water mark of John F. Kennedy's management of
the nation's security was uneven and unorthodox. Moreover, it served as
something of a prologue for the Company's fall from grace.

Having fired both the CIA's director and his heir apparent, Kennedy
intended to make the agency "his" company, not Eisenhower's let alone
Truman's. He was the first president to receive a daily briefing on the
most current intelligence. Initially called the President's Intelligence Check
List (PICL), this "book," sometimes comprised of "raw" traffic as well as
"finished" analysis, is now well known as the President's Daily Brief (PDB).[1]
Kennedy's appointments also reflected his vision for the agency. OSS
veteran and Wisner's deputy Richard Helms succeeded Bissell as deputy
director for plans; but Kennedy appointed John McCone to replace Dulles.
McCone, a conservative, fiercely anti-Soviet Republican and successful

The Hidden Hand: A Brief History of the CIA, First Edition. Richard Immerman.
© 2014 John Wiley & Sons, Ltd. Published 2014 by John Wiley & Sons, Ltd.

corporate executive who had served as undersecretary of the Air Force and chaired the Atomic Energy Commission under Eisenhower, had only indirect experience with intelligence. That was what Kennedy wanted. The president expected his new DCI to help win the administration support from across the aisle by personifying the ideal that the CIA was above politics even as, in stark contrast to Allen Dulles, his contributions to the CIA were primarily managerial.

In addition, McCone, who was trained as an engineer, was the opposite of Dulles in that his priority for the agency was to improve the quality and coordination of intelligence analysis. That also suited Kennedy. The Bay of Pigs tragedy was above all a failure of intelligence. Further, and at this point probably more important for the president, he intended to run covert operations directly out of the White House to the extent that he could without jeopardizing its capacity for plausible deniability. Operation MONGOOSE, the program to assassinate Castro and through sabotage and subversion otherwise undermine his regime, is the most notable example. Although CIA personnel participated in MONGOOSE, Attorney General and "Brother Protector" Robert Kennedy was the de facto director of the project. Moreover, the connection to the CIA of Edward Lansdale, the field commander, was highly ambiguous. Although he worked *with* the CIA, Lansdale, whose title was assistant secretary of defense for special operations, did not necessarily work *for* the CIA. As the agency's director, McCone was particularly skillful at quarantining the president from MONGOOSE's potential contagion.[2]

A suggestion by the President's Foreign Intelligence Advisory Board (PFIAB), an enhanced and renamed version of the President's Board of Consultants on Foreign Intelligence Activities that Eisenhower had created in 1956 to advise the Executive Office, further complicated the relationships among the administration's bureaucratic elements. In October 1961, Kennedy followed the PFIAB's advice and created the Defense Intelligence Agency (DIA). The DIA's purpose was to facilitate and institutionalize the transfer to the Pentagon of many paramilitary and other covert intelligence-related activities associated with the CIA. The agency's position as the vanguard of America's capacity for shadow warfare was, hearkening back to the debates of the late 1940s, once again contested. A half-century later, it has yet to be resolved.[3]

Neither Kennedy nor McCone could have foreseen in 1961 how the collision of these dynamics—the bifurcation within the CIA between the directorates of intelligence and plans, the agency's problematic capacity and responsibility for paramilitary operations, America's campaign against Cuba and Castro, and Kennedy's personalized style of decision making— would the next year propel the world toward a potential Armageddon. With Operation MONGOOSE in full swing and the Castro regime entrenching itself solidly in the Soviet camp, by 1962 Washington's relations with Havana had deteriorated to the point that a crisis appeared all but inevitable. As CIA director, McCone's contribution to MONGOOSE was limited and peripheral. He did pay close attention to Cuba. But he concentrated on its capability to threaten the United States, not America's capability to threaten Cuba by overthrowing or assassinating Castro. During three consecutive meetings with Kennedy's chief advisors in August 1962, two of which the president attended personally, McCone underscored that intelligence reporting indicated that it was probable, not merely possible, that Castro was concealing the installation of medium-range ballistic missiles (MRBMs) on the island nation. In "at least a dozen reports" prior to the detection of the installations on October 15, the DCI wrote two days later, he had judged the likelihood very high that the Soviet were establishing a medium-range nuclear strike capability in Cuba.[4]

13 Days in October

McCone's warnings caused little alarm. He was hardly an expert in intelligence analysis; his judgments appeared to almost all security officials as an overreaction driven by inexperience and anxiety. Conversely, the lessons of the bomber and missile gap controversies made veteran intelligence analysts wary of once again overestimating an adversary's capabilities. And there existed no precedent or, according to the CIA, incentive for the Soviets to accept this kind of risk. Because, as is so often the case, the evidence was ambiguous, analysts interpreted it to corroborate their assumptions and expectations. Even McCone's chief deputy in the CIA, General Marshall "Pat" Carter, concluded that the Cubans were installing defensive surface-to-air missiles (SAMs), not offensive MRBMs. The Office of National Estimates and its legendary leader, Sherman Kent, who directed ONE and chaired its nerve center, the Board of National Estimates, concurred. Kent's office had produced a series of National Intelligence Estimates in 1962 that used virtually the same words to rebuff McCone's supposition: "We believe it unlikely that the Bloc will provide Cuba with strategic weapon systems or with air and naval capabilities suitable for major independent military operations overseas."[5]

Sporadic U-2 flights in fall 1962 failed to confirm McCone's suspicions or influence the CIA's assessments. Consequently, with memories of the Gary Powers shoot-down still fresh, the Kennedy administration had insufficient confidence in the plane's invulnerability to approve multiple missions. Finally, on October 9 McCone received Kennedy's approval for U-2s directly to overfly suspected SAM sites. The first of three missions flew on October 14. By late in the evening of Monday, October 15, "the latest readout from Cuban U-2 photography indicated initial deployment of Medium Range Ballistic Missiles" at San Cristobal. As Secretary of State Dean Rusk commented to the National Security Council the next day, "Mr. McCone had predicted such a possibility back in mid-August."[6]

Because the next thirteen days were among the most dramatic in modern American—and world—history, they have been studied and restudied in the United States, the Soviet Union, Cuba, and elsewhere across the globe. McCone invariably receives high marks for his insight, foresight, and not insignificantly, persistence. The CIA as an institution, however, receives little credit for the outcome. Whether fan or critic of the administration's crisis management, scholars, journalists, and others who write about the Cuban Missile Crisis overwhelmingly stress the roles played by President Kennedy, Attorney General Kennedy, and the members of Excomm, the Executive Committee of the National Security Council that the president established to debate the options and decide upon a response. Students of the crisis have likewise scrutinized Nikita Khrushchev's motives, attitudes, and behavior and, increasingly, those of Castro. That a succession of U-2 missions that overflew Cuba throughout the crisis and National Security Agency eavesdropping operations provided the members of Excomm with a steady stream of intelligence on the number and probable operational state of the missile sites, on Soviet and Warsaw Pact military preparations, and on the progress made by Soviet ships headed toward the quarantine line receives scant if any attention. What does receive attention is the one failed U-2 mission: on October 27 a SAM missile shot down a U-2, killing the pilot and almost driving the crisis over the brink. In sum, during the Cuban Missile Crisis the CIA was more responsible, or so it would seem from much of the literature, for intensifying the crisis than for resolving it.[7]

Such a characterization is misleading. True, analysts were slow to detect the Soviet emplacement of offensive missiles in Cuba because they were not looking for them. McCone, with less training and less expertise and prone to imagine the worst when it came to either the Soviets or Cubans, relied more on his "gut instincts." What is more, the exodus of sympathetic Cubans to the United States following Castro's victory over Fugencio Batista, and the communists' increased vigilance after the Bay of Pigs, produced a woeful lack of clandestine operatives to collect human intelligence, HUMINT, within Cuba. Its capacity for HUMINT collection within the Soviet Union was historically poor.

Nevertheless, in contrast to the lead-up to the crisis, in October the CIA and the rest of the US Intelligence Community performed well. U-2 photography revealed six MRBM and three IRBM (intermediate-range ballistic missiles; McCone had limited his warnings to MRBMs) sites that collectively enveloped some three-dozen launch pads. Based on this imagery, and plans for descriptions of the sites that the defector Oleg Penkovsky provided the CIA, the agency inferred that nuclear warheads as well as missiles had arrived. It was right.[8] This imagery also provided Adlai Stevenson with the necessary ammunition to demolish Valerian Zorin's protestations of innocence during their public debate in the UN Security Council. Juxtaposed with the aerial photographs, the National Security Agency's signals intelligence allowed for careful monitoring of Soviet and Warsaw Pact military communications, which was pivotal for Kennedy and his advisors as Excomm argued over US options and Soviet ships approached the quarantine line. What is more, McCone continued to contribute throughout the crisis. He briefed the principals, wrote insightful memoranda, and participated (normally taking a hawkish position) in Excomm debates.[9]

In the final analysis, it was the combination of US nuclear superiority and political resolve, Soviet concessions, backchannel exchanges, Kennedy's judgment and leadership, and his determination, along with that of Khrushchev, to find a way to avoid a nuclear confrontation that was responsible for the peaceful resolution of the Cuban Missile Crisis. The detection of the sites by the CIA provided the administration with a critical window to frame its response, and the subsequent intelligence the agency provided militated against an impetuous employment of US force. This additional time and information was that much more vital in light of the number of Excomm participants and other advisors who advocated the employment of force. Kennedy's ordering of more photographic reconnaissance flights on October 16, in fact, effectively put the brakes on the Joint Chiefs of Staff's recommendation that the president authorize an immediate air strike against the missile sites and other targets in Cuba.

CIA experts interpreted U-2 photographs on a daily basis and displayed them for Excomm viewing. Kent's Office of National Estimates largely atoned for its mistakes, moreover, by producing two Special National Intelligence Estimates (SNIEs) by October 20 that assessed the likely Soviet responses to and consequences of a variety of US actions. While driven by inference and even speculation, these SNIEs promoted rigorous discussion, debate, and, ultimately, deliberate decision making. Further, Kennedy, because of the confidence he had gained in the CIA's capacity for aerial reconnaissance, felt no need to overreact when Castro forbade on-site inspections of the dismantling of the missile bases. In stark contrast to the Bay of Pigs' Operation ZAPATA, the CIA's performance during the Cuban Missile Crisis earned from the president the comment, "very well done."[10]

Kennedy could not say the same for the CIA's efforts to rid Cuba, and the world, of Castro, and thereby remove at least one of Khrushchev's motives for installing the missiles in Cuba in the first place. The Cuban Missile Crisis did not induce the president or his brother to put the Bay of Pigs out of their minds and call off Operation MONGOOSE. To the contrary, on October 16, in the interval between two of the most significant Excomm meetings, Bobby Kennedy met with Lansdale, Helms, and others to express the "general dissatisfaction of the President" with US efforts to execute "acts of sabotage" against the Cuban regime. The attorney general then announced he "was going to give Operation MONGOOSE more personal attention." Accordingly, he continued, beginning the next day he intended to meet with MONGOOSE's "operational representatives" at 9:30 a.m. *every morning.*[11]

Bobby Kennedy did involve himself more systematically in MONGOOSE, although not for long. Neither the president nor the attorney general was ever especially concerned about the legal, let alone ethical, questions that the program in general and assassination in particular raised. But as the Cuban Missile Crisis unfolded and the need for further intelligence collection and military preparation became more urgent, officials in both the CIA and military came to perceive MONGOOSE as a loose cannon. Moreover, officials at the White House and Foggy Bottom, including Bobby Kennedy, concluded that acts of sabotage committed by agents not held on a tight leash by Washington were incompatible with the diplomacy necessary to finalize the removal of the missiles and set into place (never successfully) an inspection regime. While intermittent efforts to undermine Castro persisted, the administration in early 1963 closed down MONGOOSE as a stand-alone program. It remained closed.[12]

After President Kennedy's assassination in November 1963, Bobby could never shake the horrifying thought that MONGOOSE had contributed to his brother's death, perhaps directly, perhaps existentially. As a vice president who was far removed from Kennedy administration policymaking, Lyndon Johnson knew little if anything about MONGOOSE. Given the apparent relaxation of the Cold War that followed October 1962 and the priority Kennedy's successor placed on his domestic programs, Johnson did not perceive Castro as much more than a minor irritant. It stood to reason, therefore, that the CIA, relieved of the hair-brained activities associated with MONGOOSE and guided by John McCone's focus on the analytic side, would devote its resources to more constructive endeavors. As a consequence, it could build on the respect it earned during the Cuban Missile Crisis to bolster its standing in Washington. But soon came the Vietnam War.[13]

Vietnam

In fundamental respects, the CIA, with the notable exception of its counterintelligence operations, performed better than other arms of the US government during the conflict in Vietnam.[14] Nevertheless, during the 1960s and 1970s, the agency came to be identified both domestically and abroad as synonymous with US foreign policy, and it suffered commensurately. That it did is more than a little ironic. Vietnam, or Indochina as the French colony was called, had been a training site for a number of America's paramilitary operatives, and for that reason CIA officials were familiar with Indochina long before it was common to be so. During World War II, OSS units forged close relationships with Vietminh nationalists and the organization's leader, Ho Chi Minh, in their fight against the Japanese occupiers and their surrogate French administrators in Indochina. Following the Japanese surrender, most OSS veterans of this theater supported Vietnamese independence from France. By this time, however, the Truman administration had adopted a Cold War perspective that gave top priority to the Western alliance and defined geopolitics as a zero-sum game.[15]

In Indochina, this perspective translated into a policy of supporting the French effort to regain control of their colony in the face of indigenous opposition. Notwithstanding their predecessors' or in some cases their own connections to the OSS, CIA operatives, and its multiple contract agents, dutifully executed the Truman policy. In 1950, the CIA had, through a holding company, the American Airdale Corporation, assumed proprietary control over the Civil Air Transport (CAT). CAT had been founded by General Claire Chennault and Whiting Willauer of Flying Tigers' fame in 1946 to aid Chiang Kai-shek's Kuomintang in the Chinese Civil War. After the Communist victory in 1949, CAT pilots airlifted thousands of Chinese Nationalists to the island of Taiwan (Formosa). Subsequently, the CIA made CAT an agency asset in order to carry out operations in the Far East, just in time for its engagement in the Korean War. But it was in Indochina that CAT distinguished itself as a covert arm of the US government by its pilots' daring airdrops of supplies to the besieged French at Dien Bien Phu in 1954. One of these missions famously cost the life of James B. McGovern, nicknamed "Earthquake McGoon" after the popular comic strip.[16]

Shortly after the French surrender in May 1954 and the division of Vietnam into North and South at the Geneva Conference in July, at the urging of the Eisenhower administration the CIA dispatched Colonel Edward Lansdale, who a half dozen years later would oversee Operation MONGOOSE in Cuba, to Saigon. Lansdale, we must recall, was an OSS veteran who from 1950–1953 had played a pivotal role assisting the governments of Elpido Quirino and Ramon Magsaysay in the defeat of the communist-influenced Huk insurgency in the Philippines.[17] He was accordingly the consensus choice to lead a team of a dozen CIA agents assigned to the US Military Advisory and Assistance Group (MAAG).

Lansdale's tasks were manifold. The Geneva Accords had established Vietnam as an independent state but split it in half at the 17th parallel pending unification elections. Lansdale's initial assignment was to mount a propaganda campaign aimed to dissuade Vietnamese in the South from voting for the communists, organize the migration of non-communist Vietnamese from the north to the south, and carry out acts of sabotage in the north. His mission soon evolved, however, in part on his own initiative. First, Lansdale manipulated an election in the south to ensure Prime Minister Ngo Dinh Diem's overwhelming triumph over the former Emperor Bao Dai. Then, despite the opposition of the French and many in the US government, he orchestrated Diem's defeat of the rival Sects and consolidation of his regime. With the support of Lansdale, Diem resisted efforts to hold unifying elections scheduled for 1956. By the time the enigmatic American that the famous US journalist Neil Sheehan described as the "attending physician at the birth of South Vietnam" returned to the United States in 1957 (he would go back to Vietnam in 1965), the US government was proclaiming Diem a miracle worker. Lansdale was not, as many have claimed, the model for Alden Pyle in Graham Greene's iconic *Quiet American*. But had Greene known him, he might have been.[18]

The claim that Diem was a miracle worker was no less of a myth than that of Lansdale inspiring Greene's portrayal of Pyle. Although more capable than popularly portrayed, his regime was profoundly unpopular in South (the Republic of) Vietnam, and by Kennedy's inauguration civil wars consumed all the former French colonies that comprised Indochina.[19] The CIA remained active throughout America's involvement in these conflicts, although during the early years its presence and influence remained small. In 1960, for example, its station in Saigon was but a fraction the size of that in Cuba, let alone West Berlin ▓▓▓▓▓▓. Yet, the next year, well before the deployment of US conventional forces to Vietnam, Kennedy authorized the CIA to initiate covert, paramilitary operations against North Vietnam. By 1967, the Saigon station had become the CIA's largest, and the agency had contributed significantly to some of the great watersheds in America's deepening commitment to the war. These included the coup against Diem in 1963; OPLAN 34-A, the psychological warfare operations and sustained program of covert airborne and maritime sabotage operations directed at bridges, small islands, and storage dumps and other targets in the north that precipitated the Gulf of Tonkin incidents in 1964; and the prosecution of a secret war in allegedly neutral Laos.[20]

More notoriously, from 1967 the CIA collaborated with the Army Command in Vietnam to manage the Phoenix Program. Conceived by CIA operative and then National Security Council staffer Robert Komer but directed primarily by future DCI William Colby, who was station chief in Saigon from 1959 until he took charge of the Company's Far Eastern Division and then the US/South Vietnamese rural pacification effort, the program established Provisional Reconnaissance Units that relied on local intelligence assets to target members of the National Liberation Front infrastructure in the South. The goal was to collect intelligence on enemy operations by capturing and interrogating important communist and NLF officials, and if possible, "turning" them into US and South Vietnamese assets. But US operatives and their Vietnamese allies acted upon information that was often either inaccurate, out of date, or intentionally corrupt. As a consequence, the number of innocents who were neutralized (tortured and assassinated) overwhelmed those who actually mattered to the enemy's infrastructure or could provide useful intelligence.[21]

The CIA also ran ▓▓▓▓▓▓▓▓▓▓, which established a top-secret radar facility at Lima Site 85 in Laos that provided instructions for US bombers flying Rolling Thunder bombing missions over North Vietnam.

The US government never acknowledged the existence of this site in neutral Laos, even after enemy forces overran it in the aftermath of the Tet offensive in 1968 and no one could account for eleven of the men stationed there (all the personnel at Lima Site 85 were required to resign from the government and conceal their identities). The shield of "plausible deniability" was so effective that the families of those killed at Lima Site 85 or who still remain missing had to spend years in courts suing the US government to receive survivor benefits.[22]

Notwithstanding this catalog of CIA projects in Vietnam, which is by no means exhaustive, the agency's primary contribution to the war was intelligence collection and analysis. Because it could combine its reporting with that of the recently established DIA, the Army's G-2, and the Military Advisory Command, Vietnam's (MACV's) intelligence structure, and it could also draw on the surveillance capabilities of the National Security Agency and aerial photographic reconnaissance units, the CIA was often able to provide military commanders in the field with relatively accurate information about enemy movements and even, with notable exceptions, troop strength and disposition. But in an unconventional war, political will, psychological initiatives, irregular forces, and parallel intangibles are frequently decisive yet resistant to precise evaluation. Moreover, CIA operatives regularly lacked the area expertise or language capabilities necessary to collect intelligence on their own. They thus had to rely on indigenous assets, and too many South Vietnamese were either unreliable or more concerned with jockeying for position against political or family rivals than serving the Americans. Hence even after the establishment in 1967 of the Combined Intelligence Center Vietnam (CICV), a unit that included both South Vietnamese and American analysts, US tactical intelligence paled in comparison to Hanoi's.[23]

With regard to strategic intelligence, in Vietnam, as was generally the rule elsewhere in the world, the CIA struggled mightily to produce the National Intelligence Estimates and Special National Intelligence Estimates written to assist policymakers in making informed decisions. Throughout the war, the relationship between the producers and consumers of intelligence, especially the highest ranking customers in Washington, was far from ideal. From early on in America's involvement, the judgments of the CIA, not unlike those of the State Department's Bureau of Intelligence and Research (INR), were consistently pessimistic.[24] The consensus in Langley as well as Saigon was that the French were unlikely to prevail, and as late as the 1954 Geneva Conference, CIA analysts estimated that the chances were better than ever that the People's Republic of China (PRC) would respond forcefully to US military intervention. As America's commitment to South Vietnam increased subsequent to the 1954 Geneva Accords and Washington's decision to prop up the Diem regime, the CIA considered Chinese intervention less likely, but it remained less sanguine than policymakers about the war's prospects. Pervading its estimates were doubts about the strength and, even more important, the cohesion of the Republic of Vietnam. Yet during this time the CIA's role was largely passive. Careful not to breach the boundary between analysis and prescription, it collected intelligence from the field and played a pivotal role in providing Washington with the Intelligence Community's most authoritative finished products: National Intelligence Estimates and Special National Intelligence Estimates.[25]

This dynamic began to change following the Bay of Pigs fiasco and Kennedy's appointment of John McCone to replace Allen Dulles as director of central intelligence. McCone initially was no more optimistic than other CIA analysts, including Sherman Kent, the Office of National Estimates' chief. McCone did differ from Kent and others, however, in pinpointing the source of the problem. Previewing the self-confident and assertive temperament that he soon displayed so prominently with regard to the emplacement of Soviet missiles in Cuba, he was not bashful about expressing his judgment. In contrast to ONE's assessment, which stressed South Vietnam's internal weaknesses, McCone, consistent with his predispositions, attributed the gains made by Hanoi and the National Liberation Front (between which he did not differentiate) largely to the assistance provided by China. He agreed with the Office of National Estimates, nevertheless, that the Diem regime suffered from serious shortcomings. Consequently, in terms of the objective of creating a viable, stable bulwark against communist expansion in Southeast Asia, South Vietnam was making little progress, and America's military assistance contributed minimally toward this end. In June 1962, only a bit more than six months into his tenure and after but a single visit to Saigon, McCone told Secretary of Defense Robert McNamara point blank that the United States could not prevail in the war. In his opinion, the US and South Vietnam forces "were merely chipping away at the toe of the glacier from the North."[26]

By the end of the year McCone's refusal to defer to the highly regarded Kent and his determination to impose his will on the agency's analysts dramatically affected both his perspective on the Vietnam War and the character of the CIA's contribution to Vietnam policymaking. In the month prior to the Cuban Missile Crisis, ONE's Board of National Estimate began to draft a new NIE entitled "Prospects in Vietnam." The draft, which was congruent with previously pessimistic assessments, reached McCone some six months later. He erupted, demanding to know why the CIA's top-level analysts dissented so extensively from almost everyone in the White House, the Pentagon, and the State Department (outside of the Bureau of Intelligence and Research) "who knew Vietnam best." He insisted that Kent and his staff consult General Earle Wheeler, the chair of the Joint Chiefs of Staff, MACV commander General Paul Harkins, ambassador in Saigon Frederick "Fritz" Nolting, Assistant Secretary of State for Far Eastern Affairs Roger Hilsman, and other senior officials. Each of them maintained that the enemy had suffered severely over the past few years. McCone instructed Kent to revise the National Intelligence Estimate to take into account their input.[27]

One explanation for McCone's reversing his assessment, or at least signaling that he was in the process of doing so, might be that, as the president's chief intelligence officer, he wanted to tell his "first customer" what he thought Kennedy wanted to hear. This would not be unusual in Washington. But Kennedy had learned to value McCone's willingness to speak his mind independently during the Cuban Missile Crisis, and the Excomm debates had shown that Kennedy welcomed diverse sources of information and advice. A more likely explanation for McCone's behavior, then, is the lesson that he learned from the Cuban Missile Crisis: not to trust the CIA's analysts, or more specifically, Sherman Kent and the Office of National Estimates. They had missed the Soviet surreptitious installation of missiles and dismissed his warnings. McCone was hesitant to endorse blindly their position now, especially because the estimates of another intelligence arm over which he at least nominally presided, the Defense Intelligence Agency that Kennedy and McNamara had set up in 1961, varied considerably. In addition, McCone did trust his close friend Victor Krulak, at the time a Marine Major General serving as the Joint Chiefs of Staff's special assistant for counterinsurgency activities. Krulak reported that South Vietnam's military capabilities had "increased markedly" over the past year, whereas incidents of the enemy's aggression were "well below 1962 levels."[28]

McCone politicized national intelligence on the Vietnam War. ONE at first resisted his pressure, but barraged by optimistic reports by Krulak and many others whom McCone claimed "knew Vietnam best," CIA's leading analytic unit succumbed. "We believe that the Communist progress has been blunted and that the situation is improving," read NIE 53-63, the revised estimate on prospects in Vietnam that McCone signed off on in April 1963. The NIE did not predict victory. But it did posit that developments over the past year "indicate that the Viet Cong can be contained militarily and that further progress can be made in expanding the area of government control and in creating greater security in the countryside."[29]

NIE 53-63 marked the beginning of the CIA's, and more specifically ONE's, descent down a slippery slope. The United States would almost certainly have intensified its military efforts in Vietnam regardless of the CIA's assessment in spring 1963. The agency's influence on policymaking was never decisive. Before his assassination, as many have noted, Kennedy instructed the Pentagon to draw up contingency plans for a possible withdrawal of US forces. But the contingencies were critical. Kennedy had to win reelection in 1964, some kind of diplomatic means to avoid a communist takeover of the entire country would need to be found, and conditions in South Vietnam would have to deteriorate not only precipitously but also irreparably. The only element of the US Intelligence Community likely to reach that judgment was the CIA. But it was now on record as assessing South Vietnam's situation and military capabilities as improving. For the agency to reverse itself again would only exacerbate the loss of credibility it suffered because of McCone's successful, and in administration circles well known, intervention.[30]

Kennedy's ultimate intentions for and policies toward Vietnam can never be known for sure. What we do know is that in order to salvage South Vietnam, the president agreed to scheme with Diem's dissident generals to engineer a regime change. But a month after the CIA completed NIE 53-63, the long-simmering antagonism between South Vietnam's Buddhist majority and the Ngo (Diem's) family rule exploded in violent street demonstrations in the Imperial City of Hué. The crisis climaxed in June, when an elderly monk, encircled by others, set himself on fire before a crowd in Saigon. Diem's government responded with a mixture of contempt and further repression. On the one hand, Madame Nhu, Diem's sister-in-law, publicly dismissed the self-immolation with the comment that the Buddhists had merely "barbequed a bonze [monk] with imported gasoline." On the other hand, even as Diem instituted martial law, Ngo Dinh Nhu, her husband and Diem's brother and closest advisor, ordered the ransacking of Buddhist pagodas throughout South Vietnam and the arrest of over 1400 additional monks. An official in the US embassy later wrote that at this juncture he realized that the United States was "dealing with a government of madmen, whose words were meaningless, where nothing that was supposed to have happened had really happened."[31]

The basic cause for the CIA's long-held pessimism about South Vietnam was the unpopularity of Diem's regime and consequent instability of the state. The Buddhist crisis confirmed this diagnosis. And although it was too late to repair the distorted National Intelligence Estimate, the emergence of a cabal of South Vietnamese generals apparently prepared to oust Diem, combined with the conclusion of key administration officials — newly appointed ambassador to Saigon Henry Cabot Lodge, Jr., Assistant Secretary of State for Far Eastern Affairs Roger Hilsman, and National Security Council staffer Michael Forrestal in particular — that Diem's continuation in power was unsustainable, seemed to present an opportunity for the agency to take some "remedial" action. Responsibility fell to the covert operatives, of course, not the analysts.

The scope of the CIA's involvement in the coup remains classified (the available evidence suggests that it did not participate in the assassination; no Americans did). In fact, although the CIA has released a previously classified internal history that, notwithstanding its heavily redacted source material, demonstrates unambiguously that beginning in spring 1963 the agency was aware of the anti-Diem conspiracy and the State Department's complicity in it, the CIA has never admitted that it played a role. Surely it did. Nevertheless, the contribution of the State Department to the coup; the litany of previous CIA activities in Vietnam; the steady communications between the CIA's chief of station (COS) in Saigon, John Richardson, and the Diem regime, the US embassy, and Langley; Richardson's replacement as COS, at Lodge's insistence, because he adamantly opposed the coup; and the stream of reporting on the coup planners from the CIA station make it inconceivable that the agency's case officers in Vietnam would have remained on the sidelines. Further, Lodge used veteran CIA operative Lucien Conein as his liaison with the anti-Diem generals.[32]

Through Conein, Lodge plotted with the conspirators. Yet because Kennedy remained indecisive as to whether to approve Diem's overthrow, the ambassador never gave the generals the green light to launch the coup. On November 1, 1963, they took matters into their own hands by seizing control of vital military assets and communications systems. Diem phoned Lodge for advice — and assistance. Lodge's reply that he had not yet received instructions from Washington on the administration's position told Diem all he needed to know: he was on his own. Diem and Nhu fled the palace, sought sanctuary in a nearby church and took communion, and accepted the conspirators' offer of safe passage out of Vietnam. Both were summarily executed. "[W]e must bear a good deal of responsibility" for the "abhorrent murders," a shocked Kennedy said when he received the news.[33] In Dallas three weeks later, the president was assassinated.

Kennedy's acknowledgment of US responsibility for Diem's coup, and by extension assassination, enlarged US responsibility for the future of

South Vietnam.[34] Lyndon Johnson escalated the military commitment, and the CIA's role in Vietnam escalated commensurately. The Phoenix program, the secret war in Laos, ███████████████████ the multiple sabotage and psychological warfare activities, and so much more accompanied the intensification of the war following Diem's death.

Yet, as an institution with a core mission to serve policymakers by collecting and analyzing intelligence, the CIA became increasingly marginalized even as the number of its "boots on the ground" in Southeast Asia mushroomed. McCone facilitated this marginalization, and only partially because of his politicization of NIE 53-63. He contributed to the alienation of the CIA from policymaking on Vietnam primarily by recognizing that he had been wrong in the spring of 1963 when he corrupted the assessment process. Perhaps it was the coup against Diem, which McCone opposed, that provided the impetus for his acceptance of the pessimistic assessment to which almost all CIA experts on Vietnam subscribed. When the Office of National Intelligence wrote in 1964 that the South Vietnamese leadership was mired in "increasing defeatism" and "paralysis" and that the position of South Vietnam was steadily deteriorating, McCone did not dissent. From the perspective of Johnson and his key advisors, therefore, McCone had defected to the other side. [35]

He had not. Rather, McCone was insufficiently loyal to the administration's side. As 1964 wore on, Pentagon planners, recognizing that progress was in fact not being made, began to evaluate the impact of a program of intensified air attacks on the north. Their expectation was that such a program would bolster morale in the South, punish the North, and interdict the flow of materiel down the Ho Chi Minh trail. The product of these three phenomena would generate a climate conducive to achieving a negotiated settlement congruent with US interests.

CIA's assessments were by now predictably less sanguine. According to its analysts, the root problem was the lack of government capacity and popular support in the Republic of Vietnam. Bombing the Democratic Republic of Vietnam north of the 17th parallel would not address these deficits. Although McCone no longer imposed his views on his analysts, he did express his dissent. Air attacks, he estimated, could put an immediate stop to North aggression, thereby providing the South with the political space it needed for a new government to stabilize. But the air attacks had to be virtually unlimited from the start. In McCone's judgment, the United States should target industrial centers and POLs (Petroleum, Oil, and Lubricant supply centers) wherever they were located, and must not allow possible retaliation from an external power such as the People's Republic of China to serve as a deterrent.[36]

But President Johnson was deterred by the possibility of PRC retaliation. He remembered all too well the price the United States, and Harry Truman, had paid when General Douglas MacArthur underestimated the risk of Chinese intervention in Korea. Having just won an overwhelming mandate to continue his ambitious domestic program, moreover, Johnson was not prepared to "Americanize" the war to the extent that accepting McCone's recommendations would require. Not until March 1965 did the United States launch Rolling Thunder, the sustained aerial bombardment of the north, and even then, the implementation was gradual and carefully bounded. By this time, Johnson had stopped inviting McCone to his Tuesday luncheons and otherwise had frozen him out of his deliberations. Concurrently, the CIA director's relations with the Pentagon had deteriorated beyond the point of repair. The "bureaucrats in the Pentagon are trying to screw things so that no one can run the intelligence business," McCone exploded. "I think the thing I should do is call up the President and tell him to get a new Director of Central Intelligence."[37]

Developments were not that direct, but essentially McCone did just that. In the words of Richard Helms's official CIA biographers, McCone "found resignation preferable to being ignored."[38] At his last meeting of the National Security Council, the outgoing DCI predicted that by choosing to pursue the Pentagon-designed military program, the United States would "drift into a combat situation where victory would be dubious and from which we could not extricate ourselves." Then, on April 28, 1965, he turned the CIA over to its new director, Vice Admiral William F. Raborn, Jr. Raborn had proven his organizational mettle by leading the project that developed the Polaris submarine–launched ballistic missile three years ahead of schedule. But he had minimal background in intelligence, and he served as DCI only long enough to witness the administration ignore his advice and the United States to increase dramatically its commitment of US forces into Vietnam. In 1966, after it became evident that Raborn could not gain the confidence of either the White House or Langley, Johnson requested his resignation. The president had neither the time nor inclination to conduct an extensive search for a replacement. He appointed Richard Helms, Raborn's deputy, as his successor.[39]

"Vietnam was my nightmare for a good ten years," reads Helms's memoir. Doubtless it was. What is more, Helms's history mirrored that of US intelligence. As a veteran of the OSS who had worked for the CIA in a variety of capacities since its start and had risen through its ranks, he well understood its politics, both internally and in relation to the other branches of government. He thus knew enough to keep his distance from Johnson when it came to Vietnam policy. Helms delegated much of the responsibility to George Carver, whom he appointed his special assistant for Vietnam affairs (SAVA). Reborn had created the SAVA position, filling it initially with former Saigon station chief Peer de Silva, who had returned to Washington after he suffered a serious injury in the March 1965 bombing of the US embassy. Carver, whose father once headed the English Department at the University of Shanghai, had graduated Phi Beta Kappa from Yale and then earned the Ph.D. from Oxford University. Although he had only served as a case officer in Saigon, he was much more familiar with the estimative process than had been de Silva. By the time of his appointment as SAVA, he had served as an "eloquent" analyst of Southeast Asia by his participation in the production of a number of NIEs and SNIEs. Even though Carver was on record as sharing the pessimistic assessment that was almost universal in the agency, he had the reputation for expertise, insight, political savvy, and loyalty to the CIA that Helms sought.[40]

After 1968 Carver's reputation would never be the same; Helms's nightmare became his, too, as well as that of the CIA writ large. In terms of its contributions to policy and strategy toward Vietnam, the agency was still reeling from the controversial 1963 NIE on the prospects for Vietnam and the resistance of McCone and Kent's Office of National Estimates to the Pentagon's assessments in 1964 and 1965. The latter dispute intensified and then, in the context of the finger pointing in Washington that attended the fallout from the January 1968 Tet offensive, it exploded.

The tipping point can be traced to the end of 1966. At that time, more than a year prior to Hanoi's launching of the Tet offensive, Sam Adams, one of the CIA's most "diligent" researchers who was about to be assigned to Carver's SAVA office, began to sound alarms that the estimates of the enemy's strength reported by the US Military Assistance Command, Vietnam were dangerously low. Using signals intelligence in contrast to MACV's interrogations and captured documents, and supplementing the number of the communists' "conventional" forces with "irregulars," by which he meant guerrillas, administrative support units, secret self-defense forces, and political cadres, Adams assessed the enemy's strength as numbering some 600,000 forces, double MACV's estimate. While many in the CIA dissented from Adams's number, most, including Carver, judged it closer to the mark than MACV's "guestimate." By 1967, Secretary of Defense McNamara had also come to doubt the military's estimates and to rely on the CIA's intelligence. But MACV, commanded by General William Westmoreland, insisted that its estimates were right. Seeking to breach the divide, in fall 1967 Helms dispatched a CIA team led by Carver and including Adams to Saigon to hammer out an agreement. [41]

Demanding a consensus on an intelligence estimate is often a counterproductive undertaking. It can easily lead to diluting the judgments or concealing, even suppressing, dissents. In this case, the consequence was even worse. The team of CIA collectors and analysts encountered an "MACV brickwall." On September 14, Carver, whose previous assessments differed only marginally, if at all, from that of his colleagues, unconditionally surrendered. Although the evidence is ambiguous, he may have been instructed by Helms to determine if there was flexibility in MACV's estimate and, if not, drop the CIA's challenge to it. More likely, Carter was persuaded by the arguments of Westmoreland, Ellsworth Bunker, the US ambassador in Saigon; the head of Civil Operations and Revolutionary Development Support, Robert ("Blowtorch Bob") Komer; and other ranking officials that accepting Adams's estimate would signal that progress had not been made in degrading the enemy's capabilities. Such an admission would seriously undermine the US effort at a critical juncture in the war. Westmoreland at the time was advocating a more aggressive military strategy that would include an invasion of the north. Carver had conceded to what one CIA veteran called the "politically correct" compromise. [42]

In November 1967, after twenty-two drafts, Helms approved Special National Intelligence Estimate (SNIE) 14.3-67, "Capabilities for the Vietnamese Communists for Fighting in South Vietnam." By tabulating enemy losses (the notorious Body Count) and excising the numbers for "irregulars," the SNIE estimated the total of the enemy's forces to number between 224,000 and 249,000, fewer than MACV's initial estimate. "Circle now squared" Carver reported, but he exaggerated. Shortly thereafter, the US Military Assistance Command, Vietnam, publicly announced an estimate of 208,000. [43]

CIA operatives in the field never accepted the Order of Battle estimate, and the Tet offensive revealed that they were right. They were also right in sending a succession of intelligence reports in November and December 1967 warning of an impending enemy offensive. In retrospect and in combination with intelligence provided by the National Security Agency, this field reporting, according to General Bruce Palmer, then the Army's deputy commander in Vietnam and soon its vice chief of staff, constituted "an uncannily accurate forecast."[44] It made little impression on the administration or MACV, however. Small wonder, therefore, that Johnson and the "Wise Men" that he summoned for advice were so surprised not only by the Tet Offensive itself but also by its aftermath. During the February–March 1968 debate over Westmoreland's request for an additional 205,000 troops which, he claimed, would deliver the knock-out punch to the North Vietnamese Army, these Wise Men received a uniformly discouraging briefing presented by intelligence experts, especially General William Dupuy of the JCS staff and, ironically, the CIA's Carver. "Someone poisoned the well," complained Johnson. Candidates for the "someone" included Helms, Carver himself, Westmoreland, and the others who, like McCone earlier, had politicized the intelligence on Vietnam.[45]

Most CIA analysts resisted this politicization. They never received credit for doing so either in Washington or with the public, however, nor for being more right than wrong during those pivotal years of the Vietnam War. To the contrary, notwithstanding the agency's overwhelming dissent from the military's estimates of the enemy's strength, the public and many in Washington identified the CIA with and blamed it for the Tet debacle, a distortion that gained greater traction when it failed to predict the August 1968 Soviet invasion of Czechoslovakia. Lyndon Johnson withdrew from the 1968 presidential contest largely because he recognized that he had lost public and congressional support. So had the CIA.

Nixon, Ford, and the Year of Intelligence

The agency's fortunes did not improve with the succession of Richard M. Nixon to the White House. Indeed, the Company, which Nixon was certain had fed information to Kennedy that contributed to the young Massachusetts' senator's victory in the 1960 election, was on the new president's "enemy list" from the start. Nixon took office convinced that the Intelligence Community was not only disloyal, but it also had grown too large and too expensive. At the same time, nevertheless, he insisted on improving the IC's capability to produce accurate estimates on the Soviet Union and China. These two countries emerged as the foci, on the one hand, of a détente that depended heavily on agreements on nuclear arms limitation and an antiballistic missile system, and, on the other hand, of the triangular diplomacy that would distinguish the grand strategy he along with Henry Kissinger would formulate. For that reason, Nixon supported a restructuring of the analytic architecture heavily influenced by a report produced in the Office of Management and Budget under the direction of James Schlesinger, the OMB's assistant director. This process led to replacing the Senior Research Staff (SRS) on International Communism, the Office of National Estimates, and the Board of National Estimates with an Office of Political Research (OPR) and a system of 12 National Intelligence Officers (NIOs). Instead of a College of Cardinals there were Twelve Apostles, said those who walked the long corridors of the CIA's Langley headquarters.[46]

While Nixon identified these reforms as cost-saving measures as well as pillars of an improved estimative process, truth be told they reflected Nixon's lack of confidence in the agency. The president perceived the CIA as "those clowns out at Langley" and a "refuge for Ivy League intellectuals," equally damning descriptions from his vantage point. He never trusted or respected Helms, and although he allowed him to remain as DCI through the first term, he kept their personal meetings to a minimum. As an independent source of intelligence, Nixon firmly believed, the CIA "counted for little," infected as it was by the "liberal Georgetown social set" that had historically opposed him. "Give Helms unshirted Hell for this!" the president instructed Kissinger early in the administration after the *New York Times* claimed that the CIA's intelligence challenged the premise that the Soviets had developed or were on the verge of developing a capability to deliver multiple independently targeted warheads (MIRVs). This estimate undercut the White House position on the "growing SS-9 [ICBM] threat." Nixon continued by ordering Kissinger to "tell him [Helms] to crack down … [on] his Georgetown underlings."[47]

The president preferred to rely on sources over which he had more control, especially the staff of Kissinger's National Security Council. To Nixon, and Kissinger wholeheartedly agreed, the usefulness of the CIA had declined steadily since the resignation of Allen Dulles. "Intelligence has been wrong on the Soviet projections since 1962," he thundered at a meeting of the National Security Council in June 1969. Perhaps even worse, in his opinion the CIA had not changed its stripes since it betrayed him during the 1960 election. Nixon was sure that the agency continually leaked "misleading information" to his opponents in Congress and the press. Nixon did not expect his restructuring of the CIA to improve its performance dramatically, nor for that matter to make it a great deal more cost-effective. But he fully expected that the reforms "will do a helluva lot for my morale," he confided to his chief of staff, H.R. ("Bob") Haldeman. In a classic example of understatement, Helms described Nixon's relations with the CIA as "cranky."[48]

Still, owing to both his experience as Eisenhower's vice president and his secretive personality and mode of behavior, Nixon was predisposed toward covert operations. And for these he was content to rely on the CIA as his primary instrument, so long as he could exercise total control over it. The result was a sharp dichotomy in terms of the agency's role and influence. For example, the CIA played virtually no role in Nixon's Vietnam endgame.[49] Even more to the point, Nixon and Kissinger made little effort to conceal their contempt for the agency's "murky and confused" analytic contributions to the Strategic Arms Limitation Talks (SALT) I negotiations or other fundamental tenets of the policy of détente. The president and his national security advisor agreed that there were "serious limitations in the process by which estimates are made. This process is an inadequate means for providing basic analysis of Soviet strategic developments and prospects for the future." But because of its responsibilities for covert projects, the CIA did contribute in a large way to Nixon's foreign policies. Both the agency and the president suffered as a result.[50]

The chief target of the administration's shadow war, and thus the CIA's paramilitary operations, was Chile. For decades Washington perceived Chile as an ally and major bulwark against communism, and American multinationals identified it as a hospitable place to do business. For that reason, in the context of Castro's successful revolution in Cuba and the increased attention the Soviet began to pay to the Third World, the CIA became immersed in Chilean politics. During the country's 1964 presidential election, the agency funneled to Eduardo Frei, the opponent of the Marxist candidate Salvadore Allende Gossens, several million dollars of covert funding. Frei won. But in September 1970, on his third attempt, Allende, heading a united front ticket known as Unidad Popular (Popular Unity), achieved a plurality among the voters. Nixon reflexively categorized him as a Chilean Castro.[51]

The year of Allende's election Henry Kissinger famously remarked, "I don't see why we need to stand by and watch a country go Communist due to the irresponsibility of its own people."[52] And the administration did not stand by and watch. Authorized by the "40 Committee," the CIA spent another $1 million to prevent Allende's triumph. In this effort, it received cooperation and additional funds from private American businesses, particularly International Telephone and Telegraph (ITT), whose chairman was former DCI John McCone. ▬▬▬▬▬▬▬▬▬▬▬▬▬▬ ▬▬▬▬▬▬▬▬▬▬▬▬▬▬▬▬▬▬▬▬▬ Signaling an underestimation of the prospects of an Allende victory, the total sum, nevertheless, did not approach the millions available in 1964. What was more, as was often the case with such covert operations, coordination between CIA station chief ████████████████ and US ambassador Edward Korry of the anti-Allende campaign was far from perfect.[53]

Nixon refused to concede defeat. Because Allende won by a plurality, Chile's Congress would decide the election's outcome at the end of October. The president now sought to pull out all the stops. He authorized Helms to spend up to $10 million and accept all necessary risks to reverse the September results. Nixon approved a two-track assault. Track I concentrated on manipulating the political process. Track II called for orchestrating a coup. The CIA focused on Track II. It set up a special task force at Langley that, rather than rely on the CIA's station in Chile, supervised a dedicated team of agents who operated under deep cover.[54]

The evidence remains ambiguous as to whether the CIA encouraged let alone was complicit in the assassination by indigenous military officers of Réné Schneider, the commander of the Chilean armed forces who refused to subvert the constitutional process. Regardless, the coup that the CIA sought to engineer never occurred. On October 24, two days after Schneider's assassination, Allende assumed the presidency. As promised, he rapidly initiated the nationalization of US-owned properties. When he did, the CIA just as rapidly intensified covert projects directed against him.

Even as the United States halted economic assistance to the Allende administration, prevented its receipt of loans from the World Bank and other multilateral institutions, and instituted a variety of economic sanctions, the CIA channeled funds to the Chilean military. Over time, many of its officers came to identify Allende as a liability. Meanwhile, Chile's population, the middle class especially, increasingly blamed him for its North American aggravated, if not induced, travails. Within this polarized environment in fall 1972, Chile's truckers accelerated the economic distress by initiating a series of national strikes that disrupted internal transportation—for months. Evidence is not available to support the allegation that CIA funding allowed the truckers to sustain the strikes for a year, but the allegations persist and they are congruent with the contours of the CIA effort. The agency's goal was for Chile's economy to deteriorate and its political tensions to escalate. Both did. [55]

Still, protected by Schneider's successor, General Carlos Prats, who shared the slain commander of the Armed Forces' respect for the constitution, Allende survived. In fact, his Popular Unity party gained seats in the March 1973 elections for Congress. Prats resigned, however, following a demonstration outside his home by the wives of his officer corps. His successor, General Augusto José Ramón Pinochet Ugarte, viewed Chile's constitution, the interests of the country and the military, and Allende very differently. In September 1973, Pinochet led a successful coup. Allende died in the assault on the Le Moneda presidential palace. Helms, by then having been removed as DCI and appointed ambassador to Iran, testified in 1973 that the CIA had never sought the overthrow of Allende. For this testimony, Helms four years later pleaded no contest to a charge of perjury.

Pinochet took over the reins of government as head of a junta. Declaring a state of siege, he turned his military loose. It killed or "disappeared" thousands of Chileans, and, probably with some US culpability, at least two Americans, Charles Horman and Frank Teruggi. Subsequently, with ████████████████ and right-wing allies in Latin America, Pinochet ran Operation Candor, assassinating opponents who had fled Chile. One victim, Allende's former foreign minister Orlando Letelier, along with his American assistant Ronni Moffitt, died when his car exploded in Washington, D.C. Pinochet ruled Chile until 1990, two years following his defeat in a plebiscite on his continuing in power. In 1998, he was arrested in London on a warrant issued in Spain, where Pinochet was under investigation for his role in the deaths of Spanish citizens. In 2000, while Pinochet was still fighting extradition, the British released him after deciding that he was too ill to stand trial.[56]

The CIA's operations in Chile accelerated the Company's downward spiral precipitated by the Vietnam War. The reason was not the bloodbath that followed Allende's death and Pinochet's ascent to power. The CIA played a more direct role in the coup that overthrew Arbenz in Guatemala, for example, the catalyst for even greater slaughter.[57] The difference is that whereas PBSUCCESS remained for decades largely insulated from public scrutiny by the doctrine of plausible deniability, Chile became the focus of a Congressional investigation. And while the American people and much of the international community never lost confidence and trust in Eisenhower, Nixon's penchant for secrecy and duplicity, and his disregard for the Constitution, led to his disgrace and in 1974 his forced resignation of the presidency. Reflecting what one scholar labeled a "double whammy," the CIA's fall accompanied that of Nixon. Already widely in disfavor because of its identification with the Vietnam War, both fairly and not, the CIA for much of the American public became inseparable from the labyrinth of dirty tricks that in aggregate the world calls "Watergate."[58]

That the CIA became ensnared in Watergate's web is in equal parts ironic and just. As early as 1967, when many Americans still considered Richard Nixon politically dead, first the *New York Times* and then *Ramparts* magazine published articles revealing the Company's own dirty tricks, and domestic ones at that. In particular, Neil Sheehan, Sol Stern, and other investigative journalists exposed the CIA's covert funding of a variety of foundations, student organizations, intellectuals and artists, labor leaders, journalists, university professors and research centers, clerics, and citizen groups—a remarkable range of front operations. Although she would regret it, even the feminist icon Gloria Steinhem took agency money after she accepted the directorship of the Independent Service for Information in 1959.[59] Most famously, almost since its origin, the CIA, treading on the fine line that distinguished foreign from domestic intelligence activities, began secretly to channel money to the United States National Student Association (NSA) for the purpose of both neutralizing communist youth fronts and collecting information. The results were meager. Similar to other independent organizations that the CIA funded, the National Student Association took the money but pursued its own agenda. "The CIA might have tried to call the tune," writes Hugh Wilford, the foremost student of the agency's covert funding of citizen groups, "but the piper did not always play it, nor the audience dance to it."[60]

Two years after these revelations, Nixon took office with a take on the relationship between student activism and politics far different from that expressed in the American press. In his view, it was not the CIA but enemies of the United States—and himself personally—who were playing dirty. Nixon was convinced that foreign agents were posing as domestic radicals and infiltrating antiwar, civil rights, and parallel organizations intent on doing damage to US society and his presidency. The escalating protests on campuses and in the streets that confronted Nixon from the start of his administration confirmed the president's beliefs. His problem was that the FBI could not uncover any evidence. So, in 1970, Nixon turned to the Intelligence Community. Disregarding their charters and mandates, the CIA, National Security Agency, and Defense Intelligence Agency all signed onto a plan designed by Tom Charles Huston, Nixon's internal security aide. This Huston Plan authorized the IC to intensify domestic surveillance by opening mail, electronically eavesdropping on phone conversations, entering homes and business illegally, and more.[61]

FBI Director J. Edgar Hoover, fearful that a massive project involving so many actors not under his control would expose his own agency's decades-long history of violating the law, refused to go along. The damage to his legacy, carefully constructed over a half-century, could prove irreparable. Recognizing that Hoover's support was essential, Nixon withdrew his approval; the Huston Plan was stillborn. The entire matter may well have remained secret, or at least relegated to an unsavory footnote in US history and the history of the CIA, were it not for the September 1971 burglary of the office of Daniel Ellsberg's psychiatrist and, more prominently, the June 1972 break-in at the Watergate office complex. Ellsberg was the former defense official who had leaked the "Pentagon Papers" to the *New York Times*, and the Watergate complex housed the headquarters of the Democratic National Committee. Among those caught were CIA veterans Howard Hunt and James W. McCord, Jr., and Cuban exiles with whom the CIA had contracted for the Bay of Pigs invasion. Although both McCord and Hunt had retired from the agency, each, especially Hunt, retained multiple connections with former colleagues. DCI Helms's resistance to interposing the CIA between the White House and FBI investigators was for Nixon the last straw. In February 1973, he replaced Helms with James Schlesinger. Schlesinger, worried about the implications of the involvement of Hunt and McCord, instructed his deputy, William Colby, to survey agency personnel to compile a record of past behavior that was not authorized by its charter. The resultant report, which chronicled CIA transgressions dating to the Eisenhower administration and ran to hundreds of pages, came to be called the "Family Jewels."[62]

Schlesinger and Colby, who succeeded him as DCI when Nixon appointed Schlesinger secretary of defense in September 1973, intended the report to remain secret. But Watergate not only forced Nixon to resign on August 8, 1974,[63] it also served as a foundation and prelude for 1975—the "Year of Intelligence." Exacerbating the political polarization, "credibility gaps," and general distrust of government and its institutions generated by the Vietnam War and the spectrum of protest movements it spawned or bolstered, the Watergate hearings raised fundamental questions about the viability of the US constitutional system and the integrity of its public sphere. In this drama over the apparent threat to America's social contract, the CIA was both villain and victim.[64]

For the CIA, the rubber met the road in the last month of December 1974. Following in the wake of the Watergate hearings, the indictment of White House officials, and the resignation of the president of the United States, Seymour Hersh, a Pulitzer Prize winner for his exposé of the March 1968 massacre of perhaps as many as 500 unarmed villagers in My Lai, Vietnam, published an article in the *New York Times* under the four-column headline, "Huge CIA Operation Reported in US Against Antiwar Forces, Other Dissidents in Nixon Years." Drawing on information from the Family Jewels report as well as his informants, Hersh revealed not only the existence of the aborted Huston Plan but also Operation MHCHAOS, a program run by the long-time and many suspected paranoid head of the agency's counterintelligence unit, James Jesus Angleton. Begun by Lyndon Johnson and expanded by Nixon, MHCHAOS, according to Hersh's description, was a "massive, illegal, domestic intelligence operation" that violated the CIA's statutory authority by targeting the "antiwar movement and other dissident groups." Hersh claimed that he likewise had evidence of illegal CIA surveillance of suspected foreign intelligence agents in the United Stated that dated to the 1950s. Writing that a "possible Watergate link is but one of many questions posed by disclosures about the CIA," Hersh concluded that only a congressional hearing could "unravel" the web of deceit.[65]

Hersh's exposé cost Angleton his job, which many in the agency applauded. The chain-smoking, sallow-complexioned counterintelligence guru's unshakable belief that every Soviet defector was a double agent and practically every CIA operative a mole had in the opinion of many agency veterans crippled the Soviet division's ability to recruit assets and otherwise collect intelligence. In addition, it had cast a sinister pale over the entire agency.[66]

But aside from Angleton's dismissal, for the Company Hersh's revelations were devastating. The muckraker had written another article in the *New York Times* a few months earlier on the CIA's efforts to subvert the Allende government in Chile. Primed by the Vietnam War and Watergate hearings to reassert, or in this case finally assert, its prerogatives, Congress at long last jumped to institute oversight measures. Before the end of 1975, the House of Representatives had approved the [Harold] Hughes – [Leo]Ryan Act, an amendment to the Foreign Assistance Act of 1961 that required the president to report and describe all covert operations conducted by the CIA to one if not more congressional committees and prohibited the expenditure of CIA funds unless authorized by a presidential "finding." The Hughes – Ryan Act, accurately observes the political scientist and former Church Committee staffer Loch Johnson, was "the first measure since the creation of the CIA in 1947 to place formal controls on the Agency."[67]

But the Hersh articles and the imposition of some semblance of congressional oversight, episodic and superficial as it was, turned out to be but the beginning of the grief that would befall the CIA. With the agency's illegal domestic surveillance now public knowledge, President Gerald Ford, Michigan's long-time congressman who in less than a year's time had succeeded the disgraced Spiro Agnew as vice president and then the disgraced

Nixon as president, established a blue-ribbon commission under Nelson Rockefeller, whom Ford has appointed his vice president, to investigate Hersh's allegations. Having received a copy of the Family Jewels report from DCI Colby, Ford hoped to preempt a more extensive and probably more hostile congressional probe that could easily end up airing the CIA's dirtiest laundry. The overwhelmingly Democratic Senate, which included ten freshmen elected to fix the mechanics and culture of a government that Watergate signaled were both broken, dashed his hopes. In January 1975 it established a Select Committee to Study Governmental Operations with Respect to Intelligence Operations, chaired by the Democrats' senator from Idaho, Frank Church. The next month the House followed suit. The House Select Committee on Intelligence was initially chaired by Lucien Nedzi (Dem., MI)), but five months later it was reconstituted and New York Democrat Otis Pike replaced Nedzi. By this time, public approval of the CIA had plummeted to less than 15%.[68]

Ford committed his administration to restoring confidence in the presidency and healing the wounds of Watergate. Events conspired against him. On April 30, 1975, the government of South Vietnam surrendered, forcing the United States to withdraw under humiliating conditions. In May Cambodians seized the US merchant ship *Mayaguez* in international waters. Rather than accept another blow to America's credibility, Ford, relying on the CIA's intelligence, ordered a three-pronged military mission to rescue the crew. Over 40 Americans died in the operation, but not a single captive was rescued. Meanwhile, a civil war erupted in Angola. Ford approved a CIA covert mission, ███████████ to combat the Cuba-assisted pro-Marxist forces, the MPLA (Popular Movement for the Liberation of Angola). ███████████ accomplished little other than exacerbate tension between the White House and Congress. The enactment of the [Iowa Democratic Senator Richard "Dick"] Clark Amendment to the Arms Export Control Act prohibited US assistance to any faction in Angola and confirmed Congress' authority to oversee intelligence operations.[69]

Prior to the fall of Saigon, the Church Committee began to call witnesses—a who's who of CIA and government officials—and its staff began to pore through thousands of pages of classified materials. Then in June, seeking to get out ahead of the rapidly unfolding story, the White House released portions of the Rockefeller Commission's report. It confirmed and elaborated upon the CIA's domestic spying exposed in Hersh's article, and it included additional insights on covert operations, surreptitious drug testing on human subjects, and parallel abuses. What it omitted was any reference to planned assassinations. That proved a tactical blunder. In a television broadcast in February 1975, the journalist Daniel Schorr had broken the news that the Family Jewels report contained explosive material on US plots to assassinate foreign leaders. Ford had inadvertently leaked this information, but he had also instructed Rockefeller's committee to keep it classified. Schorr had let the cat out of the bag. Because he had made public the plots' existence but the Rockefeller Commission had suppressed this information, the Church Committee added assassinations to the list of the CIA's misdeeds it investigated. [70]

As was consistent with the committee's charge and with the CIA's history, the hearings made no effort to evaluate the agency's performance in collecting and evaluating intelligence. They did, however, uncover robust evidence of covert operations that pushed against and frequently trespassed over the limits of the law — domestic and international. Testimony and documentation left no doubt that the agency had engaged in a seemingly continuous series of efforts to overthrow or subvert governments; had penetrated multiple arenas of American civil society; had made a practice of deception and spreading misinformation; had conducted experiments to determine the effects of mind-altering and mind-controlling drugs on unsuspecting Americans (Project MKULTRA), which in one case resulted in a suicide; and otherwise had conducted itself in ways inimical to US ideals and values but in line with the betrayals of those ideals and values linked to Vietnam and Watergate. [71]

The congressional investigations likewise determined that the CIA was complicit in assassination plots. A photograph of Senator Church holding up a pistol designed to shoot poison darts point made the front pages. But the conclusions Church and his colleagues reached were ambiguous. The effectiveness of the 40 Committee and its predecessors in constructing a shield of plausible deniability left no evidence that any president had explicitly authorized an assassination. That was fine with Frank Church. The highest value target had of course been Castro. Highly partisan with presidential ambitions, Church had no interest in dragging Kennedy through Nixon's mud. When it came to assassinations, therefore, his committee reported that the CIA operated as an out-of-control "Rogue Elephant." The House's Pike Committee, however, challenged the rogue elephant metaphor by placing responsibility for CIA deeds and misdeeds squarely in the Oval Office. But that committee became so politicized that, after it decided by a split vote to reject more than one hundred deletions from its report insisted on by the CIA, the full House voted against its public release. Having received a copy from Daniel Schorr, on February 16 the *Village Voice* published the entire report.[72]

The publication of the Church Committee's multivolume reports in December 1975 and April 1976 was therefore anticlimactic. Their most sensational revelations had already become public, and they failed to provide a systematic evaluation of America's intelligence assets and effectiveness. The unauthorized release of the Pike Committee Report undermined its legitimacy. Further, the December 23, 1975, assassination of Richard Welch in Athens, Greece, the first CIA station chief murdered in US history, reminded congressional and public critics of the dangers confronted by agency personnel even as it hardened attitudes against exposés.[73]

Consequently, the "Year of Intelligence" produced remarkably moderate reforms. The Senate established its permanent Select Committee on Intelligence (the SSCI) in 1976. That same year Ford issued Executive Order 11905, US Foreign Intelligence Activities. Its provisions included the creation of a Committee on Foreign Intelligence to prepare and manage the budget and otherwise supervise the National Foreign Intelligence Program (NFIB), and an Intelligence Oversight Board. A year later, the House stood up its Permanent Select Committee on Intelligence (the HPSCI). The Foreign Intelligence Surveillance Act (FISA) of 1978 mandated strict procedures for electronic surveillance and other methods of collecting information on suspected agents of foreign powers operating on US soil. Then, in 1980, President Jimmy Carter signed the Intelligence Oversight Act, making the Intelligence Community responsible for ensuring that the SSCI and HPSCI receive timely and comprehensive notification about significant intelligence activities, particularly covert actions. But within the CIA, the Directorate of Plans (which Colby had renamed the Directorate of Operations to reflect its true mission) continued to reign supreme; the agency's analytic capacities and structure were left untouched.[74]

Notes

1   Richard Kovar, "An Interview with Richard Lehman," *Studies in Intelligence* 9 (Summer 2000), accessed on January 4, 2013, at https://www.cia.gov/library /center-for-the-study-of-intelligence/csi-publications/csi-studies/studies /summer00/art05.html. The name "President's Daily Brief" notwithstanding, today's briefers present the PDB to a range of national security principals.

2   David M. Barrett and Max Holland, "McCone's Telcon Gaffe," *Washington Decoded*, August 11, 2012, accessed on August 22, 2012, at http://www .washingtondecoded.com/site/2012/08/mccone.html; Christopher Andrew, *For the President's Eyes Only: Secret Intelligence and the American Presidency from Washington to Bush* (NY: HarperCollins, 1995), 271–77; James W. Hilty, *Robert Kennedy: Brother Protector* (Philadelphia, PA: Temple University Press, 1997), 412–31.

3   Jeffrey T. Richelson, *The U.S. Intelligence Community* (Cambridge, MA: Ballinger Publishing Co., 1984), 35–41.

4   McCone, Memorandum for the File, August 21, 1962; McCone, Memorandum of the Meeting with the President at 6:00, August 22, 1962; McCone, Memorandum of Meeting with the President, August 23, 1962; McCone, Memorandum for Discussion Today, October 17, 1962, "The Cuban Situation," all in *CIA Documents on the Cuban Missile Crisis, 1962*, ed. Mary S. McAuliffe (Washington, DC: Central Intelligence Agency, 1992), 21–29; 161.

5   McCone, Memorandum, "Soviet MRBMs in Cuba, 31 October 1962," in McAuliffe, *CIA Documents on the Cuban Missile Crisis*, 13–17; Memorandum, "U-2 Overflights of Cuba, 29 August through 14 October 1962," February 27, 1963, in McAuliffe, *CIA Documents on the Cuban Missile Crisis, 1962*, 127–37; NIE 86-2-62, "The Situation and Prospects in Cuba," August 1, 1962, in McAuliffe, *CIA Documents on the Cuban Missile Crisis*, 9–12; NIE 85-62, "The Situation and Prospects in Cuba," March 21, 1962, *FRUS, Cuba: 1961-62*, X, accessed on December 24, 1962, at http://history.state.gov /historicaldocuments/frus1961-63v10/d315.

6   CIA memorandum, "Probable Soviet MRBM Sites in Cuba," October 16, 1962, in McAuliffe, *CIA Documents on the Missile Crisis*, 139–44; Carter, Memorandum for the Record, October 17, 1962, in McAuliffe, *CIA Documents on the Missile Crisis*, 145–47.

7   The literature on the Cuban Missile Crisis is voluminous. Among the most authoritative studies are Raymond L. Garthoff, *Reflections on the Cuban Missile Crisis* (Washington D.C.: Brookings Institution Press, rev. ed. 1990); Mark J. White, *Missiles in Cuba: Kennedy, Khrushchev, Castro and the 1962 Crisis* (Chicago, IL: Ivan R. Dee, 1997); Alexandr Fursenko and Timothy Naftali, *"One Hell of a Gamble": Khrushchev, Castro, Kennedy, 1958-1964* (NY: Norton, 1997); Graham Allison and Philip Zelikow, *Essence of Decision: Explaining the Cuban Missile Crisis*, 2nd ed. (NY: Longman, 1999); Robert Weisbrot, *Maximum Danger: Kennedy, the Missiles, and the Crisis of American Confidence* (Chicago, IL: Ivan R. Dee, 2001); Sheldon M. Stern, *Averting 'The Final Failure': John F. Kennedy and the Secret Cuban Missile Crisis Meetings* (Stanford, CA: Stanford University Press, 2003); and Michael Dobbs, *One Minute to Midnight: Kennedy, Khrushchev, and Castro on the Brink of Nuclear War* (NY: Knopf, 2008). See also *The Kennedy Tapes: Inside the White House during the*

Cuban Missile Crisis, ed. Ernest R. May and Philip D. Zelikow (Cambridge, MA: Harvard University Press, 1998).

8   President's Foreign Intelligence Advisory Board Memorandum for the President and Report, February 4, 1963, in McAuliffe, *CIA Documents on the Missile Crisis*, 361–71; McCone, Memorandum for the President and Conclusions, February 28, 1963, in McAuliffe, *CIA Documents on the Missile Crisis*, 373–76; Ray Cline, "DDI notes for DCI for NSC Briefing at 3 PM in Cabinet Room," October 22, 1962, in McAuliffe, *CIA Documents on the Missile Crisis*, 271–73.

9   Len Scott, "Espionage and the Cold War: Oleg Penkovsky and the Cuban Missile Crisis," *Intelligence and National Security* 14 (Autumn 1999): 23–47; McCone, Memorandum of Discussion Today, October 17, 1962, "The Cuban Situation," October 17, 1962, in McAuliffe, *CIA Documents on the Missile Crisis*, 161–65.

10 Kennedy quoted in Andrew, *For the President's Eyes Only*, 292; Robert A. Caro, *The Years of Lyndon Johnson: The Passage of Power* (NY: Knopf, 2012), 208–18. The most detailed account of the CIA's role from start to finish during the Cuban Missile Crisis is Raymond L. Garthoff, "U.S. Intelligence," in *Intelligence and the Cuban Missile Crisis* (Portland, OR: Frank Cass, 1988), 18–63. See also Special National Intelligence Estimate (SNIE) 11-18-62, "Soviet Reactions to Certain U.S. Courses of Action on Cuba," October 19, 1962 (Excerpt); SNIE 11-19-62, "Major Consequences of US Courses of Action in Cuban," October 20, 1962, in McAuliffe, *CIA Documents on the Missile Crisis*, 197–202; 211–20.

11 Richard Helms, Memorandum for the Record, "Mongoose Meeting with the Attorney General," October 16, 1962, in McAuliffe, *CIA Documents on the Missile Crisis*, 153–54.

12 MSC [Carter], Memorandum for the Director, "MONGOOSE Operations and General Lansdales's Problems," October 25, 1962, in McAuliffe, *CIA Documents on the Missile Crisis*, 311–12; McCone, "Memorandum of Mongoose Meeting in the JCS Operations Room," October 26, 1962, at 2:30 p.m., October 29, 1962, in McAuliffe, *CIA Documents on the Missile Crisis*, 319–21.

13 Caro, *Passage of Power*, 573–75.

14 Michael Warner, "'US Intelligence and Vietnam': The Official Version(s)," *Intelligence and National Security* 25 (October 2010): 611–37.

15 Mark Atward Lawrence, *Assuming the Burden: Europe and the American Commitment to War in Vietnam* (Berkeley: University of California Press, 2005); Kathryn C. Statler, *Replacing France: The Origins of American Intervention in Vietnam* (Lexington: University Press of Kentucky, 2007); and especially on the early role of the OSS, Archimedes L. Patti, *Why Vietnam?: Prelude to America's Albatross* (Berkeley: University of California Press, 1980).

16 On the evolution of the Flying Tigers to the CAT and ultimately Air America, see, William M. Leary, *Perilous Missions: Civil Air Transport and the CIA Covert*

Operations in Asia (Birmingham: University of Alabama Press, 1984). Chapter 13 provides an account of CAT's exploits at Dienbienphu. A CAT archive is housed at the Eugene McDermott Library at the University of Texas, Dallas.

17   Andrew E. Lembke, *Landsdale, Magsaysay, America, and the Philippines: A Case Study of Limited Insurgency* (Fort Leavenworth, KA: Combat Institute Studies Press, 2001).

18   Cecil Currey, *Edward Lansdale:The Unquiet American* (NY: Houghton Mifflin, 1989); Jonathan Nashel, *Edward Lansdale's Cold War* (Amherst: University of Massachusetts Press, 2005); Frederik Logevall, *Embers of War: The Fall of an Empire and the Making of America's Vietnam* (NY: Random House, 2012), 609–93. Neil Sheehan's description of Lansdale appears in *A Bright Shining Lie: John Paul Vann and American in Vietnam* (NY: Random House, 1988), 8. Graham Greene first published *The Quiet American* in 1955.

19   Seth Jacobs, *Cold War Mandarin: Ngo Dinh Diem and the Origins of America's War in Vietnam, 1950-1963* (Lanham, MD: Rowman & Littlefield, 2006); Jessica Chapman, *Cauldron of Resistance: Ngo Dinh Diem, the United States, and 1950s Southern Vietnam* (Ithaca, NY: Cornell University Press, 2013); Edward Miller, *Misalliance: Ngo Dinh Diem, the United States, and the Fate of South Vietnam* (Cambridge, MA: Harvard University Press, 2013).

20   John Prados, "Impatience, Illusion, and Asymmetry: Intelligence in Vietnam," in *Why the North Won the Vietnam War*, ed. Marc Jason Gilbert (NY: Palgrave Macmillan, 2002), 157; Anne Blair, *Lodge in Vietnam: A Patriot Abroad* (New Haven, CT: Yale University, 1995); Edwin Moise, *Tonkin Gulf and the Escalation of the Vietnam War* (Chapel Hill: University of North Carolina Press, 1996); Timothy Castle, *A War in the Shadow of Vietnam: U.S. Military Aid to the Royal Lao Government, 1955-1975* (NY: Columbia University Press, 1993); William J. Rust, *Before the Quagmire: American Intervention in Laos, 1954-1961* (Lexington: University Press of Kentucky, 2012).

21   Frank Leith Jones, *Blowtorch: Robert Komer, Vietnam, and American Cold War Strategy* (Annapolis, MD: Naval Institute Press, 2013); Thomas L. Ahern, Jr., *Vietnam Declassified: CIA and Counterinsurgency in Vietnam* (Lexington: The University Press of Kentucky, 2009); Dale Andrade, *Ashes to Ashes: The Phoenix Program and the Vietnam War* (Lanham, MD: Lexington Books, 2009).

22   Timothy Castle, *One Day Too Long: Top Secret Site 85 and the Bombing of North Vietnam* (NY: Columbia University Press, 1999).

23   Prados, "Impatience, Illusion, and Asymmetry," 138–39.

24   An internal study by the State Department in 1969, which parallels the Department of Defense's *Pentagon Papers*, provides a remarkably illuminating digest of the Department's analyses on a range of issues pertaining to the Vietnam War. The study, along with a useful introduction by John Padros, is available as a National Security Archive electronic briefing book. See "Intelligence and

Vietnam: The Top Secret 1969 State Department Study," accessed on May 1, 2013, at http://www.gwu.edu/~nsarchiv/NSAEBB/NSAEBB121/index.htm.

25 Harold Ford, *CIA and the Vietnam Policymakers: Three Episodes, 1962-1968* (Washington, DC: Center for the Study of Intelligence, 1968), vii, 12–14; Special National Intelligence Estimate (SNIE) 10-4-54, Communist Reactions to Certain US Courses of Action with Respect to Indochina, 15 June 1954, in *Selected Estimates of the Soviet Union, 1950-1959*, ed. Scott S. Koch (Washington, DC: Center for the Study of Intelligence, 1993), 101–08; SNIE 13-66, Current Chinese Communist Intentions in the Vietnam Situation, 4 August 1966, in *Tracking the Dragon: National Intelligence Estimates on China During the Era of Mao, 1948-1976*, ed. John K. Allen, Jr; John Carver, and Tom Elmore (Washington, DC: National Intelligence Council, 2004), 405–12.

26 Ford, *CIA and the Vietnam Policymakers*, 6, 12–14.

27 Ford, *CIA and the Vietnam Policymakers*, 2–3, 12–15.

28 Ford, *CIA and the Vietnam Policymakers*, 15.

29 NIE 53-61, "Prospects in South Vietnam," April 17, 1963, in *Estimative Products on Vietnam 1948-1975*, ed. John K. Allen, John Carver, and Tom Elmore (Washington, DC: Government Printing Office, 2005), 186.

30 John M. Newman, *JFK and Vietnam: Deception, Intrigue, and the Struggle for Power* (NY: Warner Books, 1992); Ronald Steel, "The World: New Chapter, Old Debate; Would Kennedy Have Quit Vietnam?" *New York Times*, May 25, 2003; Fred Logevall, *Choosing War: The Lost Chance for Peace and Escalation of War in Vietnam* (Berkeley: University of California Press, 1995), 395–400; Gary R. Hess, *Vietnam: Explaining America's Lost War* (Malden, MA: Blackwell Publishing, 2008), 57–64.

31 John Mecklin, *Mission in Torment: An Intimate Account of the U.S. Role in Vietnam* (Garden City, NY: Doubleday, 1965), 205. A video of the comments by Madame Nhu (Tran LeXuan) following the self-immolation of Thich Quang Duc, the Buddhist monk, is available on youtube, accessed on accessed on July 11, 2012 at http://www.youtube.com/watch?v=d_PWM9gWR5E.

32 Thomas L. Athern, Jr., *CIA and the House of Ngo: Covert Action in South Vietnam, 1954-1963* (Washington, DC: Center for the Study of Intelligence, Approved for Release February 2009), 168–223, accessed on July 11, 2012 at http://www.gwu.edu/~nsarchiv/NSAEBB/NSAEBB284/2-CIA_AND_THE _HOUSE_OF_NGO.pdf; Sheehan, *Bright Shining Lie*, 361–63.

33 Quoted in David Kaiser, *American Tragedy: Kennedy, Johnson, and the Origins of the Vietnam War* (Cambridge, MA: Belknap Press, 2000), 277.

34 Howard Jones, *Death of a Generation: How the Assassinations of Diem and JFK Prolonged the Vietnam War* (NY: Oxford University Press, 2003).

35 Ford, *CIA and the Vietnam Policymakers*, 65–66.

36 Ford, *CIA and the Vietnam Policymakers*, 77–78.
37 Transcript of a Telephone Conversation between DCI McCone and Assistant Secretary of Defense Eugene Fubrini, *Foreign Relations of the United States, 1964-1968: Organization and Management of Foreign Policy; United Nations* (Washington, DC: Government Printing Office, 2004), XXXIII: 420–21.
38 Robert M. Hathaway and Russell Jack Smith, *Richard Helms As Director of Central Intelligence, 1966-1973* (Washington, DC: Center for the Study of Intelligence, 1993), 2, accessed on November 28, 2012, at http://www.foia.cia.gov/docs/DOC_0001342704/DOC_0001342704.pdf.
39 Ford, *CIA and the Vietnam Policymakers*, 78–80.
40 Peer de Silva, *Sub Rosa: The CIA and the Uses of Intelligence* (NY: Times Books, 1978); Thomas Powers, *The Man Who Kept the Secrets: Richard Helms & the CIA* (NY: Knopf, 1979); Richard Helms with William Hood, *A Look Over My Shoulder: A Life in the Central Intelligence Agency* (NY: Random House, 2003), 309–25; Ford, *CIA and the Vietnam Policymakers*, 33. Helms's in-house biography, Hathaway and Smith, *Richard Helms As Director of Central Intelligence*, was declassified in 2006.
41 Ford, *CIA and the Vietnam Policymakers*, 85–89.
42 Ford, *CIA and the Vietnam Policymakers*, 89-102; C. Michael Hiam, *Who the Hell Are We Fighting? The Story of Sam Adams and the Vietnam Intelligence Wars* (Hanover, NH: Steerforth Press, 2006), 74–129; Sam Adams, *War of Numbers: An Intelligence Memoir* (Hanover, NH: Steerforth Press, 1994), 139; George W. Allen, *None So Blind: A Personal Account of the Intelligence Failure in Vietnam* (Chicago, IL: Ivan R. Dee, 2001), 243–54.
43 SNIE 14.3-67, "Capabilities of the Vietnamese Communists for Fighting in South Vietnam," in *Estimative Products on Vietnam*, 427–55; Tim Weiner, *Legacy of Ashes: The History of the CIA* (NY: Doubleday, 2007), 268. For a more sympathetic assessment of Helms and Carver, see Brian D. Blankenship, "A Deceptive Estimate? The Politics of Deceptive Irregular Troop Numbers in Vietnam," *Journal of Intelligence* 12 (2013): 93–112.
44 Palmer quoted in Ford, *CIA and the Vietnam Policymakers*, 108–21.
45 Richard H. Immerman, "'A Time in the Tide of Men's Affairs': Lyndon Johnson and Vietnam," in *Lyndon Johnson Confronts the World: American Foreign Policy, 1963-1968*, ed. Warren Cohen and Nancy Bernkopf Tucker, (NY: Cambridge University Press, 1994), 78–79.
46 Andrew, *For the President's Eyes Only*, 350; Douglas F. Garthoff, "Analyzing Soviet Politics and Foreign Policy," in *Watching the Bear: Essays on the CIA's Analysis of the Soviet Union*, ed. Gerald K. Hanes and Robert E. Leggett (Washington, DC: Government Printing Office, 2003), 77–80; Although the CIA's restructuring under Nixon began during Helms's tenure with the 1971

Schlesinger Report, implementation took place in 1973 when Schlesinger himself and then William Colby succeeded Helms as DCI. See "A Review of the Intelligence Community," March 10, 1971, accessed on November 17, 2012, at http://www.gwu.edu/~nsarchiv/NSAEBB/NSAEBB144/document%204.pdf.

47 Anne Hessing Cahn: *Killing Détente: The Right Attacks the CIA* (University Park, PA: Pennsylvania State University Press, 1998), 74; Andrew, *For the President's Eyes Only*, 350–54; Robert M. Gates, *From the Shadows: The Ultimate Insider's Story of Five Presidents and How They Won the Cold War* (NY: Simon & Schuster, 1996), 30; *Foreign Relations of the United States, 1969-1972: National Security Policy* (Washington, DC: Government Printing Office, 2011), XXXIV: 117n.3.

48 Editorial Note, *FRUS, 1969-72*, XXXIV: 133–34; Helms, *A Look Over My Shoulder*, 394–95.

49 See for example the documents available in *Foreign Relations of the United States, 1969-1976: Vietnam, October 1972-January 1973* (Washington, DC: Government Printing Office, 2010), IX.

50 Memorandum from Laurence Lynn of the National Security Council Staff to Kissinger, June 30, 1969, *FRUS, 1969-72*, XXXIV: 155; Memorandum for Kissinger to Nixon, November 26, 1969, *FRUS, 1969-72*, XXXIV: 370. Derogatory comments by Nixon and Kissinger about Helms and CIA run throughout this FRUS volume and the one on SALT 1, *Foreign Relations of the United States, 1969-1972: SALT 1* (Washington, DC: Government Printing Office, 2010), XXXII.

51 Tanya Harmer, *Allende's Chile and the Inter-American Cold War* (Chapel Hill: University of North Carolina Press, 2011). For other studies with contrasting interpretations, see Kristian Gustafson, *Hostile Intent: U.S. Covert Operations in Chile, 1964-1974* (Washington, DC: Potomac Books, 2007); Lubna Z. Qureshi, *Nixon, Kissinger, and Allende: U.S. Involvement in the 1973 Coup in Chile* (Lanham, MD: Lexington Books, 2009).

52 Kissinger's quote appeared subsequently in the *New York Times* on September 11, 1974.

53 Powers, *The Man Who Kept the Secrets*, 220–31.

54 Gregory F. Treverton, *Covert Action: The Limits of Intervention in the Postwar World* (NY: Basic Books, 1987), 124–43.

55 For extensive documentation on the CIA's campaign against Allende, see Peter Kornbluh, *The Pinochet File: A Declassified Dossier on Atrocity and Accountability* (NY: The New Press, 2003). For a denial of U.S. complicity, see William D. Rogers, "Mythmaking and Foreign Policy," *Foreign Affairs* 83 (January/February 2004): 160–65. Rogers was responding to a positive review of the Kornbluh volume in the previous issue. See Kenneth Maxwell, "The Other 9/11: the United States and Chile, 1973," *Foreign Affairs* 82 (November/December 2003): 147–51. Maxwell resigned as a book reviewer for the

journal to protest its refusal to print his rebuttal because, he claims, *Foreign Affairs* succumbed to pressure from Kissinger. The editors selected Princeton professor Jeremy Adelman as a replacement, but after initially agreeing he withdrew because of the controversy. See Diana Jean Schemo, "Dispute Over Pinochet Book Claims Another Casualty," *New York Times*, June 16, 2004.

56   Larry Rohter, "New Evidence Surfaces in '73 Killing of American in Chile," *New York Times*, March 13, 2004; Vernon Loeb, "The CIA had Covert Tie to Letelier Plot," *Washington Post*, September 21, 2000; BBC News, "The Pinochet Case: Time Line," accessed on November 18, 2012, at http://news .bbc.co.uk/2/hi/special_report/1998/10/98/the_pinochet_file/232499.stm. For the links between the CIA, Pinochet's coup, and Operation Condor, see Kornbluh, *The Pinochet File*. Documents are also available at the National Security Archive at http://www.gwu.edu/~nsarchiv/news/20001113/.

57   Susanne Jonas, *The Battle for Guatemala: Rebels, Death Squads, and U.S. Power* (Boulder, CO: Westview Press, 1991); Greg Grandin, *The Last Colonial Massacre: Latin America in the Cold War* (Chicago, IL: University of Chicago Press, 2004).

58   Cahn: *Killing Détente*, 71–72.

59   Hugh Wilford, *The Mighty Wurlitzer: How the CIA Played America* (Cambridge, MA: Harvard University, 2008), 141–48.

60   Neil Sheehan, "A Student Group Concedes It Took Funds from C.I.A.," *New York Times*, February 14, 1967; Sol Stern. "A Short Account of International Student Politics & the Cold War with Particular Reference to the NSA, CIA, Etc." *Ramparts* 5 (March 1967), accessed on July 20, 2012, at http://www.cia-on-campus.org/nsa/nsa.html; Tity de Vries, "The 1967 Central Intelligence Agency Scandal: Catalyst in a Transforming Relationship between State and People," *Journal of American History* 98 (March 2012): 1075–92; Quenby Olmstead Hughes, *"In the Interest of Democracy": The Rise and Fall of the Early Cold War Alliance Between the American Federation of Labor and the Central Intelligence Agency* (Oxford, England: Peter Lang, 2011); Wilford, 141–8.

61   United States Senate, 94th Congress, 2nd Session, *Final Report of the Select Committee to Study Governmental Operations with Respect to Intelligence Activities* (Washington, DC: Government Printing Office, 1976), Book III: 921–82. (Hereafter, *Church Committee Report*)

62   Stanley I. Kutler, *The Wars of Watergate: The Last Crisis of Richard Nixon* (NY: Knopf, 1990); Karen DeYoung and Walter Pincus, "CIA to Air Decades of its Dirty Laundry," *Washington Post*, June 22, 2007; John Prados, *The Family Jewels: The CIA, Secrecy, and Presidential Power* (Austin: University of Texas Press, 2013). The "Family Jewels" report is available at http://www.gwu .edu/~nsarchiv/NSAEBB/NSAEBB222/family_jewels_full_ocr.pdf (accessed October 6, 2011).

63   Ironically in light of Nixon's relationship with the CIA and his policy of détente with the Soviet Union, the day Nixon resigned, the *Glomar Explorer*, built under the cover of Howard Hughes's Deep Ocean Mining Project, secured within its cavernous hold portions of a sunken Soviet submarine. The submarine's salvage culminated the CIA's six-year Project Azorian, approved by Nixon personally and labeled by one of its participants as the agency's "greatest covert operation." At a cost estimated as high as $500 million, Project Azorian sought to raise a Soviet K-129 submarine, along with its cargo of nuclear missiles and torpedoes, that had sank in 1968 some 1500 miles northwest of the Hawaiian Isles, in order to discover its secrets it. The rewards probably were not worth the CIA's time, effort, and expense. For the fullest account of this history, see David A. Sharp, *The CIA's Greatest Covert Operation: Inside the Daring Mission to Recover a Nuclear-Armed Soviet Sub* (Lawrence: University Press of Kansas, 2012).

64   *America in the Seventies*, ed. Beth Bailey and David Farber (Lawrence: University Press of Kansas, 2004); Laura Kalmon, *Right Star Rising: A New Politics, 1974-1980* (NY: Norton, 2010).

65   Seymour M. Hersh, "Huge C.I.A. Operation Reported in U.S. Against Antiwar Forces, Other Dissidents in Nixon Years," *New York Times*, December 22, 1974.

66   Tom Mangold, *Cold Warrior: James Jesus Angleton: The CIA's Master Spy Hunter* (NY: Simon & Schuster, 1991); David Wise, *Molehunt: The Secret Search for Traitors That Shattered the CIA* (NY: Random House, 1992); Michael Holzman, *James Jesus Angleton, The CIA, and the Craft of Counterintelligence* (Amherst: University of Massachusetts Press, 2008).

67   Seymour M. Hersh, "C.I.A. Chief Tells House of $8 Million Campaign Against Allende in '70-73," *New York Times*, September 8, 1974; Loch K. Johnson, *America's Secret Power: The CIA in a Democratic Society* (NY: Oxford University Press, 1989), 207.

68   Kathryn S. Olmstead, *Challenging the Secret Government: The Post-Watergate Investigations of the CIA and FBI* (Chapel Hill: University of North Carolina Press, 1996), 19, 48–58. See also Loch K. Johnson, *A Season of Inquiry: The Senate Intelligence Investigation* (Lexington: University Press of Kentucky, 1985).

69   Robert J. Mahoney, *The Mayaguez Incident: Testing America's Resolve in the Post-Vietnam Era* (Lubbock: Texas Tech University Press, 2011); John Stockwell, *In Search of Enemies: A CIA Story* (NY: Norton, 1979); Piero Gleijeses, *Conflicting Missions: Havana, Washington, and Africa, 1959-1976* (Chapel Hill: University of North Carolina Press, 2002); Robert David Johnson, "The Unexpected Consequences of Congressional Activism: The Clark and Tunney Amendments and U.S. Policy toward Angola," *Diplomatic History* 27 (April 2003): 215–43.

70   Olmstead, *Challenging the Secret Government*, 53–6; 82–85; Cahn; *Killing Détente*, 78–81.

71 Olmstead, *Challenging the Secret Government*, 85–167; Nicholas, M. Horrock, "C.I.A. Data Shows 14-Year Project on Controlling Human Behavior," *New York Times*, July 21, 1977; "Project MKULTRA, the CIA's Program of Research in Behavioral Modification," U.S. Senate, *Joint Hearing Before the Senate Committee on Intelligence and the Subcommittee on Health and Scientific Research of the Committee on Human Resources*, 95th Cong., 1st Sess., August 3, 1977, accessed on November 27, 2012, at http://www.nytimes.com/packages/pdf/national/13inmate_ProjectMKULTRA.pdf; James Risen, "Suit Planned Over Death of Man CIA Drugged," *New York Times*, November 27, 2012.

72 Gerald K. Haines, "Looking for a Rogue Elephant: The Pike Committee Investigations and the CIA," *CSI* (Winter 1998–1999), accessed on October 7, 2011 at http://bss.sfsu.edu/fischer/ir%20360/Readings/pike.htm.

73 Laurence Stern, "CIA Agent's Murder Spurs Accusations," *Washington Post*, December 25, 1975; Weiner, *Legacy of Ashes*, 334.

74 Douglas F. Garthoff, *Directors of Central Intelligence as Leaders of the U.S. Intelligence Community* (Washington, DC: Potomac Books, 2007), 295–96; Executive Order 11905: United States Foreign Intelligence Activities, accessed on October 7, 2011, at http://www.ford.utexas.edu/library/speeches/760110e.htm #SEC. 6; Johnson, *America's Secret Power*, 209.

4

A Time of Troubles: 1977 – 1987

William Colby was at the top of the CIA's list of most enigmatic and controversial figures until his body washed ashore on the banks of Maryland's Wicomico River on May 6, 1996. (No evidence of foul play surfaced; Colby apparently suffered a heart attack while canoeing, although predictably suspicions remain.) His prowess as a covert operative dated to his OSS service during World War II. Like so many of the CIA's legends who joined the agency at its birth and went on to hold positions of leadership, Colby had been with the OSS's Special Operations branch. He had in fact been one of the very few to survive the rigorous training and subsequent selection process for Operation Jedburgh. The Jedburghs were the three-person teams composed of American, British, and French (resistance) operatives that were clandestinely inserted into France to prepare for and then assist the Allied cross-channel invasion and liberation of the country. His feats of heroism were but the start of Colby's illustrious career in intelligence, one that few in the CIA's history could match.

But as a means-justifies-the-ends kind of patriot, Colby had also directed the CIA's operations in Vietnam. Most notably, Colby was the official most identified with the Phoenix Program that generated so much criticism — and opprobrium. It was also because of his fierce patriotism, and his personal and, some would argue, sui generis system of values and priorities, that he had agreed to disclose the secrets of the Family Jewels and otherwise cooperate with the congressional investigations in the mid-1970s. For many in the CIA, most of all those of Colby's generation, his cooperation was unforgivable. The Company lived by a code of secrecy; what took place in the CIA stayed in the CIA. Richard Helms had pleaded no contest to the charge of misleading Congress because he had refused to violate that

The Hidden Hand: A Brief History of the CIA, First Edition. Richard Immerman.
© 2014 John Wiley & Sons, Ltd. Published 2014 by John Wiley & Sons, Ltd.

code because he had refused to violate that code and tell the whole story of Chile at the hearings to confirm his appointment as ambassador to Iran in February 1973. The Church and Pike Committees, while falling short of their potential, generated a healthy impulse for reform. But as far as the agency was concerned, they revealed Colby as a traitor.[1]

From Gerald Ford's perspective, Colby, with whom his relationship had never been more than distant, had become a liability. He was distrusted by the president's key aides, especially Kissinger. The Church Committee hearings had spun out of control, and for that the West Wing held Colby complicit, if not responsible. Further, even though Colby personally had not been charged with misdeeds, even in the press, as DCI he represented them. Then there was Colby's association with Vietnam and assassinations, wounds on America's soul that Ford pledged to do whatever it took to mend. Yet the CIA's 1975 covert intervention in Angola's civil war to assist the alliance opposing the Fidel Castro–supported MPLA (People's Movement for the Liberation of Angola), which ironically Ford approved but Colby opposed, aggravated those wounds. Because Colby had become so toxic to almost everyone across the political and bureaucratic spectrum, sidelining him was one step Ford could take that would not cost him or the Republicans anything. In November 1975, shortly before Congress enacted Democratic Representative from Iowa Dick Clark's amendment to the Arms Export Control Act that banned funds for the CIA operation, Ford fired Colby, along with Secretary of Defense and former DCI James Schlesinger. At the same time he stripped Kissinger of his position as national security advisor. The other half of the "Nixonger" foreign policy team, however, would continue to wear what in theory was his principal hat: secretary of state. Kissinger, the *New York Times* reported about this massive shake-up of Ford's national security apparatus, agreed to give up the executive office post that he had exploited so successfully in his rise to prominence in return for the departures of Schlesinger and Colby.[2]

The president's motives went beyond assessments of Colby's performance, loyalty, or values—and for that matter his respect or lack thereof for Schlesinger and even Kissinger. More salient in Ford's calculations was the political context, in particular his own future. By the end of 1975 Ford had begun to gear up for a challenge from the political right for the Republican presidential nomination. Ronald Reagan, the sitting governor of California, was highly inexperienced in foreign affairs. And notwithstanding his appointment to the Rockefeller Commission that Ford hoped would deter Congress from initiating an investigation of CIA abuses, he knew very little about intelligence or the Intelligence Community (even though Reagan appears to have well understood the allegations against the CIA, he rarely attended the Commission's meetings).

But Reagan had a visceral hatred of all things communist, and he instinctively found persuasive the charges of hard-line conservatives (and burgeoning neoconservatives) that the Nixon–Ford–Kissinger strategy of détente with the Soviets, especially its twin centerpieces—the Anti-Ballistic Missile (ABM) and SALT I treaties of 1972—were fatally flawed. They therefore presented, individually as well as together, a clear and present danger to the United States. For placing America at such risk, this growing circle of Reagan advisors—the group included some key members of the President's Foreign Intelligence Advisory Board (PFIAB) as well as such well-respected members of the national security establishment as former State Department official and primary author of NSC 68, Paul Nitze, and RAND Corporation and University of Chicago political scientist Albert Wohlstetter—held accountable not only the Republican leadership (now personified by Ford and Rockefeller) but also the CIA. Especially in its National Intelligence Estimates but also in other products, the CIA, from where they sat, had consistently and dangerously underestimated Soviet nuclear capabilities by understating the pace and scope of its missile production, its military spending, and most importantly, its aggressive intentions. Wohlstetter had virtually summoned Cold War hawks to wage war against both détente and the CIA in his 1974 article, "Is there a Strategic Arms Race?" published in *Foreign Policy*, a must-read journal of the national security establishment and political elite.[3]

Justifiably feeling at risk, Ford appointed George H. W. Bush to replace Colby as DCI (Donald Rumsfeld became the new secretary of defense, and Lieutenant General Brent Scowcroft, the national security advisor). In doing so, he aggravated the agency's instability and therefore its vulnerability. Including Helms, Bush was the fourth director of central intelligence between 1973 and 1976, the same number that had run the agency and community over the previous twenty years. Ford's appointment of Bush also continued and exacerbated, albeit somewhat unintentionally, the politicization of intelligence that the Vietnam War had generated. Directors of central intelligence had historically been commendably apolitical; Allen Dulles and Richard Helms had served both Republican and Democratic presidents. Bush was anything but. The son of Prescott Bush, the longtime Republican senator from Connecticut, he had served two terms in the House representing the 7th district of Texas, where he had moved after graduating from Yale. In 1970 he ran unsuccessfully for the Senate, losing to a rising star among the Democrats, Lloyd Bentson. Nixon then appointed Bush America's ambassador to the United Nations, after which he chaired the Republican National Committee through the Watergate hearings and Nixon's resignation. Subsequently, Ford appointed Bush the US envoy to China (officially the chief of the US Liaison Office) in the lead-up to American recognition. In short, Bush was exceptionally politically connected, and exceptionally politically experienced and sensitive. That is what Ford wanted in a DCI: his job description for Bush was not so much to lead the Intelligence Community as to deflect the right-wing attack that his (Ford's) administration was allowing the agency to undermine US security.[4]

Bush knew what to do. For months a proposal by the President's Foreign Intelligence Advisory Board (PFIAB) had circulated throughout the White House and Capitol Hill to launch an exercise in competitive analysis. Reflecting the predispositions of most members of the PFIAB, the purpose would be to challenge the CIA to defend its allegedly "soft" analyses of Soviet intentions and capabilities. The rationale was to firm up US assessments prior to continuing the current negotiations with the Soviets let alone reaching agreement on the second stage of an arms control treaty: SALT II. Although vulnerable to manipulation, in a value-neutral environment such an exercise could prove salutary by requiring the CIA to make more explicit its assumptions, to provide more insight into its sources and underscore its intelligence gaps, and even to stipulate alternate interpretations of the same information.[5]

But given that conservatives had already attacked the CIA's estimates, this environment was highly politicized—anything but value-neutral. In addition, the exercise was inherently flawed. It pitted one side against the other in essentially a winner-take-all contest. There was no "Team C" charged with representing the "center." Moreover, Team B's primary goal was to critique the CIA's estimate as opposed to presenting an alternative of its own. The "two teams were playing different games."[6] Consequently, Colby, appreciating the threat that this exercise posed to the professionalism of his intelligence analysts by essentially coercing them into defending themselves or surrendering to a predetermined ideologically driven position, refused, some would argue heroically, to cooperate (to improve the estimative process by encouraging a diversity of judgments and expanding the breadth of expertise, Colby had replaced the Office/Board of National Estimates with National Intelligence Officers and a National Intelligence Council in 1973). Although warned explicitly of the potential pitfalls, Bush did not stand on principle. In May 1976, shortly after Ford suffered a string of defeats in Republican state primaries, he authorized initiating the exercise with a brief note to his deputy, "Let her fly. OK. GB."[7]

The new director of central intelligence established an analytic "Team B" to face off against the CIA in dueling assessments. Its judgments were a foregone conclusion. Bush selected to chair Team B the Russian historian and rabid anti-Soviet Richard Pipes, already on record for his denunciations of CIA analyses. Pipes charged that the agency's Soviet experts failed to take sufficient account of Russian culture and Kremlin irrationality. His colleagues, among whom was the longtime critic of the CIA's estimates and Reagan advisor Lt. General Daniel Graham, were uniformly sympathetic to Pipes's ideological and strategic perspective. Graham had worked for the Office of National Estimates and directed the Pentagon's Defense Intelligence Agency. Further, Pipes' staff of consultants included Nitze and an emerging luminary among critics of America's arms control regime who had been mentored by both Nitze and Albert Wohlstetter, Paul Wolfowitz.[8]

Team B's report (which relied heavily on open sources, not the Intelligence Community's intelligence, to which it had access) was unsparing in its criticism of agency analysts' assessment of Soviet capabilities, intentions, and doctrine, as Bush and Ford knew it would be. The report indicted the CIA for failing adequately to account for the terrifying technological advances in Soviet weaponry, for underestimating how much Moscow spent to fund these advances and the resultant weapons systems, and for downplaying the Kremlin's quest for global hegemony. It also challenged the agency's tradecraft by arguing that both analysts and collectors placed such a premium on and faith in satellite imagery and signals intelligence that they neglected what the Soviet leaders and their proxies actually said and did. This criticism was not totally without validity (although the Team B report omitted any reference to the damage done to the CIA's HUMINT capacity by James Angleton's witch hunt) and would have resonance in the future. Still, the consensus among scholars and experts is that Team B's conclusions, which judged Soviet capabilities as much greater than did the CIA and rapidly increasing in size and accuracy, and which predicted that the Soviets intended to provoke a direct confrontation with the United States, were wildly off the mark.[9]

Fortunately, for both the CIA and Soviet-American relations, by the time Team B completed its assignment in 1976, Ford was too preoccupied with the campaign to do anything with it. What was more, while the incumbent president wanted to allow his conservative challengers the opportunity to influence, or at least to appear to influence, assessments of the Soviet Union, he did not want their extreme position to become the prevailing one. Ford had been a proponent, not critic, of détente and the SALT negotiations. Hence, illustrating what the political scientist Joshua Rovner labels "indirect politicization," while providing the CIA's critics a chance to place the CIA on the defensive, neither the administration nor Bush (also a "moderate" compared to the hawks on Team B) pressured the CIA to revise its fundamental judgments. As a result, submitted in October 1976, the Team B report's impact on the end-of-the-year National Intelligence Estimate on Soviet Forces for Strategic Nuclear Conflict through the mid-1980s (NIE 11-3/8-76), albeit not negligible, was minimal.[10]

In retrospect, a detached observer might judge the behavior of Ford and Bush as politically shrewd were it not for the impact of Team B on the CIA and the long-term consequences. That impact was significant, and the consequences were serious. As Colby had predicted, simply by approving the exercise in the context that they did and in the manner that they did, the president and his director of central intelligence corrupted the process of producing the vital National Intelligence Estimate on Soviet nuclear capabilities. Perhaps even more corrosive to the future of US security policy, the Team B exercise further undermined the credibility and authority of America's Intelligence Community. It is one thing for professional intelligence analysts to solicit input from scholars and others in the public sphere, and for that matter for qualified experts from outside the IC to review the analysts' products and evaluate their tradecraft. Although often reluctant to do so, they should. Such a process in fact became required and standardized after the debacle of the 2002 National Intelligence Estimate on Iraq's weapons of mass destruction program.

It is another thing, however, and an intolerable one, to encourage the input of those from outside the IC, no matter how expert, to replace or substitute for as opposed to inform judgments of professional analysts. This is what the administration did when it sanctioned the exercise, even if it did so only implicitly. By blessing a competition between the CIA and the members and staff of Team B, Ford, with Bush as his agent, signaled policy makers that they need not and perhaps should not pay attention to or even respect the CIA's analytic products. What is more, although the Team B report remained classified (not until 1996 was it declassified), at least one of its members leaked its criticisms to the press.[11] For an agency still reeling from the congressional hearings, this public condemnation of its competency, not just its methods or its behavior, could have caused irreparable damage to its reputation and therefore its effectiveness. This is particularly true because the disparagement did not target only the cowboys but also the intellectuals, not only the operatives but also the analysts.

The CIA weathered the storm, but not well and not by much. Ford did manage to distance himself somewhat from the Nixon-Kissinger policy of détente, and he did fight off Reagan's challenge for the Republic nomination. It is difficult to gauge the relationship between the two, and close to impossible to determine how consequential the Team B exercise was. What is more, in the near-term it did not much matter. Ford won the nomination but lost the election. And Frank Church, who also hoped to use the "intelligence wars" as a path to the White House, did not even secure the Democratic nomination. The party chose and Americans elected as president Jimmy Carter, a Washington outsider who pledged to right the country's moral compass and conduct a foreign policy consistent with America's ideals as well as interests. By definition and tradition, covert operations, let alone assassinations, were incompatible with those ideals, and their report card on serving the national interest was mixed at best. While Carter aligned himself with the agency's experts in their battle with Team B ideologues over estimates of the Soviet Union's capabilities and intentions, and thus the threat that the Soviets posed, he signaled during the campaign and the interregnum that he was no friend of the CIA. Neither was his vice president, Minnesota Senator Walter Mondale. Identified closely with the liberal icon Hubert Humphrey, whom he replaced in the Senate when Humphrey became Lyndon Johnson's vice president, Mondale had been a vocal critic of the agency since his service on the Church Committee. Carter and Mondale made CIA management, abuse, and accountability an issue in the 1976 presidential campaign.[12]

The Carter Calamity

The day that Carter took office, photographs from the newest generation of US spy satellites, the KH-11 ▉▉▉▉▉▉▉▉▉▉▉▉▉▉▉▉▉▉▉▉▉ ▉▉▉▉▉▉▉▉▉ reached Washington. Unlike previous images, these were digitalized transmissions. The process, called electro-optical digital imaging, did not require film to retrieve and develop. In "near real time," computers received and converted the coded data into pictures, which could be readily manipulated and enhanced. This success excited the new president, a technology enthusiast who recognized how valuable the KH-11 could be in pushing forward the SALT II negotiations.[13]

Yet Carter's skepticism about the CIA remained undiminished. He seemed to give credit for this achievement to the National Reconnaissance Office (NRO), which Eisenhower established in 1960 to manage the CORONA program, more than to the agency. Indeed, as if to signify the dawning of a new day for the DCI, Carter took the unprecedented step of dismissing Bush. It was not so much that Bush was a Republican who as DCI had served a Republican president. Of greater salience, Bush was tied to policies, programs, and priories from which Carter wanted to divorce himself— and America. Carter's preferred successor to Bush, Thomas Hughes, who had headed the State Department's Bureau of Intelligence and Research, declined the offer. The president's alternative choice was John F. Kennedy's advisor, speech writer, and alter ego, Theodore Sorensen. Sorensen accepted the nomination, but Carter withdrew his name from consideration amid criticism that Sorensen was too dovish and a potential security risk to boot. The president then turned to Admiral Stansfield Turner.

Although more extensive than Carter's, Turner's experience with intelligence was also limited—he described himself as an "outsider to the intelligence profession." Carter was confident, nevertheless, that his former Annapolis classmate and Rhodes Scholar (Carter almost won one as well) could revolutionize the CIA's culture. Congruent with this goal, and much to the chagrin of Carter's more hawkish national security advisor, Zbigniew Brzezinski, Turner requested a budget that allocated the lowest funding for covert operations since Truman's first term. He revealingly entitled his 1985 memoir, *Secrecy and Democracy: The CIA in Transition*.[14]

In 1977, during the first year of Carter's presidency and Turner's tenure as CIA director, Richard Helms pleaded no contest to the charge of perjury. Helms explained that at the hearing to confirm his appointment as ambassador to Iran, he had responded to "trick questions" about the role of the CIA in the campaign against Allende in a way appropriate for an intelligence officer. Essentially he had finessed and stonewalled; at the worst he had deceived. In legal terms, that meant he had lied to Congress, and Helms received a two-year suspended sentence and a $2000 fine. Still smarting from what they perceived as Colby's betrayal, their treatment by the Church and Pike Commissions, the establishment of the Senate Select Committee on Intelligence and House Permanent Subcommittee on Intelligence to institutionalize congressional oversight, and the Team B challenge to their expertise, many CIA veterans were horrified. Helms had been with the CIA in good times and bad, he had served as director of central intelligence longer than anyone other than Allen Dulles, he was one of them, and he had responded in the way expected of an intelligence officer: he had kept the secrets. Helms's former colleagues at the agency paid his fine.[15]

From the perspective of these veterans, Carter and Turner were piling on the insults, and of greater consequence, the injuries. Turner had directed the Chief of Naval Operations' Systems Analysis Division and presided over the Naval War College; he shared the president's distrust of and distaste for the CIA's ways of doing business. Not surprisingly, therefore, he brought with him to Langley a team of personnel that longtime CIA officials labeled the "Navy Mafia" and suspected of comprising a fifth column that would subvert the Company's culture.

The new CIA director, moreover, focused his attention on improving the agency's capabilities for collection, which along with analysis he considered the Intelligence Community's central responsibility. For this purpose, he made clear that he intended to place his faith in technology and data points. In short order, Turner pared the budget for clandestine projects and cashiered longtime operatives as relics of an irrational Cold War mindset that encouraged risky and often counterproductive adventurism. Indeed, notwithstanding what many in the CIA believed was a desperate need rapidly to expand HUMINT collection capacity in the Soviet Union after years of Angleton-induced ravages, Turner ordered the shutdown of covert operations in Moscow. By relying on SIGINT (signals intelligence, the responsibility primarily of the National Security Agency) and imagery intelligence (IMINT, imagery collected by the National Reconnaissance Office), he explained, this measure would help "put the CIA's much criticized past behind us." Turner also supported Carter's abolition of the President's Foreign Intelligence Advisory Board (Ronald Reagan revived it). In both of their views, historically the PFIAB had been too conservative institutionally and politically, too liberal with its recommendations to execute paramilitary projects, and in general of little value to the president. Carter wanted to signal that he intended to rely on his DCI, not the PFIAB, for advice, and Turner was only too happy to accommodate him.[16]

Finally, Turner once again reorganized the CIA's analytic architecture in order to further his goal of improving its estimative capability. In his view, the analytic reports, particularly the National Intelligence Estimates, were too shallow, frequently unrepresentative of the spectrum of elements that comprised the Intelligence Community, and very often either incorrect or not relevant to the needs of the IC's customers, particularly the president.

In addition, Turner concluded that in terms of producing national intelligence, his priority, there was too much redundancy between the National Intelligence Officers (NIOs) that comprised the National Intelligence Council (NIC) established by Colby and the CIA's Directorate of Intelligence. Therefore he reconfigured the DI by establishing a new entity, the National Foreign Assessment Center (NFAC). The NFAC included a Center for Policy Support, the DI's Offices of Regional and Political Analysis, Scientific Intelligence, and Weapons Intelligence, and the National Intelligence Officers.[17]

To head the NFAC, Turner appointed Robert R. Bowie, whom the new DCI had already brought into the administration to chair the National Intelligence Council. Bowie was the highly respected director of Harvard University's Center for International Affairs. Prior to his selection to head the fledgling center, he had served under Eisenhower as the assistant secretary of state for policy planning and the State Department's representative to the National Security Council's Planning Board. The acuity of Bowie's mind was legendary, his contrarian nature and love of debate a virtual guarantee against least-common denominator judgments, and like Turner, he lacked any instinctive or inherent loyalty to the CIA. Although the National Intelligence Officers and their staffs were heavily dependent on the CIA for both expertise and information, within the National Foreign Assessment Center the NIOs received "pride of place." CIA analysts interpreted Turner's reforms and selection of the outsider Bowie, even if sound in theory, as an affront to their past performance.[18]

Turner's combative leadership style and ill-concealed premise that the CIA was a broken agency in urgent need of his kind of fixing certainly contributed to the declining morale that pervaded all components of the agency during the Carter years. It is doubtful, however, that this poor morale had much to do with the Company's dismal record during the late 1970s. The reasons were more elemental and structural. Even as the Carter administration achieved some hard-fought and significant achievements during its first three years in office, culminating in 1978 with the approval of two Panama Canal Treaties and, in 1979, the signing of the Egyptian-Israeli Peace Treaty (Camp David Accords) and SALT II Treaty with the Soviets, its foreign policies lacked the coherence and consistency that are prerequisites for producers and collectors of intelligence to serve their customers effectively. Carter's incoherence deprived the Intelligence Community of the cues it required in order to know what to collect and what to assess. In part, the problem evolved from Carter's inexperience and his inability to articulate a vision that embraced both containment and the promotion of human rights. No less responsible, and inseparable, were the conflicting views between Secretary of State Cyrus Vance, a proponent of détente who preferred diplomacy to force, and National Security Advisor Zbigniew Brzezinski, an ardent and muscular Cold Warrior.[19]

In this battle for Carter's heart and mind, Brzezinski ultimately gained the upper hand, a "victory" over Vance that he owed in no small part to his control over the intelligence that Carter received. As national security advisor, he insisted that he, not DCI Turner, deliver the president's "intelligence briefing," which he pointedly renamed the "national security briefing." Brzezinski goes so far as to boast in his memoir about how successfully he limited Turner's direct contact with Carter, even though Carter had persuaded Turner to accept the appointment of director of central intelligence by promising that he would meet regularly with him alone and without a gatekeeper. Brzezinski writes that "throughout the four years [Turner had] practically no one-on-one meetings with the President, and all CIA reporting was funneled to the President through me."[20]

Nevertheless, the administration's internal pathologies and the upheavals within the CIA cannot be blamed for the grief that befell it and America at large in the latter half of Carter's presidency. History, or the international environment, conspired against Carter as events took place for which he was not responsible and over which he had no control. But because of the combination of its dysfunctional national security architecture and ill-equipped IC, the administration managed the events poorly, and arguably aggravated them.

The catalyst for the international crises that Carter confronted in his final two years in office was the growing unrest in Iran. By 1978, a quarter of a century had passed since TBAJAX had restored Shah Muhammad Reza Pahlevi to the Peacock Throne. During that time, for the United States the shah had turned Iran into an oasis of stability in the Middle East, the linchpin of American efforts to contain communism and preserve ready access to the region's vital resources, oil above all. Since the Eisenhower years, with the possible exception of the John F. Kennedy presidency, successive US administrations had also perceived Iran as a developmental model for its neighbors and for that matter the Third World in general. In addition, Iran became a vital staging and refueling base for aerial surveillance of the Soviet Union, that much more so following the Johnson administration as US relations with Pakistan steadily deteriorated in the late 1960s.[21]

For his part the shah, appreciating his value to US strategy, saw no reason to heed advice to relax the repressive regime he had methodically constructed over the decades. For their part, American policymakers and analysts accepted his iron-fisted authority as an immutable dimension of

Iran's political environment. Further, they applauded the shah's efforts to expand the middle class by instituting top-down economic and social reforms, the so-called White Revolution, believing, mistakenly, that such "modernization" would increase support for the regime and for the West in general. Its contacts limited to the shah's inner circle, armed forces, and internal police (the dreaded SAVAK, Sazamane Etelaat va Amniate Kechvar), the administration, as had its predecessors and congruent with Turner's preferences, relied almost exclusively on signals and imagery intelligence for reports and assessments. The CIA's station in Tehran was severely understaffed. At Langley, the agency dedicated only two political analysts and two economic analysts to Iran. They rarely interacted with one another. Even more rarely did they consult with academics or other outside experts, and when they did the discussions were uniformly sterile because the analysts were so careful not to divulge the agency's sources or methods. With no one to challenge their long-held beliefs, the CIA held to an insular consensus. That any substantial segment of Iran's population took seriously the 81-year-old Ayatollah Ruhollah Khomeini's calls to arms from Paris seemed too far-fetched to consider seriously.[22]

Khomeini, a senior *marja* (a scholar and authority on Shi'a Islam, the religion's second largest denomination) had been in exile from Iran for almost fifteen years because of his political activism, living in Iraq for most of that time. He summoned his fellow Shi'as to rise up against the shah in a popular revolution aimed at establishing in Iran a theocratic state that strictly followed Sharia law, the moral code and religious tenets of Islam. The CIA knew little about him or his influence on the population, and for that matter the influence of other of Iran's religious leaders or more secular groups opposed to the shah's regime. The possibility that the aging ayatollah's clatter from Paris would amount to anything was inconceivable. The worldview of Washington, to which CIA analysts subscribed, could not accommodate the possibility. Further, if confronted by a potentially dangerous popular revolt, whether sparked by Khomeini or not, the shah, in the consensus judgment of the CIA's analysts, would not hesitate to employ massive force to crush it. That he had not was interpreted by both these analysts and administration officials as evidence that there was no substantial threat. After a year in office Carter was still toasting the shah as "an island of stability in a turbulent corner of the world." The president could make this toast comfortably based on the intelligence estimates he received. According to the CIA (and the National Foreign Assessment Center's National Intelligence Estimate), Iran was "not in a revolutionary or even a prerevolutionary situation." Only the State Department's Bureau of Intelligence and

Research dissented, insisting in a mild footnote that it judged the shah's prospects as "somewhat less favorable than portrayed in some parts of this NIE."[23]

The assessment was fatally flawed; its underestimation of Khomeini bordered on criminal negligence. Close to 100% of Iranians are Muslims, and more than 75% of these are Shi'as. A large number of both the Shi'as and Sunnis (Islam's largest denomination) in the 1970s were conservative, often fundamentalist, in their beliefs. Their disaffection with the shah's secular regime and conduct had reached a breaking point as the end of the decade approached. Middle class youth produced by Iran's US-financed modernization (many of whom were educated in the United States or Europe) were equally resentful of his disregard for civil liberties and refusal to provide them a voice in his government. United only in their opposition to the Shah's rule, these very different constituencies, for whom Khomeini became a symbol even by those who rejected his extreme views, allied first to oppose and then to overthrow it.[24]

Outbursts of violence began in early 1978 and continued to intensify over the succeeding months. A turning point was reached in September, when the shah declared martial law in Tehran and eleven other cities. When that decision fueled more unrest, and worse, the killing of hundreds of demonstrators by the Shah's forces, he appointed a civilian government headed by the moderate Shahpour Bakhtiar. It was too little too late. On January 19, 1979, the shah, who unbeknownst to the CIA had been diagnosed with cancer, announced he was taking an extended vacation; he left undetermined when it would end. Less than a month later, on February 1, Ayatollah Khomeini returned to Iran; less than two weeks after that he replaced Bakhtiar as prime minister with Mehdi Bazargan. Even though from the ayatollah's perspective Bazargan was insufficiently devout, Khomeini could claim him as his appointee. On February 19, 1979, Khomeini triumphantly proclaimed the establishment of the Islamic Republic of Iran. In March the new republic, with the ayatollah as supreme leader, was approved by a popular referendum.[25]

Carter rejected Brzezinski's recommendation that the United States dispatch military forces in order to restore, for a second time, the shah to power. Yet negotiating with the new Islamic state was no more attractive an option. Thus, the administration surrendered to America's loss of influence over Iran, which including losing two sites vital to the National Security Agency's ability to monitor Soviet missile testing even as mounting opposition in the Senate to ratifying the SALT II treaty heightened the urgency of such monitoring. Then the CIA further undermined the prospects for ratification by "discovering" a Soviet Brigade in Cuba, which turned out to be a legacy of the Cuban Missile Crisis and permissible under the agreement between Kennedy and Khrushchev.[26]

As the administration struggled to decide what should be its next step, the shah, who had fled Iran (or gone on vacation) without any specific destination, struggled to identify a country that would accept him. On Vance's advice Carter decided that the United States would not be that country. But in October 1979, the president learned that the shah was receiving chemotherapy for malignant lymphoma while in Mexico, and he was not responding to the treatment. Now accepting the advice of Brzezinski, backed by Henry Kissinger and Chase Manhattan Bank's David Rockefeller (Rockefeller, who had multiple contacts in Iran owing to the extensive business he had conducted with the shah for decades, was evidently the source of information on the shah's illness and treatment, not the CIA), the president reversed himself. He invited the shah to come to the United States for medical treatment. Khomeini immediately denounced the invitation as evidence that the shah was conspiring with the United States, popularly referred to in Iran as the "Great Satin," to stage a comeback. On the morning of November 4, 1979, Carter awakened to news that thousands of Iranian "students" had seized the U.S. embassy in Tehran and taken fifty-two American hostages, whom they paraded blindfolded for the world to see.[27]

For Carter, his administration, Congress, and much of the American nation, the world was an unrelentingly hostile place throughout the 444 subsequent days required to gain the release of the hostages. The CIA could take credit for the most notable exception, even if only a very few knew enough to credit it. In a rare example of a successful covert operation, on January 28, 1980, the Company rescued six of America's Foreign Service personnel in Iran who had managed to escape the American embassy. Two found refuge in the official residence of Canada's ambassador to Iran, Kenneth Taylor, and the other four hid out in the home of John Sheardon, one of the Canadian embassy's senior staff. Although a number of ranking agency officials expressed reservations about the cover story, Carter approved the project; the Canadians offered their full cooperation. In what came to be called the "Canadian Caper," Anthony Mendez, a CIA operative, arranged to spirit all the Americans out of the country on counterfeit Canadian passports by providing them with false identities as members of Studio Six Productions. Studio Six Productions was a fake

Canadian film company that was purportedly on location in Iran shooting a scene for "Argo," an imaginary science fiction movie.[28]

Carter could make no progress, however, toward reclaiming the U.S. embassy and freeing the hostages imprisoned within it. In Iran, Khomeini ousted the Bazargan government that he had installed and replaced it with a Revolutionary Council composed of militant clerics. In the United States, Americans marked the days of captivity by adorning their property with yellow ribbons and watching Ted Koppel's updates on *Nightline* (originally called *The Iran Crisis: America Held Hostage* and anchored by Frank Reynolds) each evening. Few events in American history short of war have focused the attention of the American public for such a lengthy period.[29]

The Hostage Crisis consumed time that the White House, the State Department, nor the CIA could ill afford to give it. To the surprise of all three, on Christmas Eve of 1979 the Soviet Union invaded Afghanistan to secure its communist client against a loosely aligned insurgent opposition, the *mujahideen*, led by disparate warlords who fought in the name of their own fiefdoms and jihad—the struggle for Islam. Three days later, KGB forces assassinated President Hafizullah Amin, enabling Babrak Karmal to declare himself president and prime minister of the Democratic Republic of Afghanistan and general secretary of the People's Democratic Party of Afghanistan. The Carter administration had underestimated the power of Islamic fundamentalists in Iran and appeared helpless to do anything to contain, let alone combat it. Now the president admitted publicly that his assessment of the Soviet leadership was no more accurate. On January 3, 1980, Carter suspended his effort to gain Senate ratification of the SALT II treaty. Then in April he announced that the United States would boycott that summer's Olympics, which Moscow had received the privilege of hosting.[30]

Less than a month into the crisis, Carter, behind the closed doors of the Oval Office, had authorized National Security Advisor Brzezinski to take the lead in developing a contingency plan for a rescue mission to free the hostages should negotiations prove ineffective. Brzezinski put together a steering committee, composed of DCI Turner, Secretary of Defense Harold Brown, and Air Force General David C. Jones, the chairman of the Joint Chiefs of Staff. Brzezinski insisted that he chair the committee personally. The rescue mission would by definition need to be covert; hence, the principal role played by the CIA—or at least Turner. The group decided early on that the training and skill level required exceeded the capacity of the Directorate of Operations. The model would be the successful raid in 1976 at the airport in Entebbe, Uganda, by commandos of the Israeli Defense Force, which had freed the some 100 Jewish or Israeli passengers on an Air France aircraft taken hostage by Middle Eastern and German hijackers (the hijackers released the non-Israel and non-Jewish passengers.) The operation had succeeded at the cost of the lives of only three hostages and one commando (the unit commander and older brother of current Israeli Prime Minister Benjamin Netanyahu). Turner enthusiastically embraced the premise that if the president approved a rescue operation, it would be carried out by the Army's newly created Delta Force under the direction of the Department of Defense's Special Operations Command. The contributions of the CIA would be limited to gathering intelligence and supporting the Delta Force.[31]

The outline of the plan that evolved, Operation EAGLE CLAW, was remarkably simple in concept. ███████████████ operatives on the ground would collect detailed information on the potential landing strips, the layout of the embassy compound, and the location of the hostages. Once the operatives had completed their collection effort, a minimum of six helicopters would surreptitiously fly into Iran, landing at a predetermined staging site in the remote Persian Desert, code-named Desert One. They would be met there by Delta Force commandos, led by the unit's founder Charles Beckworth, and refueled by the C-130 transport aircraft which had ferried the commandos to the site. The helicopters would then carry the Delta Force to a hideout near Tehran, code-named Desert Two. From this hideout they would be transported to the US embassy under the cloak of darkness by trucks driven ███████████████. Once at the embassy they would penetrate the compound and cut off its electricity, overpower the guards, and escort the hostages to an athletic stadium just across the main street in front of the embassy. They would rendezvous there with helicopters that had lifted off from the Desert Two site. The helicopters would transfer them to planes waiting at a nearby airport so that they could be flown out of the country.[32]

Carter, encouraged by Secretary of State Vance, resisted approving the mission in the hope that the combination of the ongoing negotiations and a series of economic sanctions that he imposed would be sufficient to produce a settlement. As winter turned to spring, that hope evaporated. In early April the president learned that US intelligence had identified a landing site from which Delta Force could launch the operation. Less than a week later he severed diplomatic relations with Iran. Shortly thereafter, while Vance was away from Washington, Carter approved the mission. It began on April 24 and rapidly turned into a disaster. An unexpected dust storm and other mechanical failures crippled three of the eight helicopters that had been offloaded at Desert One. With a minimum of six helicopters required to execute the evacuation, Carter, on the advice of Beckworth, aborted the mission. But during the withdrawal, one of the helicopters crashed into a C-130, killing eight Americans and an Iranian interpreter. Now known to the world, the operation was no less of a calamity than the Bay of Pigs. Secretary of State Cyrus Vance, whose opposition to it had never waned, resigned his office.[33]

The CIA played a relatively minor role in the tragedy. The intelligence it provided was far from perfect, but under the circumstances, it performed satisfactorily ███████████████████████████████████ ██ No intelligence service could have predicted the dust storm. Nevertheless, its association with Vietnam and Watergate still fresh in many Americans' minds, its history tied inextricably to covert operations, and its reputation still severely damaged because of its inability to provide warning about the embassy takeover in the first place, the CIA's image suffered another blow.

But the greatest casualty of Operation EAGLE CLAW was Jimmy Carter. The failed mission took its place at the top of a seemingly endless catalog of the president's miscues and examples of his alleged incompetence. During the 1980 campaign, Republican challenger Ronald Reagan pledged to restore America's strength, its honor, and its pride. In November he won the presidency by more than eight million votes. As a lame duck, Carter succeeded on January 19, 1981, to secure a settlement that would restore freedom to the hostages. The operative word is the conditional "would." After some literally last-minute haggling with a negotiating team led by Deputy Secretary of State Warren Christopher, the Islamic Republic of Iran released them to US custody only on January 20, even as Reagan in Washington, DC, was delivering his inaugural address. It was former President Jimmy Carter who met the fifty-two hostages (one had taken ill) on January 22, 1981, at the military hospital in Wiesbaden, Germany, where they stayed for a couple of days after leaving Teheran. But it was President Ronald Reagan who welcomed them at the White House on January 27 after they returned to the United States.[34]

The Reagan Revival

Reagan had been willing to excuse CIA abuses when he served on the 1975 Rockefeller Commission that Ford established to investigate the CIA's

Family Jewels, even though he was rarely able to find the time to attend its meetings. As president a half-dozen years later, however, he was unwilling to excuse what he considered the agency's deplorable performance not only in Iran but, more important, also with regard to an array of intelligence matters concerning the Soviet Union. Drawn to the Team B critique of the relevant National Intelligence Estimates (Richard Pipes directed the National Security Council's East European and Soviet desk during Reagan's first two years in office) and the Committee on the Present Danger (CPD)'s warning that since Nixon and Kissinger the United States had become faced with an ever widening window of vulnerability against a nuclear attack (Reagan recruited many CPD members to his national security team), Reagan took office convinced that the CIA had grossly underestimated the Soviet's military power, military spending, and aggressive ambitions.[35]

Worse, the CIA according to Reagan had grossly underestimated the Soviet success in paralyzing the United States by practicing nuclear blackmail while it expanded its global influence through proxies in the Third World. During the interregnum, the president-elect assembled a transition team to recommend measures to enhance the CIA's capabilities across the board. It advised wholesale reforms, including bolstering the director's authority over all the elements of the community. In Reagan's judgment, however, improving the CIA required a change in leadership more than an institutional adjustment. It needed a DCI who appreciated that the United States was in danger, knew about intelligence but was not infected with the CIA's complacent culture, and was willing to take risks to secure the national interest. It needed William Casey. Reagan would follow in Carter's footsteps at least in one respect: he replaced the incumbent DCI with his own choice.[36]

Although their personalities contrasted sharply and their relationship was never an intimate one, Casey and Reagan saw eye to eye on the severity of the Soviet threat and the role the CIA must play in first combating and then eliminating it. To neither was improved intelligence collection and analysis the issue. Much like the members of Team B had concluded when critiquing the CIA, they adamantly believed that Soviet behavior and intentions could be assessed by what any attentive individual could observe or read in open sources; spies and advanced technologies were not necessary to reach the most basic judgments. The president and director of central intelligence, therefore, did not require a National Intelligence Estimate to tell them what they already knew: that the Soviet Union could not be trusted, that its goal was to develop the nuclear capability to hold the populations of both the United States and its European allies hostage, and that it relentlessly sought to extend its evil empire to Central America, Africa, the Middle East, and everywhere across the globe. The United States had to respond more aggressively to the Kremlin's geopolitical challenge. It should return to the era of Frank Wisner and Allen Dulles and "unleash" the CIA. Effective covert operations would roll back the gains made by the Soviets since the end of the Vietnam War and, sooner rather than later, put the Kremlin back where it belonged, on the defensive. Containment and détente were strategies based on an underestimation of US strength. America possessed the capabilities actually to secure victory in the Cold War, and the CIA must play a vital role in achieving that goal.

Casey was Reagan's immediate choice to head the CIA. He had served in the OSS during World War II as the head of the Secret Intelligence Branch in Europe. Subsequently, he enjoyed an extremely successful career as a New York City lawyer, investor, and entrepreneur, which led to Richard Nixon's appointing him chair of the Securities and Exchange Commission. After the Republicans lost the presidency in 1976 with Ford's defeat, Casey cofounded the conservative think tank, the Manhattan Institute for Policy Research. These credentials were certainly sufficient for his appointment as director of central intelligence. But Casey's resume was more attractive, still. He was intimately familiar with the president-elect. Casey had managed Reagan's presidential campaign and advised him on national security issues.

Casey would have preferred the position of secretary of state, but he was notoriously disorganized and inarticulate. He was also a risk-taker with a reputation as a rule-stretcher if not a rule-breaker, attributes which seemed more appropriate for the seventh floor of the CIA's headquarters than the State Department's (the offices of the CIA director and secretary of state are both on the seventh floor of their respective buildings). Signaling the prominent position that his former campaign manager would hold in his administration, Reagan made Casey the first DCI to have a seat at the Cabinet table, and he assigned him an office in the Old Executive Office Building next to the White House, now called the Eisenhower Executive Office Building (EEOB) to go along with his headquarters at Langley. That the EEOB also housed the National Security Council was an omen of things to come.[37]

Casey lost no time in seeking to recruit a new generation of personnel. This effort, the new DCI strongly believed, was a first and minimum step required to repair the damage to the CIA's morale and capabilities, especially its capacity for clandestine operations, which in his judgment Turner had inflicted by recruiting his generation of personnel. Casey expected the agency to no longer provide a home for Ivy League–educated Cold War liberals committed to public service. He recognized that, disillusioned by the

Vietnam War and the investigative hearings on the CIA of the 1970s, many had retreated to Wall Street and Madison Avenue, where they could earn lots of money to lavish on their families — as he had earlier. Even if they wanted to make the CIA their career, moreover, Casey did not want them. He preferred operatives that fit a different profile. Many case officers in Casey's CIA had fought in the Vietnam War, not protested against it. *Their* president was, or was to be, Ronald Reagan, not John Kennedy. The journalist Steve Coll captures the ethos perfectly. Throughout the CIA, Coll writes, "The tennis players were being replaced by the bowlers."[38]

By the end of the administration's first year, Casey and his bowlers had zeroed in on what they, the president, and Secretary of State Alexander Haig agreed was the front line of the Soviet attack: Central America. Supported by a White Paper issued by the State Department only a month after Reagan's inauguration (which, in fact, followed the line of thinking developed at Foggy Bottom during the final year of the Carter presidency), they were convinced that the Sandinista National Liberation Front, which had wrested control of the government of Nicaragua in July 1979 from Anastasio Somoza Debayle, the last in the country's dynasty of US-supported authoritarian rulers, was in the thrall of Fidel Castro. That was bad enough. But worse, the Sandinistas were funneling Cuban arms to the rebellious Faribundo Martí National Liberation Front (FMLN) in El Salvador. Their ambition was to gain dominion over all of Central America, from where they would move up north through Mexico to the United States proper.[39]

In November 1981, Reagan approved a covert project to arm and train anti-Sandinistas based in Honduras, soon to be called Contras or, in Reagan's parlance, Freedom Fighters. Reagan did sign a written "finding" on December 1, as required by the 1974 Hughes-Ryan Act. Nevertheless, the administration misled Congress by claiming that that the aim of the operation was to interdict weapons traffic to the FMLN in El Salvador. In the event, the purpose was to liberate Nicaragua from the yoke of communism. The price tag was $19 billion, and Casey oversaw the planning.[40]

Then, on December 4, Reagan issued Executive Order 12333, which allocated responsibilities within the Intelligence Community and directed all federal agencies to cooperate fully with it. Reagan wanted to ensure that the locus of all intelligence activities was firmly centered in the executive office. Among EO 12333's provisions was the granting to the CIA of exclusive authority to conduct covert operations "unless the President determines that another agency is more likely to achieve a particular object." The implication was that, notwithstanding the CIA's poor record at the Bay of Pigs, in Vietnam, and elsewhere, the president wanted to stipulate unequivocally that the CIA was in charge of America's paramilitary activities, although he would reserve the right in exceptional circumstances, such as was the case with the Iran hostage crisis' EAGLE CLAW, to call on the Delta Force or another of the military's special operations units. It turned out that EO 12333 was more than misguided. It provided a loophole that the staff of the National Security Council would soon exploit.[41]

A year later the project had achieved little other than to attract press attention. A covert operation, remarkably, had become a front-page story. The administration could not plausibly deny its involvement with the Contras, but it could and did deny that it sought the overthrow of the Sandinista regime. Reagan's replacement of Secretary of State Alexander Haig, a retired Army general who has served Nixon as chief of staff, by the less bellicose George Schultz, a Ph.D. in Economics and Nixon's former secretary of labor and the treasury as well as director of the Office of Management and Budget, did not diminish public and Congressional suspicions that the administration's anticommunist crusade continued unabated. Reagan's and Casey's commitment to the Contras appeared messianic in nature, consistent with the president's identification of them as the moral equivalent of the Founding Fathers and definition of the Vietnam War as a noble cause.[42]

Congress, which still held onto the inflated sense of power that it had developed after taking down the Nixon presidency and calling the CIA on the carpet during the Church Committee hearings, put both the president and the DCI on notice that it would not trust their words alone. On December 8, 1982, the House passed the [Massachusetts Democratic Representative Edward] Boland Amendment as a rider to the Defense Appropriations Act for fiscal year 1983. The amendment prohibited the CIA and the Pentagon from using funds appropriated for use by the Department of Defense to furnish military equipment, military training or advice, or other support for military activities to any group or individual that was not formally associated with a country's recognized armed forces for the purpose of overthrowing the government of Nicaragua. Initially attached to the classified 1983 Intelligence Authorization Bill in April by the House Permanent Select Committee on Intelligence, which Boland chaired, the amendment did allow the CIA to carry on operations intended to interdict the export of Nicaraguan arms. What is more, by specifying explicitly that the prohibition applied to the CIA and Pentagon, it tacitly allowed other agencies or offices, such as the National Security Council, to use Defense Department funds for this purpose, or so one could interpret the amendment's meaning.[43]

Unwilling to be deterred, the administration interpreted the Boland Amendment in precisely this way in order to circumvent it.[44] And it interpreted global events in a way to make doing so that much more imperative—and urgent. The attempted assassination of the Polish-born Pope John Paul II in 1981 by the Turkish ultra-nationalist Mehmet Ali Ağca, for which Casey held the KGB responsible despite the lack of evidence, Moscow's crackdown on the Solidarity Movement in Poland and declaration of martial law by General Wojciech Jaruzelski later that year, and the Soviets' downing in September 1983 of a South Korean airliner, KAL 007, because, it alleged, the plane was on a spy mission for the United States, buttressed the perception that the Evil Empire was flexing its muscle worldwide and had to be destroyed without delay.

The first steps were the CIA's. In early 1984 the agency, disregarding the Boland Amendment, began to mine Nicaraguan harbors. Casey misled Congress and attributed the mining to the Contras. Again the press uncovered the true story. The response of Senator Barry Goldwater was to write to Casey that he was "pissed off."[45] The response of the International Court of Justice was to rule that the United States was guilty of violating international law. The response of the Senate Select Committee on Intelligence was to demand an apology from Casey and his agreement to inform it in advance of *any* covert actions. The response of the House of Representatives was to enact an amendment to the Fiscal 1985 Continuing Appropriations Act, a second Boland Amendment, essentially prohibiting any organ of the US government from providing any type of support to the contras for any reason. This more draconian prohibition laid the foundation for the Iran-Contra scandal that was to consume the administration during its final years.[46]

Iran-Contra paralleled Watergate in its unconstitutionality and blatant abuse of executive power. It was qualitatively more farcical, however, and the fallout quantitatively less dramatic. The motive behind the administration's behavior was simple: President Reagan and DCI Casey refused to deprive the Contras of US support; the rebels' manifest ineptness and the two Boland Amendments were to them irrelevant. Notorious for his inattention to details, Reagan's familiarity with the particulars of the intersecting projects may never be known. The president approved it because he supported its aims. Characteristic of his leadership style, his concern was with the ends, not the means.

Regardless of what the president knew and when he knew it, Casey, who worked for and answered directly to Reagan, was more deeply involved. Nevertheless, the director of central intelligence skirted Congress's prohibitions and obfuscated his participation by "delegating" responsibility for its management to the National Security Council, which was explicitly mentioned in neither of the Boland amendments. For this reason, National Security Advisor Robert C. McFarlane and his deputy and then successor, Admiral John M. Poindexter, supervised the operation. From the basement of the White House, Marine Lt. Colonel Oliver North, a low-level NSC staffer, directed it. North's woeful ignorance of the global environment explains a great deal about how the Contras came to be linked with Iran in the scheme, and in the public consciousness. And his woeful ignorance of covert operations explains a great deal about how poorly the project was planned and executed. North's qualifications had nothing to do with competence or experience. He was daring, he was deceptive, and he was a true believer in the cause.

The premise was as uncomplicated as it was absurd. The Contras required arms, but Congress prohibited the administration from supplying them. Iran, at war with Iraq at the time, also required arms, but since the Hostage Crisis the administration was prohibited from supplying them as well. Reagan felt no sympathy for the Iranians. However, he felt a great deal of sympathy for five Americans, including the CIA station chief in Beirut, William Buckley, who had been kidnapped by the pro-Iranian terrorist organization Hezbollah in March 1984 and was allegedly (the CIA lacked reliable sources) being held in Lebanon, Hezbollah's base. McFarlane convinced Reagan that by using the Iranian arms dealer Manucher Ghorbanifar as an intermediary to sell Israeli arms to Iran, such as TOW and HAWK missiles, he could strengthen a potentially powerful faction of moderate Iranians. These moderates would thereby be in a position not only to challenge Fundamentalist rule in Iran, but also to intercede with Hezbollah to secure the release of the hostages. North, meanwhile, concocted the idea of selling the arms to Iran for a profit. He would arrange to divert the profits so the Contras could use the money to purchase their own weapons.

Poor intelligence and a poorer understanding of the environment within Iran doomed the plan from the start. With virtually no human assets within Iran, the CIA knew nothing about the supposedly moderate faction or its putative influence on Hezbollah. It did have intelligence on Ghorbanifar, and judged that he was unreliable. That judgment was of no significance. With Casey remaining far in the background, McFarlane, Poindexter, and North set the plan in motion. Ghorbanifar orchestrated the sale of the Israeli missiles to Iran. He then arranged a clandestine meeting between a party of Americans that included CIA officials and was led by McFarlane (who brought with him to Tehran a birthday cake for Ghorbanifar's mother and a copy of a Bible signed by Reagan) and several mid-level Iranian officials in May 1986. Iran's hostility to the United States remained just as intense as before, however, and there is no evidence that anyone from Iran sought the release of the US hostages. Hezbollah did release some of them. But it kidnapped an equal number to compensate. CIA chief of station Buckley died after more than a year of captivity and torture, apparently in Iran. Not until December 1991 did the Iranians allow the return of his body to the United States for burial at Arlington National Cemetery.

North used a front organization, the National Endowment for the Preservation of Liberty, to siphon money from the sales of the arms to the Iranians to purchase military materiel for the Contras. But that diversion ended no more happily. In October 1986 the Sandinistas shot down a French cargo plan that was transporting arms and supplies to the Contras, and captured the sole survivor, Eugene Hasenfus. Hasenfus, an unemployed former Marine, initially admitted to working for the CIA but later retracted the statement. It did not matter. His capture and the evidence found on the wrecked plan, most notably a book of phone numbers, tied the operation to North's organization and exposed the breach of the Boland Amendments.

The next month brought more unwelcome publicity. A Lebanese newspaper published a story about the meeting of McFarlane and his party with the Iranians in Teheran. Soon, even the Bible inscribed by Reagan went on display. As North began systematically to shred or doctor documents pertaining to the multifaceted operation, the White House began to stonewall and issue incredulous statements. A barrage of public and congressional criticism forced Poindexter to resign, the administration to fire North, and Reagan to appoint a commission chaired by Senator John Tower. Tower, a retired senator, had been the first Republican elected to Congress' upper chamber from Texas since Reconstruction. Serving as Tower's "staff" were Edmund Muskie, the former senator from Maine and Democratic nominee for vice president who had succeeded Cyrus Vance as Carter's secretary of state, and Brent Scowcroft, Gerald Ford's national security advisor, to determine what had happened and under whose authority. Its investigation lasted ten weeks. The next month Attorney General Edwin Meese appointed Lawrence E. Walsh as special prosecutor. Walsh had been a justice on the U.S. Southern District Court and a deputy attorney general under Eisenhower. His investigation lasted eight years.[47]

The mountains of testimony and other evidence produced by both the Tower Commission and Walsh's inquiry led to the criminal convictions of

McFarlane, Poindexter, and North. (The latter two convictions were subsequently vacated because of immunity agreements, and North's was later vacated on appeal because the court found that witnesses may have been influenced by his congressional testimony, for which he received immunity.) The testimony also implicated Casey, but neither investigation could establish his culpability. In May 1987, just as the Walsh investigation was starting up, Casey died. According to Bob Woodward, on his deathbed the director of central intelligence (who had resigned the previous January) answered an explicit question by nodding that he knew all.[48]

The CIA's image and standing with the American public was probably never lower, even during the post-Watergate era. Neither Congress nor most Americans wanted to charge Reagan with anything more than being an amiable dunce with a poor memory and an inability to control his subordinates (an impression severely undermined by scholarship over the subsequent decades[49]). Perhaps Iran-Contra more than any other covert project illustrates the effectiveness of the institutional cocoon that allows the US president plausibly to deny complicity. Reagan emerged from the scandal remarkably unscathed, whereas the agency, whose director repeatedly and publicly responded to questions by mumbling unintelligibly, appeared more than ever as a rogue elephant.

To replace Casey, Reagan nominated Robert Gates, a career CIA analyst with a Ph.D. in Russian and Soviet History whom Casey had the year before appointed his deputy director. But during his confirmation hearings, Gates was tarred with the Iran-Contra brush. Reagan withdrew him from consideration and in his stead sent up William H. Webster, whom Carter had appointed director of the FBI in 1978. A former federal judge, Webster had reformed the FBI after the decades of J. Edgar Hoover's malfeasance. Hoping he would repair the CIA in the same way, the Senate confirmed Webster's appointment overwhelmingly, with only the upper chamber's future majority leader, Nevada Democrat Harry Reid, voting against.[50]

Notes

1   William Colby and Peter Forbath, *Honorable Men: My Life in the CIA* (NY: Simon & Schuster, 1978); John Prados, *Lost Crusader: The Secret Wars of CIA Director William Colby* (NY: Oxford University Press, 2003); Randall Woods, *Shadow Warrior: William E. Colby and the CIA* (NY: Basic Books, 2013). In August 2011 the CIA released its official biography: Harold P. Ford, *William E. Colby as Director of Central Intelligence, 1973-1976* (Washington, DC: CIA

History Staff, 1993), accessed on December 31, 2012, at http://www.gwu .edu/~nsarchiv/NSAEBB/NSAEBB362/index.htm.

2 Piero Gleijeses, *Conflicting Missions: Havana, Washington, and Africa, 1959-1976.* (Chapel Hill: University of North Carolina Press, 2002); John Stockwell, *In Search of Enemies* (NY: Norton, 1984); Leslie Gelb, "Ford Discharges Schlesinger and Colby and Asks Kissinger to Give Up his Security Post," *New York Times,* November 3, 1975.

3 Anne Hessing Cahn: *Killing Détente: The Right Attacks the CIA* (University Park, PA: Pennsylvania State University Press, 1998); Albert Wohlstetter, "Is There a Strategic Arms Race?" *Foreign Policy* 15 (Summer 1974): 3–20.

4 Cahn: *Killing Détente,* 84; *The China Diary of George H.W. Bush: The Making of a Global President,* ed. Jeffrey A. Engel (Princeton, NJ: Princeton University, 2008), especially 397–464. See also Bush's 1988 presidential campaign autobiography, *Looking Forward: An Autobiography* (NY: Doubleday, 1987).

5 Gordon R. Mitchell, "Team B Intelligence Coups," *Quarterly Journal of Speech* 92 (May 2006): 144–73.

6 Lawrence Freedman, "The CIA and the Soviet Threat: The Politicization of Estimates, 1966-1977," in *Eternal Vigilance? 50 Years of the CIA,* ed. Rhodri Jeffreys-Jones and Christopher Andrew (London: Frank Cass, 1977), 136.

7 Joshua Rovner, *Fixing the Facts: National Security and the Politics of Intelligence* (Ithaca, NY: Cornell University Press), 124–25.

8 Cahn, *Killing Détente,* 121–140; Richard H. Immerman, *Empire for Liberty: A History of American Imperialism from Benjamin Franklin to Paul Wolfowitz* (Princeton, NJ: Princeton University Press, 2010), 200–04.

9 Tom Barry, "Remembering Team B," February 12, 2004, accessed on July 24, 2012, at http://rightweb.irc-online.org/articles/display/Remembering_Team _B; Raymond L. Garthoff, "Estimating Soviet Military Intentions and Capabilities," in *Watching the Bear: Essays on the CIA's Analysis of the Soviet Union,* ed. Gerald K. Hanes and Robert E. Leggett (Washington, DC: Government Printing Office, 2003), 158–63; U.S. Senate Select Committee on Intelligence, Subcommittee on Collection, Production, and Quality, 94th Cong., 2nd Sess., *The National Intelligence Estimates A-B Team Episode Concerning Soviet Strategic Capability and Objectives* (Washington, DC: Government Printing Office, 1978), accessed on June 22, 2013, at http://www.intelligence .senate.gov/pdfs/95nie_ab.pdf.

10 Rovner, *Fixing the Facts,* 113–36.

11 Stansfield Turner, *Secrecy and Democracy: The CIA in Transition* (Boston: Houghton Mifflin, 1985), 251.

12 Gaddis Smith, *Morality, Reason, and Power: American Diplomacy in the Carter Years* (NY: Hill and Wang, 1986), especially Chapter 1.

13 Christopher Andrew, *For the President's Eyes Only: Secret Intelligence and the American Presidency from Washington to Bush* (NY: HarperCollins, 1995),

425–31; NIE 11-1-80, "Soviet Military Capabilities and Intentions in Space," August 6, 1980, accessed on July 16, 2013, at http://www.foia.cia.gov/sites /default/files/document_conversions/89801/DOC_0000284010.pdf.

14 Turner, *Secrecy and Democracy*. Turner refers to himself as an outsider on p.3.

15 Richard Helms with William Hood, *A Look Over My Shoulder: A Life in the Central Intelligence Agency* (NY: Random House, 2003), 413–14; 439–46.

16 Turner, *Secrecy and Democracy*, 39–137. The quote appears on p.39. See also Milt Bearden and James Risen, *The Main Enemy: The Inside Story of the CIA's Final Showdown with the KGB* (NY: Random House, 2003), 64–65, 26; John Ranelagh, *The Agency: The Rise and Decline of the CIA* (NY: Simon & Schuster, 1986), 662, 683–85; Andrew, *For the President's Eyes Only*, 433–36.

17 Douglas F. Garthoff, *Directors of Central Intelligence as Leaders of the U.S. Intelligence Community, 1946-2005* (Washington, DC: Potomac Books, 2007), 131–34.

18 Garthoff, *Directors of Central Intelligence*, 142–43.

19 The most comprehensive study of Carter's diplomacy remains Smith, *Morality, Reason, and Power*. See also Burton Kaufman and Scott Kaufman, *The Presidency of James Earl Carter, Jr.* (Lawrence: University Press of Kansas, 2006); for the views of the principals, see Jimmy Carter, *Keeping Faith: Memoirs of a President* (NY: Bantam Doubleday Dell, 1982); Zbigniew Brzezinski, *Power and Principle: Memoirs of the National Security Adviser* (NY: Farrar Straus Giroux, 1983); and Cyrus Vance, *Hard Choices: Critical Years in America's Foreign Policy* (NY: Simon and Schuster, 1983).

20 Brzezinski, *Power and Principle*, 64–73.

21 James Goode, *The United States and Iran: In the Shadow of Musaddiq* (NY: Palgrave MacMillan, 1997).

22 Robert Jervis, *Why Intelligence Fails: Lessons from the Iranian Revolution and the Iraq War* (Ithaca, NY: Cornell University Press, 2010), 21–24. Jervis bases his analysis of the CIA's (especially the National Foreign Assessment Center's) analysis and reporting during the Iranian revolution on a post-mortem assessment he was commissioned to write at the time by NFAC director Robert Bowie.

23 U.S. Congress, House Select Committee on Intelligence, 96th Cong., 1st Sess., *Iran: Evaulation of the U.S. Intelligence Performance Prior to November 1978* (Washington, DC: Government Printing Office, 1979); Jervis, *Why Intelligence Fails*, 85–92; Ranelagh, *The Agency*, 648–55; Gary Sick, *All Fall Down: America's Fateful Encounter with Iran* (NY: Penguin Books, 1986), 34–35; Carter, *Keeping the Faith*, 338; Michael Donovan, "National Intelligence and the Iranian Revolution", in Jeffreys-Jones and Andrew, *Eternal Vigilance*, 148.

24 Theda Skocpol, "Rentier State and Shi'a Islam in the Iranian Revolution," Theory and Society 11 (May 1982): 265–83; Matthew Shannon, "Losing Hearts and Minds: Iranian-American Relations and International Education during the Cold War," Ph.D. Dissertation, Temple University, 2013.

25 Sick, *All Fall Down*, 50–183; Barry Rubin, *Paved with Good Intentions: The American Experience and Iran* (NY: Oxford, 1980), 217–51; David Farber, *Taken Hostage: The Iran Hostage Crisis and America's First Encounter with Radical Islam* (Princeton, NJ: Princeton University Press, 2004), 73–101; Mark Bowden, *Guests of the Ayatollah: The First Battle in America's War with Militant Islam* (NY: Atlantic Monthly Press, 2006). Extensive documentation on the evolving revolution in Iran and US policy is available on the National Security Archive's website accessed on August 6, 2012, at http://www.gwu.edu /~nsarchiv/nsa/publications/iran/iran.html. See also Jervis, *Why Intelligence Fails*, 34–122.

26 On the Soviet brigade in Cuba, see Jorge I. Dominquez, "Cuba as Superpower: Havana and Moscow, 1979," *Cold War International History Project Bulletin*, 8–9 (Winter 1996/97): 216–17; Soviet Ambassador to Cuba Vorotnikov, Memorandum of Conversation with Raul Castro, September 1, 1979, *Cold War International History Project Bulletin*, 190–92; Minutes of the CPSU CC Politiburo Meeting, 27 September 1979, *Cold War International History Project Bulletin*, 192; CPSU CC Politboro Decision, September 27, 1979, with Brezhnev-Carter Hotline Correspondence, *Cold War International History Project Bulletin*, 192–93.

27 Andrew, *For the President's Eyes Only*, 441–49; Rose McDermott, *Risk-Taking in International Politics: Prospect Theory in American Foreign Policy* (Ann Arbor: University of Michigan Press, 2001), 77–106.

28 Joshuah Berman, "How the CIA Used a Fake Sci-Fi Flick to Rescue Americans From Teheran," *American Buddha*, April 24, 2007, accessed on July 28, 2012, at http://www.american-buddha.com/cia.howciausedfakescitehran.htm. As noted in the first chapter, Ben Affleck directed and starred in the 2012 film *Argo*, which he based on this operation but used literary license liberally. See also Antonio (Tony) Mendez and Matt Baglio *Argo: How the CIA and Hollywood Pulled Off the Most Audacious Rescue in History* (NY: Viking, 2012). Mendez published his account to coincide with the release of the film.

29 Farber, *Taken Hostage*, 153–80.

30 BBC news has produced useful chronology of the Soviet invasion, including the events leading up and subsequent to it, accessed on July 28, 2012, at http://news.bbc.co.uk/2/hi/7883532.stm. Chapter 5 explores the CIA's assessment and role.

31   Brzezinski, *Power and Principle*, 487–500.

32   Charles Tustin Kamps, "Operation Eagle Claw: The Iran Hostage Rescue Mission," *Air and Space Power Journal* 21 (September 2006), accessed on July 14, 2013 at http://www.airpower.maxwell.af.mil/apjinternational/apj-s/2006/3tri06/kampseng.html; Mark Bowden, "The Desert One Debacle," *Atlantic Magazine*, May, 2006, accessed on July 29, 2012, at http://www.theatlantic.com/magazine/archive/2006/05/the-desert-one-debacle/4803/.

33   For the details of Operation EAGLE CLAW, see Charlie A. Beckwith and Donald Knox, *Delta Force: the U.S. Counter-Terrorist Unit and the Iran Hostage Rescue Mission* (NY: Harcourt Brace Jovanovich, 1983); Paul B. Ryan, *The Iranian Rescue Mission: Why It Failed* (Annapolis, MD: Naval Institute Press, 1985).

34   Farber, *Taken Hostage*, 181–84; Roberts B. Owen, "The Final Negotiation and Release in Algiers," in Warren Christopher *et al.*, *American Hostages in Iran: The Conduct of a Crisis* (NY: Council on Foreign Relations, 1985), 297–324.

35   Jerry W. Sanders, *Peddlers of Crisis: The Committee on the Present Danger and the Politics of Containment* (Cambridge, MA: South End Press, 1980).

36   On Reagan's views of the Soviet Union and nuclear balance, see Beth Fisher, *The Great Reversal: Foreign Policy and the End of the Cold War* (Columbia, MO: University of Missouri Press, 1997); James Mann, *The Rebellion of Ronald Reagan: A History of the End of the Cold War* (NY: Viking, 2009).

37   In addition to Joseph E. Persico's biography, *Casey: The Lives and Secrets of William J. Casey: From the OSS to the CIA* (NY: Viking Penguin 1990), see Bob Woodward, *Veil: The Secret Wars of the C.I.A., 1981-1987* (NY: Simon and Schuster, 1987).

38   Steve Coll, *Ghost Wars: The Secret History of the CIA, Afghanistan, and Bin Laden, From the Soviet Invasion to September 10, 2001* (NY: Penguin Press, 2004), 55–56.

39   William Legrande, *Our Own Backyard: The United States in Central America, 1977-1992* (Chapel Hill: University of North Carolina Press, 1998).

40   Harry E. Vanden and Thomas W. Walker, "The Reimposition of U.S. Hegemony over Nicaragua," in *Understanding the Central American Crisis: Sources of Conflict, U.S. Policy, and Options for Peace*, eds. Kenneth M. Coleman and George C. Herring (Wilmington, DE: Scholarly Resources, 1991), 153–66.

41   Executive Order 12333, "United States Intelligence Activities", December 1981, accessed on July 30, 2012, at http://www.archives.gov/federal-register/codification/executive-order/12333.html.

42   James Chace, *Endless War: How We Got Involved in Central America and What Can Be Done* (NY: Knopf, 1984).

43   H.AMDT.974 (Boland Amendment), December 8, 1982, accessed on July 30, 2012, at http://thomas.loc.gov/cgi-bin/bdquery/z?d097:hz974.

44   "Iran-Contra Hearings; The Testimony: On the Boland Amendment and the President," *New York Times*, published on July 17, 1987, accessed on November

28, 2012, at http://www.nytimes.com/1987/07/17/world/iran-contra-hearings -the-testimony-on-the-boland-amendment-and-the-president.html.

45 Loch Johnson, "Covert Action and Accountability: Decision-Making for America's Secret Foreign Policy," *International Studies Quarterly* 33 (March 1989): 98–99.

46 Theodore Draper, *Very Thin Line: The Iran-Contra Affairs* (NY: Hill and Wang, 1991), 15–26. The most comprehensive study of the Iran-Contra Affair, *Very Thin Line* is the source for the following account unless otherwise indicated. See also Lawrence E. Walsh, *Firewall: the Iran-Contra Conspiracy and the Cover-Up* (NY: Norton, 1997). The National Security Archive has published a compendium of documents on Iran-Contra that it acquired through the Freedom of Information Act. Peter Kornbluh and Malcolm Byrne, eds., *The Iran-Contra Scandal: The Declassified History* (NY: New Press, 1993).

47 *The Tower Commission Report: A Full Text of the President's Special Review Board* (NY: Bantam Books and Times Books, 1987); *Final Report of the Independent Counsel for Iran/Contra Matters*, Volume I: *Investigations and Prosecutions*, Lawrence E. Walsh Independent Counsel, August 4, 1993, Washington, D.C., accessed on August 6, 2012, at http://www.fas.org/irp/offdocs/walsh/.

48 Woodward, *Veil*, 504–07.

49 Fred I. Greenstein, *The Presidential Difference: Leadership Style from FDR to Barack Obama*, 3rd ed. (Princeton, NJ: Princeton University Press, 2009), 145–158.

50 John Prados, *Safe for Democracy: The Secret Wars of the CIA* (Chicago, IL: Ivan R. Dee), 572–85.

5

Victory Without Redemption:
1988–2000

Ronald Reagan escaped the Iran-Contra fiasco with his reputation and popularity mostly intact. Part of the explanation for why he avoided responsibility lay with the personality and attributes that earned him the epithet, "Teflon President." The institutional mechanisms that promote plausible deniability, the CIA's by-then historic role as lightning rod and scapegoat and widely accepted rogue elephant image, and the attention paid to Bill Casey and Oliver North likewise insulated the president from the scandal's fallout. Yet, probably the most salient reason for Reagan's evading the consequences of the set of foreign policy blunders was that the administration's breakdown over Central America and the Middle East coincided with its breakthroughs over the Soviet Union. The progress the president made during the last years of his presidency in improving relations with his erstwhile archenemies in the Kremlin distracted attention from the Iran-Contra revelations. It also laid the foundation for the end of the Cold War. That the Cold War ended so abruptly in the manner that it did, and that Reagan contributed to that outcome in the manner that he did, took practically everyone by surprise. The CIA was surprised as well, although not nearly to the extent that contemporaries believed, and many Americans still do. The CIA did not predict the end of the Cold War. That it did not, however, should not be added to the list of its intelligence failures.

The CIA's capability to collect intelligence on and produce estimates about the Soviet Union and its Eastern bloc, suspect since its origin, had been called into even greater question after the challenge of the Team B exercise during the Ford administration. Stansfield Turner's decimation

The Hidden Hand: A Brief History of the CIA, First Edition. Richard Immerman.
© 2014 John Wiley & Sons, Ltd. Published 2014 by John Wiley & Sons, Ltd.

of the Moscow station turned Carter's predisposition into a necessity. The president had no alternative but to depend overwhelmingly on technology as the sources for his estimates, estimates that, after the Soviet invasion of Afghanistan, he conceded were mistaken. By adding these missteps to the debacle over Iran and the CIA's lack of defenders, let alone champions, the agency's poor morale and the mass retirements it engendered become readily understandable. Reagan and Casey were determined to revive the Company so that they could rely on it. The CIA "has been permitted to run down," Casey wrote to the president only months into the administration. But, he quickly added, "It is a good outfit, composed of dedicated people with good spirit" who have "survived the kicking around from the press and the Congress and from Admiral Turner's wholesale firings."[1]

Casey was particularly critical of the agency's Directorate of Intelligence — equally if not more so than Turner had been. From his point of view, the DI produced analysis that with few exceptions was "academic, soft, not sufficiently relevant and realistic." In fact, Casey preferred the judgments he received from the "the streetwise, on the ground Operations staff" to those "I get from the more academic Analytical staff in Washington." The latter provided metrics that could easily be read as signs of Soviet strength: the size of the Soviet's conventional forces, the number of their strategic missiles and the throw weight of their payloads, and the like. Casey wanted to know the Soviets' weaknesses so the administration could exploit them.[2]

Consequently, one of Casey's first moves was to put John McMahon, the CIA's deputy director of operations (DDO), in charge of the National Foreign Assessments Center (by 1982 he had moved McMahon up the chain to replace Bobby Ray Inman as deputy director of central intelligence). Another early Casey innovation was to bring under his direct control the National Intelligence Council (NIC) and select as its chair Henry S. Rowen, whose ardently anti-Soviet views paralleled his own. The DCI also established an Office of Soviet Analysis (SOVA) and Office of Global Issues in order better to integrate expertise on the Soviet Union, expand the number of analysts on the Soviet account, and, he predicted, generate more hard-hitting products. Casey was encouraged by the initial results of his organizational initiatives. The May 1981 Special National Intelligence Estimate (SNIE 11/2-81), *Soviet Support for International Terrorism and Revolutionary Violence*, portrayed the Kremlin as "deeply engaged" in supporting global violence. That was Casey's belief upon taking office. It was Reagan's, too.[3]

Nevertheless, there is no evidence to suggest that the assessments of the Soviet Union were politicized—that the National Foreign Assessments Center, SOVA, or any other CIA office skewed its judgments to make them more congruent with the predispositions of the administration. By the 1980s senior analysts throughout the Intelligence Community were highly trained professionals who took pride in their performance, and none were more so than those on the NIC and the Soviet account. Moreover, although the sources and methods of intelligence collection had improved significantly since the early period of the Cold War, and the analyses were more rigorous, there remained serious gaps in information, the tradecraft was often problematic, and the conclusions were virtually always tentative and frequently equivocal. Consequently, while documentation from both the CIA and the Reagan administration is at this point insufficient to reach firm conclusions about the influence of intelligence on Reagan's policies toward the Soviet Union, and this will probably remain true even after further declassification, it is unlikely that the Intelligence Community's analyses changed policymakers' minds. Or, revising the optic, it is unlikely that these analyses significantly reduced the level of policymakers' uncertainty and deepened understanding—the primary purpose of intelligence.[4]

In part, this phenomenon was the result of the nature of the intelligence enterprise and the Reagan administration. Intelligence is almost always ambiguous, and the president and those who rallied behind his candidacy, including campaign manager and future CIA director Casey, entered office with well-formed beliefs about the "evil empire." These beliefs would have been highly resistant to the most definitive judgments had they been discordant. But not only were CIA estimates at most discordant only at the margins, but they were also hardly definitive, and in fact, in many cases they were barely estimative.[5] From inauguration day, actually from earlier than that, when during the transition Reagan and his chief advisors began to receive the Presidential Daily Brief and oral briefings, the CIA produced report after report of the failing Soviet economy, of an aged, indeed decrepit Kremlin leadership made less effectual by the jockeying going on to succeed Leonid Brezhnev, of the challenge to the empire posed by popular discontent within the Soviet borders and unrest in Eastern Europe and the Baltic, of demographic imbalances among generations and nationalities, and of multiple other related and potentially fatal flaws. Yet, while the analysts ably painted a portrait of a Soviet Union confronted by intractable problems and impossibly difficult decisions, they resisted the impulse, or the obligation, to estimate the outcome—to make a call, express how confident they were, and provide their justification.[6]

The typical analytic product identified several different possible scenarios, but it did not assess, let alone make explicit, the probability of any of them. Further, rather than systematically explain the reasoning behind or indicate the level of confidence they had in a judgment, analysts frequently peppered their reports with caveats that bordered on disclaimers. The "historical record suggests that the West has been consistently wrong, both in picking the eventual winners and in describing the policy line that they would follow," confessed the national intelligence officer for the Soviet Union and Eastern Europe in a memorandum entitled "Some Implications of the Soviet Political Succession for US Policy" that he wrote shortly prior to Brezhnev's death in 1982. He then added, "I don't think our chances for accurate predictions are much better today." Then, a month into the Yuri Andropov regime, an assessment of the Soviet Union's prospects during the decade of the 1980s included the sentence, "This type of analysis is fraught with uncertainty, very incomplete information, and widely divergent assumptions."[7]

The CIA expressed no more confidence in its evaluations of the Soviet missile defense programs, to provide another example. "It has become clear that serious uncertainties and differences of view exist both within the Intelligence Community and elsewhere in the Administration over the purpose and scope of Soviet research and development efforts in the ABM [Anti-Ballistic Missile] area," Richard Allen, Reagan's first national security advisor, wrote to Casey. He tasked the CIA director with orchestrating a "high-level interagency review and assessment of the Soviet ABM effort." Allen could not have been satisfied with the product. "Given the gaps in information and our analytical uncertainties, there are understandably many differing conclusions and opinions about the technical characteristics of Soviet ABM systems and components and supporting radars and about their capabilities to perform all the functions essential to ballistic missile defense," read the resultant National Intelligence Estimate on Soviet Ballistic Missile Defense. "We are not likely to be able to resolve many of these issues within the next several years. Moreover, we have difficulty assigning probabilities to alternative interpretations of the evidence."[8]

Estimating an End to the Cold War

Risk averse to begin with, CIA analysts lacked the incentive to present to Reagan estimates that suggested that a significant change in Kremlin policy was anything more than the most remote possibility. This was especially the case because such estimates could potentially (albeit improbably) lessen the administration's vigilance, cause a reconsideration of its plans to build up US defenses, lead to ill-conceived concessions on arms control, or produce similar outcomes. Not only could any of these outcomes prove dangerous to the United States, but individually or collectively they could also increase suspicion throughout the administration about the CIA's judgment and capability. Understandably, therefore, the analysts stayed the course established over the previous decades. Indeed, as a product of this inclination toward conservatism, they tended to veer toward the conclusions of Team B.

Consequently, if hard-line Reagan advisors such as Allen, Secretary of State Alexander Haig, Secretary of Defense Caspar Weinberger, and others required confirmation of their preexisting beliefs about the Soviets (which they probably did not), the CIA provided them with it. On the one hand, assessments suggested that conditions within the Soviet Union were approaching the tipping point, where increased external pressure could exacerbate internal strains beyond repair. The agency's analyses stressed that the decisions successive US administrations had had to make between guns and butter in the 1960s and 1970s paled in comparison with the choices confronting the current Kremlin. CIA experts also underscored that Soviet society was drowning in a sea of "apathy, cynicism, and disgruntlement" that "manifests itself in a growing consumption of alcohol, increasing labor turnover, episodic strike activity, and a flourishing black market."[9]

On the other hand, to the CIA these attitudes and pathologies did not mean a change in Soviet behavior or a diminution of the threat the USSR posed was in the offing. To the contrary, the transition following Brezhnev's death was so smooth because Andropov was widely recognized as someone who could take firm control of the situation and restore Soviet pride, reputation, and influence. With Andropov, "the US faces a new and, in many ways, far more intelligent and skillful adversary than we confronted in Khrushchev and Brezhnev," Robert Gates the CIA's deputy director of intelligence, wrote to Casey. "My money says we will face a much greater challenge from the USSR under his leadership." Estimates did suggest that concerns about an American "window of vulnerability" to a Soviet attack, a centerpiece of Reagan's presidential campaign, were overblown. Nevertheless, even prior to Andropov's promotion to party secretary, and notwithstanding the Soviet Union's political, economic, and social woes, the CIA saw "no evidence of a reduction in Soviet defense spending. Indeed, on the basis of observed military activity—the number of weapon systems in production, weapon development programs, and trends in capital expansion in the defense industries—we expect that Soviet defense spending will continue to grow." The agency judged that "the strength of the system," combined with the "patriotism and passivity of the populace," would allow the leadership to manage effectively domestic discontent while at the same time continuing to project its global power.[10]

While the CIA had followed Andropov for decades prior to his ascendency to leader of the Kremlin (as ambassador to Budapest in 1956 he played an important role in crushing the Hungarian Revolution, and he was appointed head of the Soviet intelligence and internal security organization, the KGB, in 1976), it was unaware in 1982 of how seriously ill he was. Fifteen months later, Andropov was dead. Thirteen months after that, his successor, Konstantin Chernenko, was likewise dead. On March 11, 1985, only three hours after Chernenko's death and less than two months into Reagan's second term in office, the Politburo elected Mikhail Gorbachev general secretary of the Soviet Communist Party. The CIA had identified Gorbachev as a contender to succeed Brezhnev from the start of the Reagan administration. But Soviet experts in the agency considered him too young (only fifty-four when he did take office, Gorbachev was the first party leader born after the Revolution), and insufficiently conservative for the Kremlin's old breed. They were right. Gorbachev was too young and insufficiently conservative. For this reason, the CIA underscored the implications of his elevation once the Party leadership fatefully made the decision. In June, the Directorate of Intelligence entitled its memorandum on the new Kremlin leader "Gorbachev, the New Broom."[11]

By this time the US president's stridency toward the Soviet Union had already begun to mellow. Even before the 1984 campaign, when he had to respond to Democratic challenger Walter Mondale's effort to portray him as an irresponsible saber rattler, Reagan seems to have developed second thoughts about the "Evil Empire." In the aftermath of his announcing the Strategic Defense Initiative (Star Wars) on March 23, 1983, and Abel Archer, NATO's exercise in nuclear release procedures that November, he appears to have reached the realization that the Soviets feared that the Americans were preparing for a first strike as much as he feared that they were. The CIA had been reporting the same kind of security dilemma since 1981. Now, because its reports were congruent with his evolving beliefs, Reagan began to accept its judgment. He also began to gravitate toward the CIA's position, or at least leave open the possibility that its position was valid, that Gorbachev was willing to break with the Soviet past.[12]

The CIA provided little guidance, however, as to what might be the consequences of that break. Analysts were confident that Gorbachev would concentrate on pursuing a domestic program that enveloped economic reforms, including the promotion of some private initiatives, a campaign against corruption, and perhaps even a relaxation of centralized planning. Toward this end, he would probably even risk alienating many on the Politburo. But the CIA was much less certain about whether Gorbachev might chart a different course in the international arena. It estimated that the new general secretary, worried that the Strategic Defense Initiative might reflect a technological innovation about which Soviets were not familiar, wanted greater time for ongoing programs of military modernization, and, mindful of the costs of arms racing, was likely to seek an agreement on arms limitation or even reduction. But that left the Kremlin with a spectrum of potential approaches to defense planning. CIA analysts identified them but did not assess their relative probabilities. The only firm estimate they expressed was that Gorbachev would resist making any concession that jeopardized the strategic advantages, such as its advances along the globe's periphery, which he and his colleagues in the Kremlin believed the Soviets had achieved over the previous decade. Analysts considered the evidence too unreliable to judge Gorbachev as any more prepared than his predecessors to end Soviet meddling in Central America, Afghanistan, or other targets of opportunity in the developing world.[13]

Nevertheless, as the months went by and Gorbachev began to articulate the premises and goals of his foreign policies with greater specificity, his "New Thinking" increasingly challenged the beliefs about the Soviet Union that Reagan carried with him into the White House and which framed his foreign and defense policies during the first term. In this regard, the CIA exercised little influence on him, and not just because it so frequently hedged the judgments expressed in its finished intelligence. More salient were the first customer's chief sources of intelligence, which were not Intelligence Community-generated products so much as the briefings and advice he received from his closest aides. Even after he elevated officials such as Henry Rowan and John McMahon to leadership roles, DCI Casey remained suspect of the quality of the IC's finished intelligence. He considered his own assessments, which he based often on instinct and ideology, more trustworthy than that of any element of the Intelligence Community. And Casey was predisposed to mistrust all Kremlin leaders, Gorbachev included, and highlight consistent patterns and worst case scenarios in Soviet behavior. In his judgment, therefore, by his "New Thinking," Gorbachev, especially in promoting arms control, was laying a "political trap" to ensnare Reagan's defense programs, the Strategic Defense Initiative above all.[14]

Robert Gates, Casey's deputy director of intelligence, reinforced his boss' predispositions. Gates had joined the CIA as an intelligence analyst in 1966 and served as the National Security Council expert on and the national intelligence officer for the Soviet Union under Carter. He, therefore, had the bona fides to ensure that his views mattered. And Gates's views paralleled Casey's: Gorbachev's reforms and proposals were in his view tactics designed to achieve what was now and forever the Soviet's strategic objective—the defeat of the West. Subscribing to this perspective as well was Caspar Weinberger, the powerful secretary of defense. Casey and Weinberger agreed that the Defense Intelligence Agency and other Intelligence Community elements with budgets controlled by the Pentagon should exercise greater influence on the preparation of "net assessments"—the comparison of United States to Soviet Union capabilities—than had been the case under Carter, DCI Stansfield Turner, and Secretary of Defense Harold Brown. Evidence suggests that not only did Casey's and Weinberger's advocacy of an increased role for Department of Defense intelligence analysts result in consistent attention to the magnitude of the Soviet threat, but also the voices of CIA analysts inclined to assess Gorbachev's New Thinking as credible, such as SOVA director Melvin Goodman, were subordinated if not drowned out.[15]

Reagan could not discount the pessimism of his chief advisors. After all, even the most optimistic judgments that he received from Goodman and others in the CIA did not indicate that the analysts had high confidence in their judgments. To the contrary, in almost all cases they included less sanguine estimates as well. Moreover, at the same time that the CIA and Reagan's key national security managers were debating what to make of the new breed of Kremlin leaders, the Intelligence Community was rocked by a spy versus spy scandal of fictional proportions. It enveloped the defection and reversal of that defection by KGB Colonel Vitali Yurchenko in the lead-up to the 1985 Gorbachev-Reagan summit in Geneva; Yurchenko's identification of ex-CIA officer Edward Lee Howard as a Soviet mole; Howard's escape to Moscow, where he received asylum; the FBI sting operation that resulted in the 1986 arrest in New York City of Gennadi Zakharov, a Soviet physicist who worked for the United Nations Secretariat, for purchasing classified information; and the retaliatory arrest in Moscow of the journalist Nicholas Daniloff for allegedly spying for the United States. Even as the CIA appeared that much less trustworthy, the Soviets appeared to be up to their old games. In fact, in the counterintelligence competition, the CIA was faring worse than the Americans realized. Unknown to the agency or FBI, the same year that Howard fled to Moscow, the KGB recruited Aldrich Ames, who would serve as its most valuable mole during the last years of the Cold War.[16]

Reagan nevertheless was unwilling to define Gorbachev as a closet Stalinist or otherwise to write him off. In part, this resolve was almost certainly influenced by a string of intelligence assessments. While still considering an authoritarian and militaristic resurgence, and even a right-wing takeover, possible, and conceding that the "increasingly volatile conditions" in the Soviet Union "makes an already difficult analytical problem even more uncertain," these estimates judged it likely that Gorbachev would continue and, in fact, intensify his reform efforts. Casey, Gates, and others were unmoved; Reagan's inclination was to trust but verify. Secretary of State George Schultz, who replaced Alexander Haig in 1982, also did his part in encouraging the president to at least leave open the possibility of reaching a bargain. Still, the greatest influence on the president was his personal assessment of the Soviet leader. Each time Reagan met with Gorbachev, in Geneva in 1985, in Reykjavik, Iceland in 1986, and in Washington, DC in 1987, he became more convinced that cooperation was possible. And as a product of this cooperation, Reagan certainly hoped and increasingly believed, the two leaders could bring about first an end to the nuclear arms race and then an end to the Cold War.[17]

The negotiations during the Nixon and Carter administrations that produced the two Strategic Arms Limitation Treaties (SALT I and II) were so complicated and arduous primarily because, in an environment of secrecy and mistrust, they depended heavily on the capabilities of the Intelligence Community. Reagan's agreement on the Intermediate-Range Nuclear Forces Treaty, which went into effect in June 1988, was less dependent on intelligence because it depended heavily on his relationship with Gorbachev. But because this watershed in the tortuous course of Soviet-American relations was so dependent on this personal relationship, the momentum toward the further relaxation of tension was halted by Reagan's leaving office.[18]

His successor, George H. W. Bush, the only president whose resume included the directorship of the CIA, embraced the agency more enthusiastically than did Reagan. Deeply conservative in his thinking about foreign policy and wary of changes in the international order that could produce power vacuums and instability, Bush was sympathetic to the suspicions about Gorbachev harbored by many of the CIA's analysts. In their view, Reagan had gone too far in his judgments about the newness of the Kremlin leader's thinking. As reflected in a National Intelligence Estimate prepared for Bush shortly after his inauguration, many of the agency's Soviet experts defined the changes in Soviet policy during the final Reagan years as "largely tactical, driven by the need for breathing space from the competition." This cohort of analysts "believe[d] the ideological imperatives of Marxism-Leninism and its hostility toward capitalist countries are enduring … They judge that there is a serious risk of Moscow returning to traditionally combative behavior." This assessment of course paralleled that of Gates. Reagan's chief of the CIA's Directorate of Intelligence was a more intimate advisor to President Bush than was CIA director William Webster. Gates served as Bush's deputy national security advisor before he replaced Webster as DCI. Partially because of Gates's influence, Bush was hesitant to build on Reagan's foundation. But he no more than Gorbachev could control the forces that glasnost, perestroika, and other elements of the reformist agenda had unleashed.[19]

Bush was greatly surprised when the Berlin Wall came come tumbling down in 1989, and, two years later, following the "Velvet Revolution" in Czechoslovakia, the reunification of Germany and its entry into NATO, and the collapse of Communist rule throughout the Eastern bloc, the Soviet Union imploded. While the CIA warrants some culpability for the administration's being caught off guard, its inability to predict these momentous events does not warrant inclusion in the list of complete intelligence failures, where it often appears.[20]

Over the preceding decade, the Intelligence Community had produced countless products that perceptively identified the Soviet Union's multiple and potentially fatal ailments: its economy, its society, its demographics, its nationality problems, its relations with its clients and allies, and many more. By the time that Bush moved into the White House, analysts, while confronting "too many unknowns" and "sharply divided" over the likely outcome of the crisis, or crises, consuming the Soviets, were estimating the odds of Gorbachev succeeding in implementing his reformist agenda (referred to as the "light at the end of the tunnel" scenario) as no greater than alternative scenarios that ranged from anarchy to a military-supported coup designed to restore a dictatorship to a change in regime and policy so dramatic that it was tantamount to a revolution. These estimates underscored that the concomitant development to the growing dissatisfaction with Gorbachev as he shifted from reformer to consolidator was the emergence of Boris Yel'tsin, who in 1991 became the first president of Russia (formally the Russian Soviet Federative Socialist Republic), as the standard bearer for the discontented and disillusioned.[21]

In early 1991, prior to Yel'tsin's election to the newly created position in Russia, George Kolt, the chief of the Office of Soviet Analysis, produced a remarkably perceptive and prescient report. He wrote that on the one hand Yel'tsin "has a good chance of becoming the first popularly elected leader in Russian history, acquiring the legitimacy that comes with that mandate." On the other hand, Kolt pointedly warned, the military, MVD (the institution charged with internal security), and KGB leaders, setting their sights on Yel'tsin as "their first target," were "making broad preparations for a broad use of force." This "situation of growing chaos" prevented Kolt from forecasting the near-term consequences. Nevertheless, he concluded with an uncharacteristic expression of confidence. "With or without Gorbachev, with or without a putsch," the veteran Soviet analyst judged, "the most likely prospect for the end of this decade, if not earlier, is a Soviet Union transformed into some independent states and a confederation of the remaining Republics, including Russia."[22]

While Kolt's estimate was more accurate and forward leaning than other analysts and offices, including his own subordinates in the Office of Soviet Analysis (many in SOVA vigorously disagreed with their manager), in general the CIA's portrait of the Soviet Union in the lead-up to its disintegration was well informed, insightful, and reliable. The collapse of the Berlin Wall was accidental; the agency cannot be faulted for failing to anticipate it. Perhaps analysts should have been bolder in projecting the collapse of the Kremlin regime, especially after the seismic tremors throughout its satellites. Yet they were explicit in underscoring that because of Gorbachev's dwindling support, he was losing control. By April 1991 the CIA reported that "the current political system in the Soviet Union is doomed."[23]

But they were acutely aware that history suggested, Russian as well as Soviet history, that Moscow's (or before that St. Petersburg's) ruling authorities would intervene with force before permitting the downfall of the Soviet state and empire. This was the case during the eras of the Ruriks and Romanovs, and the Communists were very likely to follow precedent. Even Kolt expected a reactionary putsch. In his judgment, it would fail, although not necessarily immediately. Indeed, no analyst in the Intelligence Community could provide the Bush administration with a timetable — the "actionable intelligence" that administrations badly desire but cannot realistically count on receiving. This does not constitute an intelligence failure; analysts do not peer in crystal balls. The blame for not identifying the fracturing of the Soviet Union as a contingency for which preparations should have been made falls on Bush and his advisors, not the CIA.[24]

Just as the conclusion of the INF Treaty and other indices of the improvement in Soviet-American relations insulated Reagan from the fallout of Iran-Contra, the reunification of Germany, the dissolution of the USSR, and other way stations in the denouement of the Cold War allowed George H.W. Bush to escape censure for a lack of strategic foresight. In both cases, as is the norm in the United States, the CIA served as the lightning rod.

On the operations side, however, the CIA's record was anything but the norm. Indeed, the CIA should have received credit, at least from those who paid close attention, for its concurrent projects in Afghanistan. Those who knew much about these operations, which because of their covert nature were primarily government officials and journalists who resided within the Beltway and scholars who followed Afghanistan, US foreign policy, or both intensely, perceived them at the time largely as a success. At least they did in February 1988, when Gorbachev announced the Soviet withdrawal which it would complete over the next year. That announcement appeared as the climax of a decade-long effort. The CIA's involvement in Afghanistan began during the Carter administration. It grew exponentially more extensive and intense, however, under the direction of Reagan and Casey. The agency's support for the resistance to the Soviet-sponsored regime helped turn Afghanistan into the Kremlin's Vietnam. History may well conclude that the CIA's contribution to the grief that befell the Soviet Union was less than its contribution to the grief that befell the United States on September 11, 2001, and has continued for more than a decade since. But that progression was hardly linear or foreordained.

Of course the CIA designs its operations so that it will not receive credit — or for that matter attribution. Despite the scale and duration of the CIA's activities in Afghanistan, and the press coverage, the project remained officially, and to a remarkable extent, covert. Indeed, prior to the Soviet withdrawal, the agency's role in the unfolding events attracted little attention from either the US or international publics. With the end of the Cold War and the dawn of what President Bush called the "New World Order," moreover, for much of the globe's population the CIA as an institution and an instrument of policy became an increasingly irrelevant afterthought. In Washington, there were even calls for its abolition.

New York Senator Daniel Moynihan led the charge. Moynihan, like many others, argued that the CIA missed all the signals pointing to the Soviet Union's collapse. This failure demonstrated its inadequacy as a collector and analyst of intelligence. No less important, he argued that the secrecy that inhered in the Company's mission and self-definition violated the ideals and values responsible for America prevailing over the Soviets. Citing Britain's master spy novelist John le Carré as his authority, Moynihan thundered, "The Soviet Empire did not fall apart because the spooks had bugged the men's room in the Kremlin or put broken glass in Mrs. Brezhnev's bath, but because running a huge closed repressive society in the 1980s had become—economically, socially and militarily, and technologically—impossible." A creation of the Cold War, the CIA had seemingly lost its raison d'être: "CNN replaced the KGB as the agency's biggest competitor." As early as 1991, Moynihan proposed folding its functions into the State Department. Then in 1995, following the arrest and sentencing to life in prison for treason of Aldrich Ames, the former head of the CIA's Soviet counterintelligence division, he sponsored the Abolition of the Central Intelligence Agency Act.[25]

Moynihan's bill generated scant support. Approaching its fortieth anniversary, the CIA was an entrenched institution; its abolition would be politically and bureaucratically much more difficult than its establishment. Virtually no one in Washington was willing to expend the requisite political capital and, if successful, literally have nothing to show for the effort. Further, especially within the Pentagon, the CIA had vigorous and highly influential defenders.

But even if abolition was not on the table, the CIA's future after the collapse of the Soviet Union was uncertain. There were those in Congress and among the public who expected and insisted on receiving a peace dividend from "winning" the Cold War. Such a benefit was likely to gain the support of the Clinton White House, with its priority on domestic concerns, economic growth, and expanding the Democratic Party. Significantly reducing the CIA's budget could contribute to such a dividend without engaging in the legislative battle an attempt to abolish the CIA would provoke. A minority in Congress saw the situation from the opposite perspective. Some senators and representative from both parties who had built their reputations as experts on security issues, such as John Warner (Rep, VA), Sam Nunn (Dem, GA), Porter Goss (Rep, FL), and Bob Kerrey (Dem, NE), worried that too drastic a reduction of the CIA budget would seriously degrade essential intelligence capabilities. The criticism that the CIA received for the role that poor intelligence played in the Black Hawk Down incident in October 1993, when close to twenty Americans died in the Battle of Mogadishu, Somalia, intensified these concerns.[26] Warner and his colleagues therefore supported proposals to reexamine the structure and mission of the CIA. Their goal was to adapt it, and the other elements of the Intelligence Community, to the post-Cold War environment.

As a consequence, in late 1994 President Bill Clinton established a commission headed by recently fired secretary of defense and current chair of the President's Foreign Intelligence Advisory Board (PFIAB — the "Foreign" was removed to produce PIAB after the George W. Bush administration declared a Global War on Terror) Les Aspin to determine how best to align the CIA with the challenges that the United States confronted now that the Soviet Union had disintegrated and communism had been discredited. Poring through thousands of pages of documentation and conducting scores of interviews, the investigation of this Commission on the Roles and Capabilities of the US Intelligence Community, as it was formally titled, went on for a year. After Aspin died, he was replaced as its head by another former secretary of defense, Harold Brown. Finally in March 1996 the commission submitted its report. It included a multitude of reforms that encompassed roles and missions; structure, coordination, and management; budget and resources; and oversight and accountability. Congruent with the ways of Washington, current and past senior officials in both the CIA and the Pentagon, bolstered by the allies of both chambers of Congress, rallied in virtually unanimous opposition. Because Clinton did not actively support the recommendations, his endorsement of them meant nothing. As a result, the CIA not only survived the end of the Cold War, it also survived essentially unchanged. [27]

The Intelligence Community's state of stasis would prove disastrous by the end of the decade. But throughout Bill Clinton's first term, reforming, improving, or otherwise adapting the CIA to better serve post-Cold War America was situated firmly at the bottom of agendas. This was not illogical. As attested to by the complimentary television series and films, if

Americans thought about the CIA at all during this time, they tended to look on it more favorably—at least compared to the previous decades.

The improved image of the CIA was based on illusion. But that is evident only in retrospect. The success in early 1991 of Operation Desert Storm, the US-led destruction of Saddam Hussein's army and forced evacuation of the Iraqis from Kuwait after less than two months of combat, was attributable in no small part to good intelligence. The CIA's responsibility for achieving the victory with so few casualties was minor compared to that of the military. Still, the agency's detection and tracking of the buildup of Iraqi forces along the Kuwaiti border had provided advance warning of Saddam's invasion. Moreover, it provided the Bush administration with insightful assessments that judged it unlikely that economic sanctions would compel Iraq's withdrawal and likely that a US military response would receive widespread international approval. Historically anomalous as it is, and despite the public criticism of the commander of US forces, General Norman Schwartzkopf, the CIA, along with America's military, received widespread credit for a job well done.[28]

Moreover, the agency received little blame for the massacre of thousands of Kurds in the Gulf War's aftermath, although in this case it was culpable. Following Saddam Hussein's defeat, the United States and its allies established an ersatz Kurdestan, a safe area for Iraqi Kurds in the "no fly zone" north of the 36th parallel. There, authorized first under the George H. W. Bush administration and then under that of Bill Clinton, the CIA embarked on a covert project to topple Saddam's regime. It funneled millions of dollars to two anti-Saddam organizations: Ahmed Chalabi's Iraqi National Congress (INC) and the Iraqi National Accord, or Wafik, led by Iyad (Ayad) Allawi, a former member of Saddam Hussein's Ba'ath Party. The organizations and their leaders were bitter rivals who refused to cooperate. The CIA shifted its support between the two sides, which resulted in acrimonious finger pointing in both the United States and Iraq. Operatives also recruited Kurds eager to establish their independence from Iraq. They, too, however, were divided between the Patriotic Union of Kurdistan (PUK) and the Kurdistan Democratic Party (KDP). Encouraged by the CIA, the two factions of Kurds united temporarily to take up arms against Iraq in 1991 and 1995. At neither time did they receive help from the Americans, regardless of who was president. Crushed militarily in the first instance, they aborted the insurrection in the second and turned for protection to either Iran or, in a sign of their desperation, Saddam himself.[29]

The Kurds' calamity did not detract from a CIA image burnished by Saddam's defeat in the Gulf War. The same can be said of the agency's involvement in the Balkan Wars during the Bush and Clinton administrations. On the positive side, along with other elements of the US Intelligence Community, the National Security Agency in particular, the CIA collected valuable evidence of Serbia's campaign of "ethnic cleansing" (albeit, manifesting a tendency that would attract widespread attention and condemnation a decade later, it frequently resisted sharing its intelligence with its IC partners and America's allies). On the negative side, its operations, designed to destabilize the regime of Serbia's president Slobodan Milošević, contributed to the escalation and expansion of the fighting. The CIA helped to fund, train, and supply first the Army of Bosnia, then the Kosovo Liberation Army, and finally extremist offshoots of the KLA who launched campaigns in Southern Serbia and Macedonia. Few knew about these covert operations, however, and even had they been brought more widely to the attention of the public, the CIA probably would have avoided criticism. Of the myriad actors in the Balkan tragedy, Milošević was widely regarded as the most evil. Much of the world's opinion supported intervention to assist his victims, and the CIA's operations preceded those of NATO. In June 1999, the agency emerged from the Kosovo War not only on the winning side, but also on the right side.[30]

Assessing Afghanistan

Assessments of the CIA's role in Afghanistan may well have been the same had it also been on the right side there. Or it is probably more accurate to write, assessments of the CIA's role in Afghanistan might have been the same had there been a right side. But for the United States, and some would say for the Soviets as well, there was not one. Afghanistan had historically existed as an acutely fractured nation, with ethnicity, ideology, and "warlordism" acting like centrifugal forces. In 1973, Sadar Mohammed Daoud Kahn, who had served as prime minister the previous decade, overthrew the monarchical rule of his first cousin and declared himself Afghanistan's first president. Daoud was something of a nationalist, at least in terms of establishing a state that represented all Pashtuns (Afghanistan's largest ethnic group). His support came largely from the Soviets and indigenous communists. Two factions fiercely divided the latter, although both claimed to represent the People's Democratic Party of Afghanistan (PDPA). Personalities (Babrak Karmal on one side, Noor Mohammed Taraki and Hafizullah Amin on the other) and rival alliances explained the divisions more than did contrasting visions or agendas. Daoud was not drawn to the Soviets or either Communist faction because of his own political sympathies. Rather, he saw them all as hostile to the patron of Afghanistan's two primary enemies—Iran and Pakistan. They were enemies of his enemies.[31]

With the United States emerging from its struggles in Vietnam and embracing détente with the Soviets, Afghanistan, never more than a tertiary strategic interest, economically without value, and culturally almost unintelligible to US policymakers, remained a low priority in Washington before and after Daoud's coup. ████████████████████████ ██ ████████████████████████████████ Ironically, Daoud became more of an intelligence target during the Carter administration, when, for reasons difficult for the CIA to judge beyond the problems he confronted trying to manage Afghanistan's warring Communist parties, the Afghan president began to distance himself from Moscow. Struggling to assess the implications, the CIA adopted a position of watchful waiting.

Although not a game changer in Washington, Daoud's assassination and the PDPA's seizure of power in April 1978 raised concerns to a previously unimaginable level. Uncertainty and discord intensified commensurately. Many in the White House, at Foggy Bottom, and on Capitol Hill assumed that the Soviet Union had orchestrated the coup. Their premise was that Daoud had become too independent; always worried about a revival of the historic Great Game and fearful that Afghanistan's large Muslim population could roil its own Central Asian appendages, Moscow required a more compliant regime.[32] However, the CIA could collect no evidence of Soviet complicity in the coup. Subsequently obtained sources revealed that the policymaking and intelligence communities were both right. The Kremlin did conspire with anti-Daoud forces to remove him. But the Soviets were surprised that the coup took place as early as it did—before a power-sharing arrangement between the two PDPA factions had been firmly put in place.[33]

The continued discord between the two Communist contenders for control in Afghanistan had dire consequences for all the parties concerned, although the respective consequences and their time frames differed dramatically. Within months of the coup, as the number of Soviet advisors in Afghanistan doubled, the PDPA coalition splintered again. The Taraki-Amin faction (the Khalqs) gained decisive control over state policy, exiling Karmal and his allies (the Parchams) to various ambassadorial posts. But the Khalq faction itself was riven by disputes and rivalries. What is more, the PDPA regime in Kabul, within which Amin exercised principal albeit contested power, launched a program to impose a socialist revolution from above throughout the country. The effort, which included land redistribution, outlawing customary privileges, and even extending new rights to women, encountered stiff resistance from tribal leaders and Muslim scholars and clerics, the mullahs. The regime's response was repression. The response of the tribal leaders and mullahs was insurrection. By the end of the year, the fighting had intensified and spread. Assisted by Pashtuns in Pakistan, the insurgents overran large swaths of territory, especially in Afghanistan's northern and eastern areas. In December 1978, Amin and Taraki flew to Moscow to request help. They left having signed a twenty-year treaty of "cooperation and friendship." In the judgment of CIA analysts, the treaty "could be invoked to justify Soviet combat intervention on behalf of the [Afghan] regime."[34]

The treaty marked a watershed for the Carter administration, although not for the CIA—at least not one discernible immediately. Throughout 1978, Secretary of State Cyrus Vance and National Security Advisor Zbigniew Brzezinski had characteristically offered the president opposing diagnoses and prescriptions. Since the April coup Vance had argued that the Amin-Taraki government was not the Kremlin's client, and because of this autonomy, the United States should pursue policies designed to contain Soviet influence. Brzezinski identified the Khalq faction in particular and Afghanistan in general as instruments the Soviets were exploiting to acquire regional hegemony. In contrast to Vance, he advised that the United States sever ties with Kabul and undertake covert operations aimed at rolling back the Soviets. Carter initially tilted toward Vance, but after the December treaty he reversed direction. According to Brzezinski, while the president stopped short of sanctioning direct US support for the oppositionist forces, he did approve the CIA's offering to cooperate with the Pakistanis to aid the insurgents. In February 1979, Carter's attitude toward Amin took a turn for the worse. After kidnapping Adolph Dubs, the US ambassador to Afghanistan, a group of antigovernment extremists proposed to trade his freedom for that of their comrades. Despite US entreaties, Amin refused the bargain. The extremists killed Dubs. Surely with his mind on the anti-Americanism of the recently installed regime in Iran, Carter pointed the finger at Kabul. He cut off all economic assistance and canceled programs to train the Afghan military, leaving Soviet influence over it unchallenged.[35]

Notwithstanding the ongoing hostage crisis in Iran, Langley made Afghanistan an equal priority. Notwithstanding Soviet assistance, the Amin-Taraki government appeared to be losing ground rapidly to the insurgents, a situation exacerbated by its continued internal strife. The question the CIA could not answer was what response the United States could expect of the Soviets. Would Moscow allow the defeat of its client, especially if the victors were Muslims? Not only were Muslims historically hostile to the Soviets, but they were also supported by a US ally, Pakistan, and perhaps the United States itself. Was this threat sufficient to drive the Soviets to commit their own combat troops to save the Afghan government?

The CIA's answer to this question has led to the inclusion of predicting the Soviet intervention in Afghanistan on lists of US intelligence failures.[36] In this case, the indictment is largely, although not entirely, justified. The CIA did not rule out the possibility that the Soviets would commit its troops to Afghanistan. The agency recognized that the Kremlin might assess certain outcomes as intolerable. Chief among these was the potential for a chain of militant Islamist states capable of destabilizing the Central Asian Republics to ally with one another on the Soviet Union's southern border.

But on balance the CIA assessed Soviet intervention in Afghanistan as unlikely. Its military leaders, the agency reported, recognized that Amin's government was highly unpopular. Parallel to the United States' experience in Vietnam, this lack of indigenous support, in combination with Afghanistan's inhospitable terrain, could readily turn the theater into a quagmire, which could take years and the commitment of resources that the Soviet state could ill afford to use up. Moreover, the very effort so blatantly to determine Afghanistan's future might well produce a backlash among Muslims, both internationally and within its borders, which could prove catastrophic. Probably the greatest deterrent to Soviet intervention, read intelligence reports, was SALT II. At this point there was no greater priority for the Brezhnev government than the conclusion of the treaty. Those negotiations would almost certainly collapse if the Soviets committed troops to Afghanistan. In the CIA's judgment, the Soviets would not allow this collapse. Rather, they would engineer the replacement of the Amin-Taraki government with one led by Karmal and his exiled Parcham faction. Once the substitute Karmal-led regime was in place, the Soviets would deploy the minimum number of military advisors necessary to secure its survival.[37]

The CIA continued to reexamine its assessment over the next six months. As Amin's control continued to erode, and indeed he survived an attempt on his life, intelligence analysts warned that the odds of Soviet intervention were increasing. Time was running out for a managed regime change. "The Soviet leaders may be on the threshold of a decision to commit their own forces to prevent the collapse of the regime and to protect their sizable stakes in Afghanistan," DCI Stansfield Turner wrote to Carter in September. Turner's and other warnings alerted the administration that developments in Afghanistan were causing the Kremlin great alarm, and the greater the alarm the greater the likelihood of the introduction of USSR forces. Nevertheless, most analysts, relying on cost-benefit calculations, adhered to their previous judgment that the Kremlin would not be willing to pay the military and political price of a major intervention. The detection in mid-December of new Soviet military deployments to Afghanistan, including motorized rifle divisions, transport and combat helicopters, fighter-bombers, and other personnel and materiel generated additional dissent from and a slight modification of this judgment. Yet its fundamentals did not change. The majority of intelligence analysts now concluded that "the Soviets were preparing to engage directly in combat operations and that this would, by itself, represent a distinct escalation of their commitment." But these operations were not a prelude to a full-fledged intervention designed to seize control of the country. The object, rather, was more modest: "Augmentation of the Afghan military effort to assist in stabilizing the situation" and "security for Soviet nationals and Soviet support operations."[38]

It was the National Security Agency, not the CIA, that notified US policymakers that the majority of America's intelligence analysts had been wrong. Actually, as many Soviet leaders at the time argued, and history would validate, this majority was not wrong when evaluated on the basis of its key judgment. The political and military cost of the Kremlin's decision to commit a massive military force to Afghanistan was intolerably high. Still, the leadership, fearing a loss of influence in the region that would benefit Iranian-inspired Islamic extremists and perhaps even the United States, chose to pay it. And congruent with the CIA's assessment of the risk, the commitment contributed to the demise of the Soviet Union itself.[39]

But as often is the case with intelligence estimates, correct assessments of the situation do not lead to correct predictions of behavior. The CIA, explained an internal postmortem, judged that Brezhnev "would act rationally in accordance with our perception of Soviet self-interest." But Brezhnev, and a small group of advisors, perceived the stakes differently. On December 24, NSA Director Bobby Ray Inman reported that within fifteen hours the Soviets would launch a large-scale intervention. The following day, Christmas, Turner warned that the Soviets had completed their preparations and the intervention may already have begun. The DCI's warning was too late; by the time he sent it, Soviet forces were surging into Afghanistan. On December 27, they killed Amin—or he may have killed himself. Regardless, broadcasting from across the Soviet border, Babrak Karmal announced that he had formed a new government. The next day Carter chaired a meeting of the National Security Council. "All knew," Brzezinski later reported, that "a major watershed had been reached."[40]

None of the principals, and certainly not the CIA, had any inkling of how major that watershed was. The Carter administration, as manifest in the doctrine that the president enunciated in his 1980 State of the Union, for reasons that extended beyond safeguarding the access of the United States and its allies to the region's oil, determined that it must deter Moscow from projecting greater power toward the Persian Gulf. Support of the mujahideen would well serve this purpose by tying down Soviet troops in Afghanistan. In light of the events in Iran, moreover, there was the possibility of deflecting Muslim animosity away from Washington and toward Moscow. Carter feared too much US involvement. But following the advice of Brzezinski, he signed a "finding" that authorized the CIA to provide the rebels with nonlethal supplies, cooperate with Pakistan's intelligence service, the Inter-Services Intelligence (ISI), and undertake propaganda and psychological warfare projects.[41]

The CIA's Afghan operations intensified dramatically with Reagan's election and the arrival of Bill Casey at Langley. To the activist director of the Company, the Kremlin's naked aggression in Afghanistan made it an attractive vehicle for mobilizing the hard line anti-Soviets. Further, the Islamist dynamic of the Afghan resistance struck a responsive chord with Casey's militant Catholicism. "More than any other American," writes the prize-winning journalist Steven Coll insightfully, "Casey saw the Afghan jihad not merely as statecraft, but as an important front in a worldwide struggle between communist atheism and God's community of believers." Disregarding the advice of such subordinates as Bobby Ray Inman, now the agency's deputy director whom Casey considered "too timid," the DCI collaborated with Defense Secretary Caspar Weinberger to manipulate the Pentagon's budget so that he could dedicate hundreds of millions of unaccountable dollars to the Afghan theater. He also reached an arrangement with Saudi Arabia's royal family by which dollar for dollar the Saudis secretly matched US funding. In addition, through closer cooperation with Pakistan's Directorate for Inter-Services Intelligence, he orchestrated the transfer to Afghanistan's mujahideen of ever more potent weaponry. By 1986, these weapons included Stinger antiaircraft missiles. Battery powered and guided by a remarkably effective yet portable heat-seeking system, the Stingers downed scores of Soviet helicopters and transport aircraft. Casey's objective went beyond "merely" making the Soviets pay for invading Afghanistan. His goal in this "largest covert operation" in US history was nothing less than to drive them out of the country and establish an indigenous government untainted by communism or communists.[42]

Many actors and factors contributed to Gorbachev's decision in 1988 to withdraw Soviet forces from Afghanistan in 1988, but the CIA's role was among the leading ones. Casey did not live long enough to witness this success. Nor did he live long enough to witness the consequences. In part because he was enmeshed in the Iran-Contra troubles, but in larger part because his priority was to cause the Soviets the greatest grief possible, Casey had given little thought to what the Kremlin would leave behind. CIA analysts were confident that without the support of Soviet troops, Afghanistan's Communist regime, headed since 1986 by Mohammed Najibullah, would collapse. They were also confident that the aftermath would be unstable and unpredictable. The mujahideen had long been divided among rival leaders, most prominently Ahmad Shah Massoud and Gulbuddin Hekmatyar. Each of these warlords had an army loyal only to him. Pakistan supported the latter; the United States equivocated. As the Islamist resistance to Soviet rule grew in the 1980s, moreover, so did the number of Muslims from other states who migrated to Afghanistan and Pakistan to join the cause. Among these was Osama bin Laden (the CIA prefers the transliteration from the Arabic alphabet of Usama bin Laden), who arrived in Afghanistan from Saudi Arabia in the mid-1980s. The CIA knew that bin Laden came from a wealthy Saudi family. It knew little else about him.[43]

Najibullah defied the CIA's predictions by clinging to power after the last Soviet troops evacuated Afghanistan in early 1989. Nevertheless, with President George H. W. Bush fixated on the rapid disintegration of the Soviet state (Bush closed the US embassy in Kabul in 1989), Germany's reunification and NATO's integrity, and Iraqi aggression, CIA operations and interest in Afghanistan fell off precipitously. The agency, as a result, followed the lead of Pakistan and backed Hekmatyar. Complicating matters, however, Bush's State Department favored Massoud, and relations with Pakistan deteriorated further when the United States cut off assistance to India's enemy in a futile effort to halt Islamabad's nuclear program.[44] Making matters worse, by the end of the Bush presidency the CIA had identified Afghanistan as a breeding ground for Islamist *jihadists*. By that time, the end had arrived for the Soviet Union as well, and with it the end of Najibullah's rule. In February 1992, Massoud's forces took Kabul and placed Najibullah under house arrest.[45]

Burhanuddin Rabbani became president of a coalition government. This compromise satisfied neither Massoud nor Hekmatyar, and within two years a civil war erupted between the two warlords. Within those same two years, Pakistan abandoned Massoud and threw its support to a united group of Islamist students, or *taliban*, from the Pashtun region that traversed the border between it and Afghanistan. Although they had dedicated their lives to studying at madrasas, schools dedicated to the Islam religion, the Taliban rapidly proved their military mettle and gathered a popular following. While Massoud and Hekmatyar fought each other, in 1996 the Taliban captured the vital city of Kandahar and then steamrolled into Kabul. They hung Najibullah, deposed Rabbani, and established their own fundamentalist government headed by Mullah Muhammad Omar.[46]

The Challenge of Counterterrorism

Foreign policy was low down on Bill Clinton's agenda when he took office. The counterterrorist policies and programs that Clinton pursued, with impetus provided by the bombings of New York's World Trade Center in 1993 and the Murrah Federal Building in Oklahoma City in 1995, concentrated on domestic terrorism. Further, since the 1980s, when stories about the bombing of the Marine barracks in Beirut (1983), the hijacking of the *Achille Lauro* cruise ship in Italy (1985), the attack on a West Berlin discotheque (1986), and the explosion of Pan Am Flight 103 over Lockerbie, Scotland (1988) started to make headlines, Washington debated whether international terrorism was a law enforcement or national security problem regardless of who was president.[47]

The CIA had established a Counterterrorism Center within the Directorate of Operations in 1986. But the agency devoted most of its attention to more state-centered problems, especially after Saddam Hussein retained power in Iraq following the 1991 Gulf War. The Taliban's march into Kabul coincided with the administration's identification of international terrorism as a grave threat to national security. The CIA's priorities began to shift accordingly. By this time, Clinton had replaced Woolsey with John Deutch. The new director of central intelligence, a professor of chemistry and provost at the Massachusetts Institute of Technology (MIT) who had served in Clinton's Pentagon and would have preferred to stay there, had much in common with Stansfield Turner. He was no fan of covert operations. But he was an enthusiastic advocate of using the most advanced technologies to collect intelligence. And like Turner, especially at first, he had the respect of the president. In June 1995, Clinton signed Presidential Decision Directive-39, "U.S. Policy on Counterterrorism." It tasked the director of central intelligence with leading the effort to reduce US vulnerabilities to international terrorism through an "aggressive program of foreign intelligence collection, analysis, counterintelligence and covert action." Concurrently, though, Deutch prohibited the recruitment of personnel with records of criminal behavior or human rights abuses. While well-intentioned, this directive devastated the CIA's indigenous counterterrorist assets. A year later, 19 US servicemen died when Hezbollah terrorists bombed the military barracks at Khobar Towers in Saudi Arabia.[48]

At the end of Clinton's first term, Deutch, having never taken to the job or the agency, returned to MIT. The president nominated National Security Advisor Anthony Lake as his successor, but Lake withdrew his name from consideration when Senate Republicans pilloried his record on both foreign policy and political fund raising. Clinton then turned to George Tenet. In contrast to Deutch, and for that matter Clinton, Tenet was an ardent booster of the CIA. He was also a skilled bureaucrat, a political centrist without party ties, and predisposed to currying favor by telling people what they wanted to hear. Prior to becoming the agency's deputy director under Deutch, Tenet had served on the staffs of the Senate Select Committee on Intelligence and the National Security Council. Tutored and championed by Oklahoma's Democratic Senator David Boren, a former chair of the SSCI, he learned to work the corridors of Congress and the White House machinery. Tenet recognized that for purposes of advancing the CIA's mission to enhance American security and restoring its reputation, budget, and élan, the agency had to reorient its emphases. Building on PDD-39, he began to position the CIA as the linchpin of what he argued had to be a much more aggressive and concerted effort to confront terrorism, the proliferation of weapons of mass destruction, and other unconventional threats to

US security far removed from dynamics associated with the Cold War. Tenet managed the CIA, he defended it, and he advocated for it.[49]

The Senate confirmed Tenet's nomination in July 1997. Seemingly overnight, the CIA's morale improved and funding increased. Tenet highlighted boosting recruitment and rebuilding the Directorate of Operation's clandestine service. Yet his success in combating the spread of terrorism was not commensurate. By 1998 Osama bin Laden and his network of terrorists, which in the late 1980s he had loosely organized to form al-Qaeda (the Base), were rivaling if not replacing Saddam Hussein as America's number one enemy. Early that year the CIA formulated and rehearsed an elaborate scheme to kidnap bin Laden from Tarnak Farms, his Afghan compound in Kandahar, and bring him to the United States. Deciding it too risky, however, Tenet called the operation off. But the hunt for bin Laden was on.[50]

On August 7, 1998, terrorists bombed the US embassies in Nairobi, Kenya, and in Dar es Salaam, Tanzania. Tenet identified Osama bin Laden as the mastermind. For the CIA, bin Laden's profile as a terrorist rose along with its concern over the Taliban turning Afghanistan into terrorism's homeland and a safe haven for al-Qaeda. In the hope of a quick fix, Clinton ordered a missile strike on Zawhar Kili in eastern Afghanistan, where the CIA thought bin Laden was attending a meeting. He was not. The Pakistanis may well have tipped off the Taliban, which warned bin Laden. Even if Clinton had succeeded in killing al-Qaeda's leader, moreover, CIA intelligence analysts strongly doubted that the terrorist threat would go away. Further, with accusations, popularized in the film "Wag the Dog," that Clinton had authorized the strike to divert attention from the Monica Lewinsky scandal (Clinton had sexual relations with a White House intern), the agency was concerned that politics might constrain its options and operations.[51]

The administration's efforts and frustration intensified during Clinton's final years in office. The president appointed Richard Clarke as the White House counterterrorism "czar" and assigned him a seat at the Cabinet table. To enhance coordination with Clarke in the White House and more effectively hunt down bin Laden and al-Qaeda, in 1999 Tenet appointed J. Cofer Black to head up the CIA's Counterterrorism Center. Black had been following bin Laden's trail since serving as the CIA station chief in Khartoum, Sudan, in 1993, and kept close tabs on the progress of the "bin Laden station." Known as the Alec Station, this was the special unit led by

Michael F. Scheuer and housed in a building separate from but close to the Langley headquarters that the CIA established in 1996 exclusively to track the wealthy Saudi.[52] Clinton signed a Memorandum of Notification (MON) authorizing the CIA to use lethal force if necessary, to cripple the terrorist organization. The agency's operatives, however, even the most highly trained personnel in the Office of External Development's "non-official cover" (NOC) program, were unable to penetrate al-Qaeda. Further, neither the Counterterrorist Center nor the bin Laden station "acquired intelligence from anyone that could be acted upon." Bin Laden remained out of harm's way.[53]

Black came to assess the Taliban as no less dangerous than bin Laden and al-Qaeda. Pursuing both targets placed terrific stresses on the CIA's resources, even as the military, mindful of the failed mission to rescue the Iran hostages during the Carter administration, demanded "actionable intelligence" before it would commit its Special Forces. What is more, the CIA's partnership with Pakistan's intelligence service, the ISI, had ruptured years earlier. The cause was primarily that Pakistan supported the Taliban as an ally in its conflict with India over Kashmir and as a prophylactic that it thought necessary to prevent unrest among its own Pashtun population. The CIA appreciated that allying with Massoud could prove useful but was deterred from aggressively reaching out to him. Because he smuggled opium and murdered civilians, Massoud, the Company recognized, would be a very unpopular partner. Despite such obstacles, the agency's counterterrorist operations dramatically expanded in the last months of the Clinton administration. Their effect was negligible. On October 12, 2000, terrorists blew up the U.S.S. *Cole*, docked in the harbor of Aden, Yemen. Seventeen Americans died. It took several months for the CIA to determine that bin Laden was responsible. By then, Clinton was a lame-duck president.[54]

President George W. Bush retained George Tenet as his director of central intelligence. The bond established between the DCI and president was immediate and strong; Tenet named the agency's headquarters compound at Langley the George [H. W.] Bush Center for Intelligence after the new president's father. But Tenet was about the only Clinton legacy that Bush did retain. Candidate Bush was advised during the campaign and transition by a band of hard line and frustrated conservatives and neoconservatives known as the Vulcans. None of them had extensive or intimate experience with the Intelligence Community, and most of them had little respect for it. Bush and his team of national security managers, notably Vice President Dick Cheney,

Defense Secretary Donald Rumsfeld and his chief deputy, Paul Wolfowitz, and National Security Advisor Condoleeza Rice, took office convinced that Clinton's foreign policies were fatally flawed.[55]

Among the most deleterious of the flaws identified by both the Vulcans and Bush's national security team (there was some overlap) was what they considered Clinton's misplaced obsession with bin Laden, al-Qaeda, and the Taliban. In their view, Saddam Hussein's Iraq, owing to its present capabilities, potential capabilities, and sponsorship of other terrorists' capabilities, represented a far more severe threat than did, in the words of Paul Wolfowitz as reported by Richard Clarke, the "little terrorist in Afghanistan." Until the attack on the Twin Towers and the Pentagon, neither Rice nor Wolfowitz publicly uttered al-Qaeda's name a single time, and each referred to bin Laden only once. Further, the new administration intended defense against nuclear missiles, not terrorism, to be the cornerstone of its national security strategy. Rice has scheduled a major speech justifying that priority for delivery on September 11, 2001.[56]

She never gave it.

Notes

1   William J. Casey, Memorandum for the President, "Progress at the CIA," May 6, 1981, in *Ronald Reagan, Intelligence, and the End of the Cold War*, DVD Produced by the CIA's Center for the Study of Intelligence, November 2, 2011 (Hereafter cited as *Reagan and End of the Cold War DVD*). The CIA declassified and made available on this DVD over 200 documents in conjunction with this publication.

2   Robert M. Gates, *From the Shadows: The Ultimate Insider's Story of Five Presidents and How They Won the Cold War* (NY: Simon & Schuster, 1996), 200–08; Casey, Memorandum for the President, "Progress at the CIA," May 6, 1981; H. Bradford Westerfield, "Inside Ivory Bunkers: CIA Analysts Resist Managers 'Pandering' — Part II," reprinted in *Strategic Intelligence: Windows into a Secret World*, eds. Loch K. Johnson and James J. Wirtz (Los Angeles, CA: Roxbury Publishing Co., 2004), 2010–11.

3   Raymond L. Garthoff, *The Great Transition: American-Soviet Relations and the End of the Cold War* (Washington, DC: Brookings, 1994), 20–26; Douglas F. Garthoff, "Analyzing Soviet Politics and Foreign Policy," in *Watching the Bear: Essays on the CIA's Analysis of the Soviet Union*, ed. Gerald K. Hanes and Robert E. Leggett (Washington, DC: Government Printing Office, 2003), 83–84.

4   Thomas Fingar, *Reducing Uncertainty: Intelligence Analysis and National Security* (Stanford, CA: Stanford University Press, 2011), 25; Richard H. Immerman,

"Intelligence and Strategy: Historicizing Psychology, Policy, and Politics," *Diplomatic History* 32 (January 2008): 16–17.

5   Or Arthur Honig, "The Impact of CIA's Organizational Culture on Its Estimates under William Casey," *International Journal of Intelligence and Counter-Intelligence* 24 (March 2011): 44–64.

6   On the DVD the CIA produced to accompany *Ronald Reagan, Intelligence, and the End of the Cold War*, the CIA's Center for the Study of Intelligence made available many such analytic products from early in the administration for the purpose of providing context for and perspective on the later years. See for example Briefing of President-Elect Reagan, December 11, 1980; Directorate of Intelligence, Intelligence Assessment, "USSR: Economic Issues Facing the Leadership," January 2, 1981; Directorate of Intelligence, Paper, "Soviet and Eastern European Economic Problems," January 1, 1982; Directorate of Intelligence, Intelligence Assessment, "The Soviet Political Succession: Institutions, People, and Policies," April 1982.

7   National Intelligence Officer for the USSR and Eastern Europe, Memorandum for DCI, "Some Implications of the Soviet Political Succession for US Policy," May 20, 1982, *Reagan and End of the Cold War DVD*; Directorate of Intelligence Research, Paper, "Soviet Society in the 1980s: Problems and Prospects," December 1982, *Reagan and End of the Cold War DVD*.

8   Interagency Memorandum on Discussion of U.S. Intelligence Needs on Soviet Ballistic Missile Defense, with Tasking Memorandum from Richard Allen, July 17, 1981, *Reagan and End of the Cold War DVD*; NIE 11-13-81, "Soviet Ballistic Missile Defense," October 11, 1982, *Reagan and End of the Cold War DVD*.

9   Special National Intelligence Estimate, "Soviet Potential to Respond to US Strategic Force Improvements, and Foreign Reactions," October 6, 1981, *Reagan and End of the Cold War DVD*; Directorate of Intelligence, Intelligence Assessment, "Soviet Elite Concerns About Popular Discontent and Official Corruption," December 1982, *Reagan and End of the Cold War DVD*.

10 Robert M. Gates, Memorandum for DCI, "Andropov: His Power and Program," November 20, 1982, *Reagan and End of the Cold War DVD*; NIE 11-4-82, "The Soviet Challenge to US Security Interests," August 10, 1982, *Reagan and End of the Cold War DVD*; Directorate of Intelligence, Paper, "The Soviet Challenge: The Determinants of Soviet Behavior," January 1, 1982, *Reagan and End of the Cold War DVD*; NIE 11-9-83, "Andropov's Approach to Key US-Soviet Issues," August 9, 1983, *Reagan and End of the Cold War DVD*.

11 National Intelligence Council, Memorandum, "After Andropov: The Coming Turbulence in Soviet Politics," February 13, 1984, *Reagan and End of the Cold War DVD*; Directorate of Intelligence, Intelligence Assessment, "The Soviet Political Succession: Institutions, People, and Policies," April 1982, *Reagan and End of the Cold War DVD*; Directorate of Intelligence, Memorandum, "Gorbachev, the New Broom," June 1985, *Reagan and End of the Cold War DVD*.

12   Don Oberdorfer, *From the Cold War to a New Era: The United States and the Soviet Union, 1983-1991* (Baltimore, MD: Johns Hopkins University Press), 65–68; National Intelligence Council, Memorandum, "Moscow and the Reagan Administration: Initial Assessments and Responses," September 1, 1981, *Reagan and End of the Cold War DVD*; Directorate of Intelligence, Memorandum, "Soviet Thinking on the Possibility of Armed Confrontation with the United States," December 30, 1983, *Reagan and End of the Cold War DVD*; SNIE 11-9-84, "Soviet Policy Toward the United States in 1984," August 14, 1984, *Reagan and End of the Cold War DVD*; Directorate of Intelligence, "Gorbachev, the New Broom."

13   Directorate of Intelligence, "Gorbachev, the New Broom;" Directorate of Intelligence, Memorandum, "The Soviet Economy in Perspective," July 1, 1985, *Reagan and End of the Cold War DVD*; SNIE 11-16-85, "Soviet Strategic and Political Objectives in Arms Control in 1985," March 1985, *Reagan and End of the Cold War DVD*; Directorate of Intelligence, Research Paper, "Soviet SDI Response Options: The Resource Dilemma," November 1987, *Reagan and End of the Cold War DVD*; Directorate of Intelligence, Intelligence Assessment, "Soviet Policy Toward Nicaragua," November 1986, *Reagan and End of the Cold War DVD*.

14   Casey letter to Reagan, September 9, 1985, *Reagan and End of the Cold War DVD*.

15   Robert Gates Memorandum, "Gorbachev's Gameplan: The Long View," November 24, 1987, *Reagan and End of the Cold War DVD*; CIA/DIA, Paper, "The Soviet Economy Under a New Leader," March 19, 1986, *Reagan and End of the Cold War DVD*; Raymond Garthoff, "Estimating Soviet Military Intentions and Capabilities," 168–72; Douglas Garthoff, "Analyzing Soviet Politics and Foreign Policy," 88–91; Christopher Andrew, *For the President's Eyes Only: Secret Intelligence and the American Presidency from Washington to Bush* (NY: HarperCollins, 1995), 494–96.

16   James Kelly, "The Spy Who Returned to the Cold," *Time.com*, accessed on October 5, 2012, at http://www.time.com/time/magazine/article/0,9171, 1050566,00.html; David Wise, *The Spy Who Got Away: The Inside Story of Edward Lee Howard, The CIA Agent Who Betrayed His Country's Secrets and Escaped to Moscow* (NY: Random House, 1988); Nicholas Daniloff, *Two Lives, One Russia* (Boston: Houghton Mifflin, 1988); David Wise, *Nightmare: How Aldrich Ames Sold the CIA to the KGB for $4.6 Million* (NY: HarperCollins, 1995).

17   Directorate of Intelligence, Intelligence Assessment, "The New CPSU Program: Charting the Future," April 1986, *Reagan and End of the Cold War DVD*; Directorate of Intelligence, Intelligence Estimate, "Gorbachev's Domestic Challenge: The Looming Problems," February 1987, *Reagan and End of the Cold War DVD*; Directorate of Intelligence, Intelligence Assessment,

"Gorbachev: Steering the USSR Into the 1990s," July 1987, *Reagan and End of the Cold War DVD*; NIE 11-18-87, "Whither Gorbachev: Soviet Policy and Politics in the 1990s," November 1987, *Reagan and End of the Cold War DVD*; Directorate of Intelligence, Memorandum, "Leadership Situation in the USSR," September 17, 1988, *Reagan and End of the Cold War DVD*; George P. Schultz, *Turmoil and Triumph My Years as Secretary of State* (NY: Scribner's 1993).

18 John Prados, *The Soviet Estimate: U.S. Intelligence and Soviet Strategic Forces* (Princeton, NJ: Princeton University Press, 1986), 225–90; Douglas Garthoff, "Analyzing Soviet Politics and Foreign Policy," 88–99; *Witnesses to the End of the Cold War*, ed. William C. Wohlforth (Baltimore, MD: Johns Hopkins University Press, 1997); Jack F. Matlock, Jr., *Reagan and Gorbachev: How the Cold War Ended* (NY: Random House, 2004), 106-328.

19 NIE 11 -4-89, "Soviet Policy Toward the West: The Gorbachev Challenge," April 1989, *Reagan and End of the Cold War DVD*; Gates, *From the Shadows*, 449–531. For an exceptionally insightful explanation of the difficulty of foreseeing the revolutionary changes of 1989 and afterward, see Mark Kramer, "The Demise of the Soviet Bloc," *The Journal of Modern History* (December 2011): 788–854.

20 Tim Weiner, *Legacy of Ashes: The History of the CIA* (NY: Doubleday, 2007), 429–35; John Diamond, *The CIA and the Culture of Failure: U.S. Intelligence from the End of the Cold War to the Invasion of Iraq* (Stanford, CA: Stanford University Press, 2008), 17–53; Uri Friedman, "The Ten Biggest American Intelligence Failures," *Foreign Policy*, January 3, 2012, accessed on January 6, 2012, at http://www.foreignpolicy.com/articles/2012/1/3/the_ten_biggest _american_intelligence_failures.

21 Directorate of Intelligence, Intelligence Assessment, "Rising Political Instability Under Gorbachev: Understanding the Problem and Prospects for Resolution," April 1989, *Reagan and End of the Cold War DVD*; NIE 11- 18-90, "The Deepening Crisis in the USSR: Prospects for the Next Year," November 1990, *Reagan and End of the Cold War DVD*. See also Douglas J. MacEachin, *CIA Assessments of the Soviet Union: The Record Versus the Charges* (Washington, DC: Center for the Study of Intelligence, 1996), accessed on November 29, 2012, at https://www.cia.gov/library/center-for-the-study-of-intelligence /kent-csi/vol40no5/pdf/v40i5a08p.pdf.

22 Directorate of Intelligence, Paper, "The Soviet Cauldron," April 25, 1991, *Reagan and End of the Cold War DVD*. For more on this paper and George Kolt, see *Russia Watch: Essays in Honor of George Kolt*, ed. Eugene B. Rummer and Celeste A. Willander (Washington, DC: Center for Strategic and International Studies, 2007).

23 Directorate of Intelligence, Paper, "Gorbachev's Future," May 23, 1991, *Reagan and End of the Cold War DVD*.

24 In a parallel contemporary episode, one of the scenarios laid out in a February 1989 CIA Directorate of Intelligent Report forecast with almost eerie prescience the explosive student protests at Beijing's Tiananmen Square and the ensuing political fall-out. Once again, however, the estimate was insufficiently precise to be "actionable." CIA Directorate of Intelligence Report, "China: Potential for Political Crisis," February 9, 1989, accessed on April 29, 2013, at http://www.gwu.edu/~nsarchiv/NSAEBB/NSAEBB47/doc2.pdf.

25 James Bamford, *A Pretext for War: 9/11, Iraq, and the Abuse of American's Intelligence Agencies* (NY: Doubleday, 2004). Moynihan's Abolition of the Central Intelligence Agency Act and his speech introducing it on January 4, 1995, accessed on September 11, 2012, at http://www.ernesthancock.com/www.dcia.com/cia2.html. See also Mary H. Cooper, "Overview: After the Aldrich Ames Spy Scandal," *The CQ Researcher* 6 (February 2, 1995), 99–106, accessed on November 30, 2012, at http://www.cqpress.com/context/articles/cqr_cia_overview.html.

26 The classic study of the Battle of Mogadishu remains Mark Bowden, *Black Hawk Down: A Study of Modern War* (NY: Monthly Atlantic Press, 1999). See also Vernon Loeb, "The CIA in Somalia," February 27, 2000, accessed on April 29, 2013, at http://www.somaliawatch.org/archivejuly/000927601.htm.

27 For a detailed study of the Aspin-Brown Commission, see Loch K. Johnson, *The Threat on the Horizon: An Inside Account of America's Search for Security After the Cold War* (NY: Oxford University Press, 2011).

28 CIA report, "CIA Support to the US Military During the Persian Gulf War," 16 June 1977, accessed on October 9, 2012, at https://www.cia.gov/library/reports/general-reports-1/gulfwar/061997/support.htm; Richard L. Russell, "CIA's Strategic Intelligence in Iraq," *Political Science Quarterly* 117 (Summer 2002): 191–207; U.S. House of Representatives Armed Services Committee, Report of the Oversight and Investigations Subcommittee, "Intelligence Successes and Failures in Operations Desert Shield/Storm," 103rd Cong., 1st Sess., (Washington, DC: Government Printing Office, 1993), 18–23.

29 Ralph McGehee, "CIA and the Kurds," September 9, 1996, accessed on October 9, 2012, at http://saintconfused.tumblr.com/post/24692434325/358; Randy Stearns (reproduced from ABC News), "The CIA's Secret War In Iraq, October 1998," accessed on October 9, 2012, at http://www.defencejournal.com/oct98/cia_secretwar.htm; John F. Burns, "Kurds, Secure in North Iraq, Are Cool to a U.S. Offensive," *New York Times*, July 9, 2002.

30 Charles Lane and Thom Shanker, "Bosnia: What the CIA Didn't Tell US," *New York Review of Books* 43, May 9, 1996, accessed on October 9, 2012, at http://www.nybooks.com/articles/1542; "The CIA role in Bosnia," n.d. [1994], *International Action Center*, accessed on October 9, 2012, at http://www.iacenter.org/bosnia/ciarole.htm; Tom Walker and Aidan Laverty, "CIA Aided Kosovo Guerilla Army," *Sunday [London] Times*, March 12, 2000, accessed on

October 9, 2012, at http://www.balkanpeace.org/index.php?index=/content /balkans/kosovo_metohija/articles/kam01.incl; Peter Beaumont, Ed Vulliamy and Paul Beaver, "CIA's Role In Causing Revolt Against Milosevic in Kosovo Revealed," March 11, 2001, accessed on October 9, 2012, at http://educate -yourself.org/nwo/nwociaroleinkosovorevoltexposed12mar01.shtml; Colonel David Hackworth, "The CIA Strikes Out Again, March 14, 2001," accessed on October 9, 2012, at http://emperors-clothes.com/docs /hack.htm.

31   Henry Bradsher, *Afghanistan and the Soviet Union*, 2nd ed. (Durham, NC: Duke University Press, 1985), 17–74.

32   On the "Great Game," the contest between the British and Russian Empires over Central Asia, see Peter Hopkirk, *The Great Game: On Secret Service in High Asia* (Oxford, England: Oxford University Press, 2001).

33   Douglas MacEachin, *Predicting the Soviet Invasion of Afghanistan: The Intelligence Community's Record* (Washington, DC: Center for the Study of Intelligence, 2002), accessed on October 8, 2012, at https://www.cia.gov/library /center-for-the-study-of-intelligence/csi-publications/books-and-monographs /predicting-the-soviet-invasion-of-afghanistan-the-intelligence-communitys -record/predicting-the-soviet-invasion-of-afghanistan-the-intelligence -communitys-record.html. MacEachin, who was appointed the CIA's deputy director of intelligence in 1993, was detailed to the Pentagon's Strategic Warning Staff in 1979. This CSI monograph draws on that experience as well as the CIA's archives. The CIA declassified two important documents subsequent to this monograph's publication: Interagency Intelligence Memorandum, *Soviet Options in Afghanistan*, September 28, 1979, accessed on October 9, 2012, at http://www.foia.cia.gov/docs/DOC_0000278533/DOC_0000278533.pdf; and Interagency Intelligence Memorandum, *The Soviet Invasion of Afghanistan: Implications for Warning*, October 1980, accessed on October 11, 2011, at http://www.foia.cia.gov/docs/DOC_0000278538/DOC_0000278538.pdf.

34   Interagency Intelligence Memorandum, *Soviet Options in Afghanistan*, 8.

35   Cyrus Vance, *Hard Choices: Critical Years in America's Foreign Policy* (NY: Simon and Schuster, 1983), 384; Zbigniew Brzezinski, *Power and Principle: Memoirs of the National Security Adviser* (NY: Farrar Straus Giroux, 1983), 426–28; MacEachin, *Predicting the Soviet Invasion of Afghanistan*.

36   Willis C. Armstrong, William Leonhart, William J. McCaffrey, Herbert C. Rothenberg, "The Hazards of Single-Outcome Forecasting," in *Inside CIA's Private World: Declassified Articles from the Agency's Internal Journal, 1955-92*, ed. H. Bradford Westerfield (New Haven, CT: Yale University Press, 1995), 253–54.

37   MacEachin, *Predicting the Soviet Invasion of Afghanistan*.

38   MacEachin, *Predicting the Soviet Invasion of Afghanistan*; Interagency Intelligence Memorandum, "Soviet Invasion of Afghanistan," 34.

39   Vladislav M. Zubok, *A Failed Empire: The Soviet Union in the Cold War from Stalin to Gorbachev* (Chapel Hill: University of North Carolina Press, 2007), 259–64.

40   MacEachin, *Predicting the Soviet Invasion of Afghanistan*; Armstrong, *et al.*, "Hazards of Single-Outcome Forecasting," 254; Brzezinski, *Power and Principle*, 429.

41   Steve Coll, *Ghost Wars: The Secret History of the CIA, Afghanistan, and Bin Laden, From the Soviet Invasion to September 10, 2001* (NY: Penguin Books, 2004), 39–50. The National Security Archive has published a large collection of documents related to Soviet and American policy toward and operations in Afghanistan. See *The September 11th Sourcebooks*: Volume II: *Afghanistan, Lessons from the Last War*, ed. John Prados and Svetlana Savranskaya, accessed on October 9, 2012 at http://www.gwu.edu/~nsarchiv/NSAEBB/NSAEBB57/.

42   Coll, *Ghost Wars*, 62–151. The quotes are on pp. 93 and 125. George Crile, *Charlie Wilson's War: The Extraordinary Story of the Largest Covert Operation in History* (Boston, MA: Atlantic Monthly Press, 2003).

43   Coll, *Ghost Wars*, 107–124; 84–88.

44   Provided impetus by India's acquisition of a nuclear capability in 1974, Pakistan in 1998 became the seventh nation successfully to develop and test a nuclear weapon.

45   Coll, *Ghost Wars*, 147–265.

46   Ahmed Rashid, *Taliban: Militant Islam, Oil and Fundamentalism in Central Asia*, 2nd ed. (New Haven, CT: Yale University Press, 2010).

47   Richard A. Clarke, *Against All Enemies: Inside America's War on Terror* (NY: Free Press, 2004), 73–84.

48   Richard A. Clarke, *Against All Enemies*, 87–92; Coll, *Ghost Wars*, 138–44; 240–335; PDD-39, "U.S. Policy on Counterterrorism," June 21, 1995, accessed on October 16, 2012, at http://www.fas.org/irp/offdocs/pdd/pdd-39.pdf, Ronald Kessler, *The CIA at War: Inside the Secret Campaign Against Terror* (NY: St. Martin's, 2003), 21–28; Seymour Hersh, *Chain of Command: The Road from 9/11 to Abu Ghraib* (NY: HarperCollins, 2004), 80.

49   Tim Weiner, "Conservatives Attack C.I.A. Nominee," *New York Times*, February 3, 1997; Weiner, "Lake Pulls Out as Nominee for C.I.A., Assailing Hearing as Endless Political Circus," *New York Times*, March 19, 1997; James Risen, "Failures on Terrorism Are Seen Shaping Tenet's Legacy," *New York Times*, June 5, 2004; Richard D. White, "George Tenet and the Last Great Days of the CIA," *Public Administration Review* 68 (May/June 2008):420–7.

50   *The 9/11 Commission Report: The Final Report of the National Commission on Terrorist Attacks Upon the United States* (NY: Norton, 2004), 111–15.

51   Coll, *Ghost Wars*, 405–11; Terry H. Anderson, *Bush's Wars* (NY: Oxford University Press, 2011), 49–50; Bill Clinton, *My Life* (NY: Alfred A. Knopf, 2004), 797–805.

52   Eric Lichtblau, "C.I.A. Officer Denounces Agency and Sept. 11 Report," *New York Times*, August 18, 2004. Scheuer cryptically refers to this group in his damning critique of U.S. policy and strategy toward bin Laden and al-Qaeda. Anonymous, *Imperial Hubris: Why the West is Losing the War on Terrorism* (Washington, DC: Brassey's, 2004).

53   Bamford, *Pretext for War*, 188–221; Peter Bergen, *The Longest War: The Enduring Conflict Between America and al-Qaeda* (NY: Free Press, 2011), 40–42.

54   Coll, *Ghost Wars*, 417–503; David Johnston and Todd S. Purdum, "Missed Chances in a Long Hunt for bin Laden," *New York Times*, March 26, 2004; Clarke, *Against All Enemies*, 209–10; 222–26.

55   Elisabeth Bumiller, "Under Fire for Sept. 11, C.I.A. Chief Gains From His Bond with Bush," *New York Times*, December 18, 2002; James Mann, *Rise of the Vulcans: A History of Bush's War Cabinet* (NY: Viking, 2004), 234–60.

56   Clarke, *Against all Enemies*, 231–2; Robin Wright, "Top Focus Before 9/11 Wasn't on Terrorism." *Washington Post*, April 1, 2004; Bergen, *Longest War*, 42–43.

6

9/11, WMD, GWOT, IRTPA, and ODNI: 2001–2004

Throughout the initial eight months of the George W. Bush presidency, no one sought more ardently than did George Tenet to impress on the national security principals that al-Qaeda was the gravest contemporary threat confronting the United States and the non-Muslim (and portions of the Muslim) world. The director of central intelligence, who in 1998 had declared that the US Intelligence Community was "at war" with terrorism, began to brief administration officials on the severity of the danger posed by al-Qaeda during the transition. The first DCI in the agency's history regularly to present the president with his morning briefing, he briefed Bush personally about Osama bin Laden some 40 times. Through July 2001 the CIA reported that "Bin Laden Planning Multiple Operations," "Bin Laden Attacks May be Imminent," and "Planning for Bin Laden Attacks Continues, Despite Delays." CIA senior officials instructed overseas station chiefs to warn their host governments that al-Qaeda planned "High Profile Attacks."[1]

Tenet did not brief the president during August 2001, when Bush was vacationing at his ranch in Crawford, Texas. It was Michael Morell, who within a decade would head the CIA's Directorate of Analysis and then earn a promotion to deputy Director of the agency. One of the items in the President's Daily Brief (PDB) for August 6, 2001, entitled "Bin Laden Determined to Strike in US," stipulated that al-Qaeda's leader "has wanted to conduct terrorist attacks in the U.S." since 1997, that he planned his operations years in advance, that sleeper cells of al-Qaeda members residing in America provided support for the operations, and that uncorroborated sources claimed that bin Laden's plans included hijacking

The Hidden Hand: A Brief History of the CIA, First Edition. Richard Immerman.
© 2014 John Wiley & Sons, Ltd. Published 2014 by John Wiley & Sons, Ltd.

US aircraft. Barbara Sude, an analyst who specialized in assessing the al-Qaeda threat, subsequently explained that its purpose was to warn Bush that, in the CIA's judgment, he should expect an attack.[2] The most recent intelligence did not provide for a specific date, but it strongly suggested that increased vigilance and preparations were essential and time sensitive. In Tenet's soon-to-be famous phrase, the agency's alert system was "blinking red." Bush, however, later characterized the briefing as "historical." In light of the personal nature of a private presidential briefing, which allows for and indeed encourages the exchange of questions and virtually guarantees clarifications, it is difficult to imagine how the president could have misinterpreted the intent of the PDB. But Bush claims he did. What is indisputable, moreover, is that the administration treated the briefing as if it presented no new information. Not until September 4 did Rice convene a meeting of the principals to discuss a strategy paper drafted in June explicitly to combat terrorism.[3]

A week later, shortly before 9:00 a.m. Eastern Daylight Savings Time on September 11, 2001, a hijacked airliner slammed into the north tower of New York City's World Trade Center. Before the morning was over, a second airliner struck the other Twin Tower, a third crashed into the Pentagon, and a fourth, en route to the Capitol Building in Washington, DC, was brought down in rural Pennsylvania by courageous passengers on board. Claiming more victims (some 3000 deaths) than the Japanese attack on Pearl Harbor that was the catalyst for the establishment of the CIA, the 9/11 disaster may prove to be equally transformative for the agency and for the Intelligence Community. It may also prove to be equally transformative for the influence of intelligence on America's society and culture as well as its national security.

Rapidly identifying al-Qaeda as responsible for the calamity, the CIA conceded the obvious—its effort to monitor bin Laden and his terrorist network had not adequately detected preparations for the attack, and the agency knew nothing about the implementation strategy. Nevertheless, with notable exceptions such as Alabama's Richard Shelby, the ranking Republican on the Senate Select Committee on Intelligence, Americans, uniting in their common grief and anger, muted their criticism of the catastrophic intelligence failure. Taking their cue from the president, they sought revenge. "[W]e're going to smoke them out," Bush told reporters at the Pentagon. "I want justice," he said. "There's an old poster out West that said, 'Wanted, dead or alive'."[4]

Global War on Terror

Within a month CIA operatives had reentered al-Qaeda's safe haven in Afghanistan. As if to fulfill the president's promise, they rapidly began to make amends. Operation ENDURING FREEDOM was the plan of the CIA, not the Pentagon. Cofer Black, who headed the CIA's Counterterrorism Center, briefed it to the National Security Council only two days after the 9/11 attacks. In but a few weeks, he boasted, the terrorists responsible for the outrage would have "flies walking across their eyeballs." Tenet provided a more detailed briefing of the plan to Bush two days later at Camp David, and on September 17 President Bush instructed the CIA to execute it.[5]

Black's prediction at first seemed not far off receding and then to an unprecedented extent collaborating closely with Special Operations Forces from the US and British militaries, the agency's paramilitary operatives (the 7-member Northern Afghanistan Liaison Team, code-named Jawbreaker and led by Gary Schroen) quickly reestablished contacts with the Northern Alliance's anti-Taliban warlords. They provided them with intelligence and, according to Bob Woodward, some $70 million in money and supplies. They also coordinated with other operatives previously stationed in Uzbekistan to direct Predator drones (unmanned aircraft) on surveillance missions over Afghanistan. Once the United States launched Operation ENDURING FREEDOM on October 7, CIA agents in the field (ultimately a total of about 110) provided vital support by collecting real-time, "actionable" intelligence, identifying and then helping to guide American bombs to designated targets, and interrogating prisoners. CIA officer Johnny "Mike" Spann became Operation ENDURING FREEDOM'S first fatality when he was killed on November 25. By that day the allied Taliban and al-Qaeda forces had lost the battles for Mazar-e-Sharif and Kabul in the north, and with CIA assistance were being pummeled, presumably along with Osama bin Laden himself, in the Tora Bora cave complex near Afghanistan's eastern border.[6]

In early December the Taliban's southern stronghold of Kandahar fell, and its leader, Mullah Omar, fled to the Tora Bora mountains to join bin Laden in hiding. In March 2002, following Operation ANACONDA's defeat of the remnants of al-Qaeda and the Taliban, major combat operations ended. By then, American bombers had steadily clobbered Tora Bora. An estimated 700,000 pounds of ordinance landed on the mountains between December 4 and 7 alone. Victory eluded the Americans, nevertheless. Reluctant to violate Rumsfeld's insistence on maintaining a "light footprint," on the one hand General Tommy Franks refused to deploy the reinforcements that Henry Crumpton, who, as director of special operations for the CIA's Counterterrorism Center commanded the agency's "forces" in Afghanistan, desperately requested for the purpose of preventing an escape.[7] On the other hand, bin Laden, his chief lieutenant Ayman al-Zawahiri, Mullah Omar, and others were able to find shelter in the tunnels and bunkers built with CIA money in the 1980s by the Afghans who fought the Soviets. The al-Qaeda and Taliban survivors therefore managed to flee over the border to Pakistan, as a bitter Crumpton predicted they would. The Bush administration was unconcerned. Already it had redirected the crusade against terrorism to target Saddam Hussein's regime in Iraq. Presuming, without reliable intelligence from the CIA or any other agency, that Saddam Hussein had assisted bin Laden in executing the 9/11 attacks, the Bush administration began to develop war plans against Iraq in early November.[8]

Former DCI James Woolsey was a leading champion of the theory that tied Saddam Hussein to bin Laden. Rumsfeld described evidence of the link as "bulletproof." But the CIA's sources did not support the claim. In Tenet's words, "the intelligence did not show any Iraqi authority, direction, or control over any of the many specific terrorists acts carried out by al-Qa'ida." The Pentagon established a two-person Policy Counter Terrorism Evaluation Group (PCTEG) to comb through the files of the CIA and the Defense Intelligence Agency. Perceiving itself as the heir to those who had challenged the CIA's analyses of the Soviet Union during the Ford years, this self-styled "Team B" claimed that it had found evidence of "consultation, training, financing, and collaboration" between Saddam and al-Qaeda." Despite this supposed evidence and the "relentless" grilling by Rumsfeld, Wolfowitz, Wolfowitz's deputy Douglas Feith, and others, the agency held to its position. Because this iteration of the 1970s Team B reported to Feith, the CIA referred to the findings as "Feith-based analysis." After winding up its investigation of the PCTEG in 2008, the Senate Committee on Intelligence was equally critical.[9]

The CIA's intelligence likewise did not support the claim that Saddam Hussein possessed chemical and biological weapons and sought actively to develop nuclear weapons. The president alleged that Saddam not only possessed (and was determined to acquire more) weapons of mass destruction (WMD), but he was also prepared to supply them to bin Laden and other terrorists. This syllogism implicated the CIA in the president's justification for a preemptive attack on Iraq as an integral front in a Global War on Terror (GWOT). Tenet played along. The director of central intelligence did not share the view that Iraq was in league with al-Qaeda. But he did share the assessment of Bush, Cheney, Rumsfeld, Wolfowitz, Feith, and Secretary of State Colin Powell that Saddam was seeking to augment a cache of WMD he had concealed since expelling UN inspectors in 1998 with a nuclear capability. Further, Tenet appreciated that his providing the president with the service that he sought for the purpose of promoting "regime change" in Iraq would cement his relationship with Bush and bolster the institutional interests of the CIA.[10]

Bereft of human assets in Iraq, the CIA relied on U-2s, drones, and parallel technological means to gather intelligence on the danger posed by Saddam. It remained unable to uncover evidence of WMD, however, let alone penetrate Saddam's inner circle. This inability was of greater consequence to the administration's efforts to gain the support of allies and the American people for an attack on Iraq than to its own policy formulation. Reflecting the unshakeable belief of Bush and his chief advisors in Saddam's guilt and the multiple benefits that inhered in fulfilling the goal of regime change in Iraq that the United States had pursued since the 1990s, policy already was set. In his January 2002 State of the Union speech, the president devoted more attention to Iraq than to any of the other states that comprised the "axis of evil." Among his many allegations, he indicted its effort "to develop anthrax, and nerve gas, and nuclear weapons for over a decade." The challenge for the CIA and other components of the Intelligence Community was to confirm that this effort continued and, moreover, that Saddam Hussein had available for his use and that of al-Qaeda the products of this effort: weapons of mass destruction.[11]

Having observed Saddam's unconscionable behavior for decades, CIA analysts strongly suspected that Saddam had hidden in Iraq at least a small stockpile of WMD. The Intelligence Community collected no disconfirming evidence. But neither did it collect confirming evidence. Consequently, in its analytic products the agency hedged if not equivocated. Such reports frustrated the administration's hawks who "shared a well seasoned antipathy" toward the agency. Chief among these was Paul Wolfowitz. Wolfowitz had served on the original "Team B" during the competitive exercise to estimate Soviet capabilities in the 1970s. As Cheney's deputy in 1990, he had faulted the CIA for insufficiently recognizing Saddam's intention to invade Kuwait even earlier than it did. Then, Wolfowitz had been a member of the Commission to Assess the Ballistic Missile Threat, which Donald Rumsfeld had chaired in 1998. In what was tantamount to another Team B exercise, that commission concluded that the CIA had underestimated the severity of the threat of a long-range missile attack posed by the very rogue states that Bush had labeled the axis of evil. Its chair was Donald Rumsfeld. Wolfowitz and Rumsfeld interpreted the CIA's hedging over Iraqi WMD as symptomatic of an enduring pathology.[12]

The Pentagon chief and his top deputy took matters in their own hands. Wolfowitz set up a small Office of Special Plans, directed by his friend from undergraduate days at Cornell and Ph.D. studies with Leo Strauss and Albert Wohlstetter at the University of Chicago, Abram Shulsky. Wolfowitz's goal was for Shulsky's shop to produce intelligence assessments on Iraq independent of—and to many observers in competition with—the CIA. Rumsfeld established the even smaller Policy Counterterrorism Evaluation Center for fundamentally the same purpose. The secretary of defense also created the position of undersecretary of defense for intelligence in order, according to the *New York Times*, to wage a "turf war for dominance over the American IC." To fill the post Rumsfeld appointed Stephen Cambone, who had served on the Commission to Assess the Ballistic Missile Threat. The press described Cambone as Rumsfeld's "most trusted troubleshooter" and "favored bureaucratic commando."[13]

Despite all the controversy over the administration's allegations, Tenet did not instruct the National Intelligence Council to produce a new NIE on Iraq's weapons programs. But in early September 2002, members of Congress, not persuaded by the administration's case for going to war, demanded one. The result was that in less than three weeks the NIC cobbled together a 92-page National Intelligence Estimate on "Iraq's Continuing Programs for Weapons of Mass Destruction." The National Foreign Intelligence Board approved the NIE on October 1, and Congress officially received it on October 3. Based on extant "off the shelf" products because of time constraints and the absence of new intelligence, the authors violated cardinal principles of analytic tradecraft. They conflated "fact" with assumptions and failed to identify gaps in intelligence. In addition, kept too much in the dark by collectors, the authors of the estimate insufficiently expressed their confidence in the reliability of their sources or challenged the credibility of those like the notorious "Curveball," the Iraqi defector to Germany who concocted evidence that Saddam had hidden mobile bioweapons laboratories from inspectors.[14]

By not reexamining their previous judgments, dwelling on their failure to detect Saddam's secret WMD programs previously, and succumbing to the logic that if Saddam had pursued such programs before he must be doing so again, the analysts, moreover, exaggerated worst case scenarios and were thus easily duped by, in the words of a CIA postmortem, "Iraq's intransigence and deceptive practices." The National Intelligence Estimate's first key judgment read, "We judge that Iraq has continued its weapons of mass destruction (WMD) programs in defiance of UN resolutions and restrictions. Baghdad has chemical and biological weapons as well as missiles with ranges in excess of UN restrictions; if left unchecked, it probably will have a nuclear weapon during this decade." It was as inaccurate as it was categorical. Comparisons are difficult, but the *New York Times* was certainly within the bounds of reason when it described the NIE as "one of the most flawed documents in the history of American intelligence."[15]

Attesting to the adage that in the political world of Washington "there are only two possibilities: policy success and intelligence failure," critics and advocates of the war alike held the National Intelligence Estimate responsible for their postures. They claimed that it either misled them by exaggerating Saddam Hussein's threat or by failing to expose the threat's hollowness. To ascribe to the estimate this much influence is to seriously distort intelligence's role in the formulation of policy, regardless of who is president. As is typical of National Intelligence Estimates, only a few in Washington read it in its entirety, and reportedly Bush was not one of them. What is more, the soundness of one of the most telling judgments of the NIE turned out to be impossible to evaluate. It was that Saddam was unlikely to use a weapon against the United States, whether a WMD or any other, unless he was attacked.[16]

Further, what most critics did read was not the National Intelligence Estimate, which waffled over a multitude of crucial points and never assessed the threat as imminent. What they read was the NIE's "Key Judgments." The White House released the judgments under great pressure from the press and the public in July 2003, by which time the invasion of Iraq had taken place. Or, or perhaps in addition, they read the unclassified White Paper which Congress had insisted that the National Intelligence Council produce but which had not been coordinated among the IC elements that contributed to the National Intelligence Estimate. Making available the Key Judgments and White Paper exacerbated the NIE's shortcomings by omitting the caveats and acknowledgments of dissents (primarily by the State Department's Bureau of Intelligence and Research) included in the original. The poor quality of the NIE must not be minimized. Given the political and security environment, the lack of a capacity to collect HUMINT in Iraq, and the poor tradecraft practices that were common in 2002, there is no reason to presume that provided more time to prepare the National Intelligence Estimate the analysts would have reached or written down dramatically different judgments. But there is also no reason to presume that different judgments would have produced different policy. Responsibility for the decision to divert resources and attention from Afghanistan and invade Iraq rests with the administration, not the CIA.[17]

Although some administration officials sought to politicize the National Intelligence Estimate, charges that they succeeded are overdrawn.[18] The mistakes made by the analysts were their own. Nevertheless, as Bush marched inexorably toward war, CIA leaders muted their reservations, and Tenet fell in line with his president. At a meeting in the Oval Office in December 2002, the director of central intelligence, without expressing concerns with the quantity or quality of current intelligence, famously predicted that the "case" for invading Iraq was a "slam dunk." Bush did not need a green light from the CIA, but Tenet's was useful to him. Policymakers strongly prefer that intelligence supports their policies, and the public demands it.[19]

The CIA appeared to have satisfied both. Referring implicitly to the well-publicized but still-classified National Intelligence Estimate in his January 2003 State of the Union address, Bush asserted unequivocally that Saddam possessed chemical and biological weapons and the capability to deliver them. The president also cited unidentified "intelligence sources, secret communications, and statements by people now in custody [that] reveal that Saddam Hussein aids and protects terrorists, including members of al Qaeda. He could provide one of his hidden weapons to terrorists, or help them develop their own." Bush then homed in on what Americans for decades identified as the world's most severe danger: nuclear weapons. Saddam Hussein recently sought to acquire "significant quantities of uranium from Africa," he told the nation.[20]

CIA analysts in fact harbored reservations about reports that Saddam Hussein had attempted to obtain raw "yellow cake" uranium, specifically from Niger. Bush and his advisors knew about their concerns. The agency had questioned the credibility of the sources since it first learned of the allegation from Italy's military intelligence agency, the Servizio per le Informazioni e la Sicurezza Militare (SISMI), in February 2002. It advised Bush to delete a reference to the yellow cake when it appeared in a draft of a speech that he delivered that October in Cincinnati. At that time the president obliged, although he did warn that for the purpose of reconstituting his nuclear program, Saddam had held "numerous meetings" with his "nuclear mujahadeen," his "nuclear holy warriors." But close aides like Rumsfeld and Wolfowitz counseled that the CIA was again placing too much emphasis on the lacunae in its intelligence and refusing to draw obvious inferences from the intelligence that was available. They received support from Cheney and Rumsfeld. "Intelligence is an uncertain business, even in the best of circumstances," the vice president remarked. By now the aphorism "the absence of evidence is not evidence of absence" had become Rumsfeld's mantra. Bush allowed the charge to remain in the State of the Union, finessing the issue by citing British intelligence as his source. This ruse proved useful. When subsequent investigations into "Iraq's Weapons of Mass Destruction: The Assessment of the British Government," the so-called September Dossier, revealed that Britain's Prime Minister Tony Blair's Joint Intelligence Committee (JIC) relied on forged documents to reach its judgment, the administration claimed that neither it nor the CIA warranted blame.[21]

Secretary of State Colin Powell omitted any reference to the yellow cake uranium when, in a major address to the United Nations' Security Council on February 5, 2003, he indicted Iraq for possessing WMD. His department's intelligence agency, the Bureau of Intelligence and Research, which, in contrast to the CIA, had dissented from the 2002 National Intelligence Estimate's first key judgment, held the report to be "highly dubious." Powell, nevertheless, was not so cautious when it came to the allegation that the aluminum tube purchases made by Saddam Hussein's regime were intended for use in hidden Iraqi uranium centrifuges. The press later disclosed that a junior CIA analyst assigned to the Weapons Intelligence, Nonproliferation and Arms Control (WINPAC) office had virtually by himself advanced that theory. Almost a year before nuclear experts, particularly those in the Energy Department, had seriously challenged if not wholly discredited the WINPAC theory. Unlike the president, Powell acknowledged unspecified sources who considered conventional rocket launchers the tubes' likely destination. But he quickly added that all experts agreed that they "can" be used for nuclear centrifuges. As an "old army trooper," he continued, logic convinced him that if the tubes can be used to reconstitute Saddam's nuclear program, they will be used.[22]

Powell's speech in front of a rapt audience in the UN Security Council, which was broadcast live over television throughout the world, more systematically than Bush's State of the Union drew on the available intelligence to close the administration's case against Saddam Hussein. With Tenet seated at this shoulder, the widely respected secretary of state, who as chairman of the Joint Chiefs of Staff had orchestrated the Gulf War in 1991, gratefully acknowledged "people who have risked their lives to let the world know what Saddam Hussein is really up to." Proclaiming that "every statement I make today is backed up by sources, solid sources," which he highlighted with unprecedented frequency but of course refrained from revealing, Powell charged Saddam Hussein, on twenty-nine different occasions according to one count, with taking extraordinary measures to conceal his possession of a range of banned weapons and continuing efforts to develop and acquire others. In what became the most notorious example, the secretary cited four different sources, including a defector "currently hiding in another country with the certain knowledge that Saddam Hussein will kill him if he finds him [Curveball]," to condemn Iraq for maintaining mobile production facilities capable of producing "a quantity of biological poison equal to the entire amount that Iraq claimed to have produced in the years prior to the Gulf War." Not only did Powell project on a screen a diagram of the facilities mounted on both a truck and a railroad car, but he also stipulated that Iraq had at least seven of these mobile "factories," some with multiple trucks. No audience could fail to be impressed with the detail of the intelligence available in the United States — and nowhere else.[23]

In a much-publicized CNN interview in 2010, Powell expressed regret for playing such a pivotal role in "making the case [for war] before the international community." But that "was my job at the time," he explained, which the president expected him to do well. He added forcefully that although he had rigorously "vetted" the intelligence and received the "assurances" that he asked for, he had been misled by the CIA and its partners in the Intelligence Community. Powell is right to be "ticked" at Tenet and his colleagues, but he should shoulder more of the blame himself. From the day he came out of retirement from the military to take over the State Department, he had believed that Saddam had suffered such a decisive defeat in 1991 that even if he did possess weapons of mass destruction, and Powell doubted that he did, the tyrant did not pose a military threat. In addition, one need not have been the experienced intelligence consumer that he was, having served in the highest ranking military positions, to have identified the multiple problems with the sources.[24]

What is more, neither in this interview nor at any other time did Powell give the CIA credit for warning about the "negative consequences" that an invasion of Iraq could well produce, including the perception of the United States as conquerors, the outbreak of sectarian violence, and the recruitment of Islamist terrorists.[25] But he was correct about the expectations that came with his job and in his self-evaluation of his performance. Powell "wanted to sell a rotten fish," a former intelligence officer commented. "His job was to go to war with as much legitimacy as he could scrape up."[26] The secretary was so outstanding in carrying out that assignment that his allegations were invulnerable to criticism. The US press expressed virtually no reservations.

Even international inspectors such as Hans Blix and Mohamed ElBaradei, who opposed Washington's rush to judgment, could not challenge the assertions about Iraq's subterfuge because they lacked the evidence to do so. Indeed, Powell succeeded in portraying the intelligence as so solid, and the community's collection capabilities as so robust, that he all but set the CIA up to take the fall when the truth came out.[27]

That took months, and for some, years. In the interim, the CIA played a significant role in OPERATION IRAQI FREEDOM the preemptive attack on Iraq that the United States launched on March 19, 2003. But it won fewer plaudits than in Afghanistan. The day of the attack, the agency provided Bush with intelligence that Saddam Hussein and his two sons, Uday and Qusay, had taken shelter in an underground bunker at the Dora Farms compound south of Baghdad. At a lengthy meeting with his key advisors, DCI Tenet stressed that if the president did not reach a decision to strike quickly, he might miss his only "target of opportunity." Bush prided himself on being decisive; he ordered US stealth fighter planes that evening to demolish the bunker. Soon it became apparent that either the CIA had incorrect intelligence on the location of Saddam and his family, or it had misinterpreted the Arabic word "bunker" for "compound" and Saddam and his sons were in a building at the outskirts of Dora Farms. The fact of the matter is that he survived. The ensuing campaign of "shock and awe" included dozens of other air strikes that targeted senior Iraq leaders. Also based on CIA intelligence, these strikes caused the deaths only of civilians. The agency's troubles had just begun.[28]

It took less than two months for Baghdad to fall; Saddam, his sons, and his lieutenants fled into hiding. Standing aboard the U.S.S. *Lincoln* in front of a banner with the words "Mission Accomplished" blazoned on it, Bush proclaimed an end to military operations in Iraq on May 1, 2003. Ironically, the swiftness and what seemed the totality of the US military success was a fundamental cause of the grief that befell the CIA. The stockpiles of WMD, the factories and laboratories that produced them, and data documenting illicit programs and activities that had eluded detection by international inspectors but that US intelligence sources had putatively uncovered over the previous months sources should have surfaced immediately. But none of the above did. In April American and Kurdish troops did locate two trailers near Mosul, Iraq. This discovery prompted the CIA to make public the next month a White Paper describing the trailers as "the strongest evidence to date that Iraq was hiding a biological warfare program." Referring to the "striking similarities" between the trailers and the diagrams Powell had projected during his February UN speech, the White Paper asserted that "BW [biological warfare] agent production is the only consistent, logical purpose for these vehicles." The CIA was "confident that this trailer is a mobile BW production plant because of the source's description, equipment, and design."[29]

That confidence was misplaced. Led by the State Department's Bureau of Intelligence and Research, other analysts in the Intelligence Community vigorously disputed the CIA's claim. They pointed out that the trailer's configuration was ill-suited to produce biological weapons, and that the trailers were devoid of any traces of biological agents. More likely uses, according to the CIA's challengers, were the manufacture of hydrogen for weather balloons, the production of rocket fuel, or the refueling of extant Iraqi missiles. President Bush backtracked. He stated that even if the trailers were not used to produce WMD, their existence demonstrated that Saddam Hussein was *capable* of producing these kinds of weapons. But the dubious connection between the trailers and the capacity to wage biological warfare paled in comparison to the failure to locate evidence of any nuclear program. Not only was Saddam's nuclear threat the foundational justification of the US invasion, but also the intelligence the CIA purportedly collected to assess the threat was the foundation for its and the Bush administration's claims that the agency's capabilities distinguished it from all the world's other intelligence services.[30]

Even as the CIA's credibility became increasingly suspect, the growing frequency and intensity of indigenous attacks on American troops in now-occupied Iraq resurrected memories of the Vietnam quagmire. As early as August 2002, in a report ominously entitled "The Perfect Storm: Planning for Negative Consequences of Invading Iraq," the agency had explicitly raised the danger of the invasion turning into a boon for al-Qaeda by destabilizing the region and providing safe havens from which to operate. Six months later, prior to the start of OPERATION IRAQI FREEDOM, the CIA contributed to two like-minded reports, "Principal Challenges in Post-Saddam Iraq" and "Regional Consequences of Regime Change in Iraq." They were even more explicit in predicting that a US invasion would generate profound factions within Iraq that likely would collide violently. This collision "probably would result in a surge of political Islam and increased funding for terrorist groups" in the Muslim world. These reports, however, were not disclosed to the public until September 2004. By this time the agency had been branded by the flawed 2002 National Intelligence Estimate. For the growing legion of CIA critics, the mounting toll of casualties spawned by post-invasion Iraq's spiral of violence not only brought to mind Vietnam but it also rekindled memories of the litany of previous intelligence failures, real or purported, ranging, from Korea to the Bay of Pigs to 9/11.[31]

The intensification of the War Iraq, moreover, affected perceptions of the more general Global War on Terror. In particular, it led to revelations of and an investigation by the agency's Office of the Inspector General in May 2004 on the CIA's use of extraordinary renditions (kidnapping suspected terrorists and spiriting them off to countries known for sanctioning torture) and enhanced interrogation techniques, which agency interrogators employed themselves on suspected al-Qaeda members or sympathizers. Most notably, these techniques included waterboarding, which involved tying the prisoner down at a slight incline, covering his nose and mouth with a cloth, and pouring water over his face to simulate drowning. The press and human rights groups publicized waterboarding as the CIA's preferred means of torture. But, waterboarding was only one of a long list of interrogation methods that were sanctioned by a team of psychologists under contract to the agency. The psychologists borrowed from a regimen developed during the Korean War to train American prisoners of war to endure the brutal treatment associated with the Communist Chinese (known as Survival, Evasion, Resistance and Escape, or SERE). The prescribed techniques included berating and threatening the prisoners; depriving them of sleep, food, and clothing; confining them to small boxes and compelling them to stand in uncomfortable positions for hours on end; and subjecting them continually to loud music, white noise, and bright lights.[32]

Whether these techniques constitute "torture" remains fiercely debated. The agency's internal Inspector General's report described them as "unauthorized, improvised, [and] inhumane," and the Detainee Treatment Act passed by Congress in 2005 banned the "cruel, inhuman, and degrading treatment" of any prisoner held by the United States. A commission headed by two former congressmen representing both parties convened by the independent, bipartisan Constitutional Project concluded in 2013 that it is "indisputable that the United States engaged in the practice of torture." Regardless of the ultimate judgment and any hair splitting, the CIA seemed to many Americans to have regressed to and even surpassed its criminal-like behavior during the pre-Church Committee hearings era. Some advocated the prosecution of agency officers who participated in the interrogations notwithstanding the Bush administration's repeated sanctioning of their behavior. As a prophylactic, the head of the Directorate of Operations (renamed the National Clandestine Service in 2005) ordered the destruction of dozens of videotapes that could identify culpable agency officers.[33]

His presidency under fire, in mid-June 2003 Bush appointed David Kay, who had led three arms inspections of Iraq for the UN in the 1990s and had repeatedly expressed his conviction that Saddam Hussein was guilty as America had charged, as a special advisor to Tenet. The president predicted that Kay and a team of experts, the Iraq Survey Group, would justify the war by discovering Saddam's hidden cache of weapons of mass destruction. It took Kay six months to render his verdict: "Iraq did not have any large stockpiles of chemical or biological weapons by the time the conflict began." The CIA had relied on both out-of-date and unreliable intelligence. Resigning his position in January 2004, Kay recommended an investigation to find out why. "Iraq was an overwhelming systemic failure of the Central Intelligence Agency," was his personal judgment.[34]

Irresistible Impulse for Reform

The CIA's reputation concurrently came under assault for additional reasons. It was tarred with the Defense Intelligence Agency's brush when, in the lead-up to the invasion of Iraq, an analyst for the Pentagon's agency, Ana B. Montes, was arrested for spying for Cuba. Shortly thereafter, in April 1993, Los Angeles businesswoman Katrina Leung, a paid informant for the FBI on Communist Chinese espionage in the United States, was arrested for funneling classified information to the People's Republic of China. Among the documents Leong copied were ones she obtained from James J. Smith, her handler with whom she had an affair. James Risen and Eric Lichtblau highlighted in a *New York Times* article that the CIA considered Leong such a valuable asset that it awarded Smith a medal for intelligence collection.[35]

But perhaps it was the revelations in 2004 that the CIA seemed to have downplayed credible evidence that North Korea was closer to developing a nuclear capability than was Iraq during the years prior to the US attack on Saddam Hussein that generated the most criticism. A link with Pakistan exacerbated the agency's problem. The pardoning of Abdul Qadeer Khan, the founder of Pakistan's nuclear program and the primary peddler of nuclear technology to Pyongyang, by long-time president Pervez Musharraf provided strong if indirect evidence that Kim Jong-il's government received assistance from a pivotal American ally in the Global War on Terror. These juxtapositions suggested to critics that the CIA, Tenet especially, had allowed the administration to politicize the intelligence process by not only "cherry picking" but, worse, also "cooking the books" for the purpose of justifying regime change in Iraq. The appointment of Iyad Allawi as Iraq's first post-Saddam prime minister added more fuel to critics' fire. Allawi had been a favorite of the CIA since his founding of the Iraqi National Accord in 1991.[36]

The fire had already been stoked by a controversy that erupted over Bush's "16 word" reference in his 2003 State of the Union to Saddam Hussein's effort to purchase uranium from Niger. It had been because of the CIA's suspicions that Bush had cited as his source "Iraq's Weapons of Mass Destruction: The Assessment of the British Government." British Prime Minister Tony Blair was the president's most supportive ally in the Iraq undertaking; his Joint Intelligence Committee had produced the September dossier in 2002. The controversy exploded on July 6, 2003, when Joseph C. Wilson, a former ambassador to Gabon and the senior director for African affairs on President Bill Clinton's National Security Council, published an opinion piece in the *New York Times*. Entitling his essay "What I Didn't Find in Africa," Wilson recounted how after a CIA-mandated investigative trip to Niger in February 2002, he had reported to the administration that intelligence concerning the alleged attempted purchase was "probably forged." Consequently, Wilson wrote in the *Times*, in light of President Bush's State of the Union address and decision to invade Iraq a year after his report, "I have little choice but to conclude that some of the intelligence related to Iraq's nuclear weapons program was twisted to exaggerate the Iraqi threat."[37]

The White House placed the blame for the error on the CIA, and Tenet fell on his sword. Within a week the DCI issued a statement explaining that the CIA had mistakenly cleared the inclusion of the reference to uranium in the speech; he, not President Bush, was responsible for the gaffe. Three days later, nevertheless, the syndicated columnist Robert Novak publicly disclosed that Wilson's wife, Valerie Plame, worked for the CIA's Directorate of Operations and specialized in counterproliferation. The public search for the source for Novak's information on Plame appeared to lead back to the White House (it turned out to be then Deputy Secretary of State Richard Armitage), providing additional support for Wilson's claim that the administration sought to discredit him. Indeed, Novak's disclosure of the identity of a CIA agent, which violated the Intelligence Identities Protection Act, was widely interpreted by the public and the press as part of a campaign to intimidate the administration's critics.[38]

Within this context the Senate Select Committee on Intelligence began to investigate, in the words of its vice chairman, the West Virginian Democrat John D. Rockefeller IV, "the accuracy of our pre-war intelligence and the use of that intelligence by the Executive." A year later the SSCI issued its report. Covering more than 400 pages, its 117 different judgments added up to a devastating critique of virtually every analytic product related to Iraq to which the CIA contributed (it glossed over those that forecast post-invasion scenarios). The committee, chaired by Kansas Republican Pat Roberts, characterized the CIA's collection of intelligence, HUMINT in particular, as bad. It characterized what the CIA did with the intelligence it did collect as worse. In the unanimous, bipartisan opinion of the SSCI, not only did the CIA insufficiently distinguish between credible intelligence, fabrication, and hearsay, not only did it repeatedly use conjecture and unsubstantiated judgments as the foundation on which to layer additional unsubstantiated conclusions and inferences which none of its analysts dared to challenge (manifesting "groupthink"), not only did it ignore contradictory evidence, but it also withheld discordant or even disconfirming intelligence from other analysts and policymakers.[39]

The Senate Select Committee on Intelligence assessed the inclusion in the 2003 State of the Union of the possible sale of Niger yellow cake uranium to Iraq as one of the CIA's less egregious offenses. A more serious transgression noted in the report was the agency's withholding testimony from the families of Iraqi scientists about the cessation of Saddam's programs to produce WMD in the years following the withdrawal of the UN inspectors. Perhaps the least excusable, and most unconscionable, was the CIA's summary dismissal, without any evidentiary basis, of the judgment of both UN and American experts that the aluminum tubes discovered in Iraq were used for conventional rockets permitted by the UN Security Council. The CIA claimed the tubes were intended to act as centrifuges in order to enrich the uranium essential for nuclear weapons.[40]

On multiple occasions, moreover, the CIA relied on a single source for information. The most prominent example was the defector "Curveball." The CIA received explicit warnings, particularly from the Defense Intelligence Agency, that Curveball, whose real name was Rafid Ahmed Alwan al-Janabi, was unreliable and probably fabricated his testimony. Yet he was the sole source for the CIA's claim that Saddam was using mobile laboratories to produce biological weapons—a centerpiece of Secretary Powell's address to the UN. This violation in analytic tradecraft was as incomprehensible as it was indefensible. Ahmad Chalabi, the leader of the exile organization the Iraqi National Congress, had introduced Curveball to the CIA. While the Pentagon championed Chalabi to head the post-Saddam Iraqi government, the CIA assessed him as a self-promoting and untrustworthy opportunist.[41]

"The Intelligence Mess" was the title of the *Washington Post*'s 2004 editorial about the SSCI report. It described the performance of the CIA as "shockingly incompetent."[42] That September, Charles Duelfer, David Kay's successor as head of the Iraq Survey Group, made this evaluation official—and unanimous. Duelfer's more than 900-page *Comprehensive Report of the Special Advisor to the DCI on Iraq's WMD* concluded that Saddam Hussein had not restarted his nuclear program after its destruction in 1991, nor had he attempted to. The last Iraqi factory that produced illicit weapons had been shut down in 1996. With regard to Iraq's weapons of mass destruction, Duelfer told a Senate panel, "We were almost all wrong."[43]

Rather than acknowledge that "almost all" of the participants in the decision to invade Iraq were not just culpable but also wrong, the Senate Select Committee on Intelligence's report pointed its finger at the CIA and the Intelligence Community, all but exonerating George Bush and the policy-making community. Tenet became the fall guy; shortly before the report's publication, he "resigned" and was replaced as acting director of central intelligence by John McLaughlin. McLaughlin, a veteran of more than three decades of service to the CIA, was Tenet's chief deputy and among the agency's most respected analysts.[44] Despite Tenet's willingness to take one for the team (he exacted his revenge three years later when he published his memoir) and the highly regarded McLaughlin's elevation to acting DCI, the CIA remained under assault from multiple fronts. Within days of the 9/11 attack, a bipartisan coalition of legislators had called on President Bush to establish an independent commission to investigate the tragedy. Hoping to avoid unpredictable judgments that could damage the administration, the White House resisted. In response, the intelligence committees of both chambers launched a joint investigation. This decision did not satisfy the families of the 9/11 victims, who insisted on total accountability. The White House surrendered. In November, Bush signed legislation creating the National Commission on Terrorist Attacks Upon the United States (the 9/11 Commission).[45]

With New Jersey's former governor, the Republican Thomas Kean, as chair, and as vice chair Lee Hamilton, a Democrat who until retiring in 1999 had represented Indiana in the House of Representatives for over three decades, the 9/11 Commission completed its organization in December 2002, just as the House-Senate Joint Inquiry issued its separate report on the terrorist attacks. Extending to more than 800 pages including appendices, that Inquiry's criticism of the Intelligence Community was withering. It centered on the dysfunctional relationship among the individual elements of the IC. They resisted sharing the intelligence that each gathered, preferring instead to funnel their reports directly up its respective chain of command (stovepipe became a ubiquitous metaphor for this behavior). This hoarding of information inhibited both warning and deterrence. The most egregious offenders were the FBI and, worst of all, the CIA. Two years earlier, the CIA had identified two of the hijackers, the Saudis Khalid al-Midhar and Nawaq Alhazmi, as al-Qaeda sympathizers who had fought in Afghanistan and consorted with jihadists suspected of participating in the attack on the U.S.S. *Cole*. But the CIA did not pass this intelligence onto the FBI or US immigration officials. This failure allowed the two to enter the United States and travel freely. The report quoted an FBI agent's testimony that the CIA's sharing its intelligence on al-Midhar and Nawaq with the FBI would have made a "huge difference" in the prospects of uncovering the 9/11 plot in time to prevent its execution.[46]

The 9/11 Commission set to work at the same time that the House-Senate Joint Inquiry into the attacks ended. Kean and Hamilton chose Philip Zelikow as the Commission's executive director. The director of the University of Virginia's prestigious Miller Center with doctorates in both law and international affairs, Zelikow had coauthored a book with Condoleeza Rice on German reunification based on their experiences together as National Security Council staffers under George H.W. Bush. He had more recently served on George W. Bush's transition team and Foreign Intelligence Advisory Board, and he had had headed the latter Bush's Markle Task Force on National Security in the Information Age. Notwithstanding Zelikow's credentials, some critics argue that Zelikow's appointment compromised the integrity of the commission by affording him the opportunity to mold its findings in a way that exonerated the administration.[47]

While one should not expect to find a smoking gun in these circumstances, the evidence does not support this criticism. With Kean and Hamilton at the helm, the commission proceeded in a way that was less partisan than the Church Committee hearings and more rigorous than the investigation into Iran-Contra. Overcoming White House opposition "at nearly every turn," Zelikow and his staff pried loose documents that the administration sought to withhold, and it heard testimony not only from Tenet, Rumsfeld, Clarke, and others whom it could subpoena but also from those it could not: Rice, Cheney, and Bush (the president insisted that he and the vice president testify together and not under oath). All told, the staff and the members of the commission examined more than 2.5 million pages of documents and interviewed over 1200 individuals from ten countries.[48]

Further, the conclusions of the 9/11 Commission stood "on the shoulders," to use Zelikow's words, of the previous House-Senate Joint Inquiry, on which Zelikow did not serve. They also dovetailed with an internal investigation conducted by the CIA's inspector general. By summer 2004, when the commission published its report, those conclusions had become the conventional wisdom in and out of Washington. The standard fare included the charge that the attacks "should not have come as a surprise" because for months, by some indices years, the alert was "blinking red" (the title of the report's eighth chapter). The intelligence was available, but the Intelligence Community, most notably the CIA, lacked the imagination necessary to connect the dots. No one "looked at the big picture; no analytic work foresaw the lightning that could connect the thundercloud to the ground," testified "John," a CIA office supervisor. In addition, too few questioned their previous assumptions or thought in terms of scenarios that were unlikely yet potentially extremely consequential. As if these individual errors were not sufficient to explain the catastrophic intelligence failure, they were compounded by structural defects that were most acute within the CIA. The agency was plagued by a "dispersal of effort on too many priorities," a "declining attention to the craft of strategic analysis," and "security rules that prevented adequate sharing of information." And of course there was information hoarding and stovepiping.[49]

What politicized the 9/11 Commission report was not the influence of Zelikow in his capacity as executive director, or even for that matter the priorities of the White House. What politicized it was timing and context. Because the commission's report and that of the Senate investigation of the US intelligence on Iraq's weapons of mass destruction came out within a month of each other in summer 2004, the two intelligence failures were linked together by politicians, pundits, and the public. With the Iraq War and its mounting casualties already framing the fast-approaching presidential election, the combination of America's political culture and its shared grief made it all but unavoidable that the twin reports would become fodder for questions and allegations about culpability on the one hand, and the use and abuse of intelligence on the other. Americans needed someone, or something, to blame. The Intelligence Community provided a shield for both Congress and the White House. That intelligence analysis is an art and not a science was dismissed as irrelevant.[50]

As if to signal that he would not tolerate a CIA that, according to both reports, had badly betrayed him as well as the United States, Bush, not unlike Kennedy after the Bay of Pigs, moved to clean house even before the 9/11 Commission published its report. Notwithstanding John McLaughlin's reputation, he, too, had to go. He has been Tenet's second in command and, before that, the agency's deputy director of intelligence. Thus, McLaughlin had headed the directorate held most responsible for the recent intelligence failures. In August 2003 the president nominated Porter Goss as the next DCI. A veteran of the CIA himself, Goss had served in the Directorate of Operations before retiring and winning election to Congress from Florida. He had been a member of the Aspin-Brown Commission and chaired the House Permanent Subcommittee on Intelligence. His credentials thus seemed impeccable. Yet, during an election season when allegations of the politicization of intelligence filled the media, Bush all but laid down a marker by daring the Senate to challenge his nomination of a staunch Republican and avowed ally to fill this apolitical position.[51]

If Bush hoped for an early political showdown over intelligence that might provide him with a campaign issue, he was disappointed. With all Republicans and most Democrats voting in favor, the Senate confirmed Goss as what turned out to be America's last director of central intelligence by an overwhelming margin of 77–17. Neither party wanted to face off over intelligence. Or put another way, there was a bipartisan interest in portraying the CIA as the "government's equivalent of Enron" and therefore culpable for the WMD in Iraq fiasco as well as the 9/11 tragedy. Republicans feared the vulnerability of the president. Democrats feared their own vulnerability: In 2002 a majority of the Democratic senators and the party's leadership of both houses had voted in favor of the joint resolution authorizing the use of American military force in Iraq. They preferred that voters perceive them as having been duped by the intelligence rather than having not rigorously examined it.[52]

This objective, coupled with genuine concern, drove the same Democrats to concentrate on devising legislation that would incorporate the list of reforms proposed by the 9/11 commission. Republicans were more ambivalent about pushing for them. Some wanted to tread lightly lest the CIA launch a counteroffensive and try more directly and aggressively to implicate the administration. Others wanted to abolish the agency altogether. The majority, however, appreciated that abolishing the CIA was a nonstarter, and failing to follow the lead of the 9/11 Commission could prove awkward. Published immediately, the report became an instant bestseller. The White House nevertheless did resist the impulse to legislate reform. Bush issued a series of executive orders in the hope that doing so would satisfy the drumbeat for reform without the fanfare sure to accompany hammering out and then agreeing on specific legislation. But again the families, especially the widows of 9/11 casualties, intervened. They vigorously advocated the most dramatic and institutionalized reforms of the Intelligence Community on the premise that more rigorous analysis and more cooperation among the IC elements may have saved the lives of their loved ones. Bush's resistance became untenable.[53]

The staffs of both the House and Senate intelligence committees faced a monumental task. The 9/11 Commission's list of proposed reforms was lengthy, complicated, and, in many cases, highly charged because of bureaucratic politics and the clash of organizational interests. Chief among the recommendations was the establishment of a cabinet-level National Intelligence Director (NID) to command all lines in the intelligence budget (which would be made public) and to which would report the director of the CIA as well as comparable heads of the other intelligence agencies. This would include those elements of the Intelligence Community that previously reported to the secretaries of defense and state: for example, the Defense Intelligence Agency, the National Security Agency, and the Bureau of Intelligence and Research, or those domestic ones, like the FBI, which reported to the Attorney General. Indeed, this Office of the National Intelligence Director, housed in the Executive Office of the President, would oversee all sixteen elements of the Intelligence Community and its personnel. It would also replace the DCI as the president's principal advisor on intelligence.[54]

Enhancing the power of an executive to manage the intelligence community was not a new idea. It has been proposed multiple times previously, dating to the 1950s. The reason is readily understandable. To quote a report written for William Colby, "The DCI is in effect a feudal lord over four baronies." In January 1989 Pennsylvania's Republican Senator Arlen Specter had introduced legislation to create a new position he called the "Director of National Intelligence," the same title that James Schlesinger had used when he had called for the creation of a similar position in his report to Richard Nixon. The Senate Select Committee on Intelligence held a hearing on the idea; Specter garnered little support except from William Odom and Bobby Ray Inman, both former directors of the National Security Agency. Still, the concept resurfaced soon thereafter during the Aspin-Brown Commission in the mid-1990s, and an inquiry shortly after 9/11 led by the former two-time national security advisor and the current chair of the President's Foreign Intelligence Advisory Board, Lt. General Brent Scowcroft. Sandwiched between these two studies, a 1998 commission chaired by the former vice chairman of the Joint Chiefs of Staff, Admiral David Jeremiah (USN, ret.), to investigate the Intelligence Community's failure to detect India's nuclear test that year likewise recommended vesting more authority over the IC in a single official in order to improve community management. Jeremiah, as did other reformers, recommended the director of central intelligence as that official. He would receive more statutory control over the other agencies, most notably those who answered to the secretary of defense. But the concern that combining the roles and responsibilities of DCI and DCIA created an inherent conflict of interest was longstanding. What had been lacking previously was the incentive and political will to wage a turf war. The 9/11 tragedy provided both.[55]

The 9/11 Commission advanced a number of other proposals for reform, most of which likewise had antecedents. The creation of a National Counterterrorism Center, for example, would address the "stovepipe problem" by unifying the agencies responsible for strategic intelligence and operational planning related to terrorism, institutionalizing the sharing of intelligence among them, and as a consequence of both and without violating any laws, piercing the boundary between foreign and domestic intelligence. This innovation, while dramatic, was less revolutionary than would have been the case had there not been recent precedents. The recognized value of integrated centers with complementary missions drove the establishment of the Department of Homeland Security in 2002 and the joint CIA-FBI "Terrorist Threat Integration Center" the next year. The CIA had not been enthusiastic about these initiatives because of their potential to erode the agency's clout. Its personnel also had reservations about the training and thus capabilities of the agency's partners. Yet for political reasons, the leadership muted its opposition.

This was not the case with the 9/11 Commission's recommendation that the CIA relinquish control over covert, particularly paramilitary, operations to the military. Reviving an issue that had seemingly been laid to rest when Frank Wisner and Allen Dulles trumped Walter Bedell Smith during the agency's infancy, the Commission recommended that the CIA concentrate its efforts on improving its analytic and intelligence gathering capabilities. The latter would include placing more emphasis on HUMINT collection and developing greater proficiency in such critical languages as Arabic, Persian, Pashto, and Urdu. The CIA would remain involved in covert action by its efforts to recruit indigenous agents and otherwise collecting intelligence on the ground. Yet building on the foundation laid in the aftermath of the failed Operation EAGLE CLAW to rescue the Iranian Hostages in 1980 and activation of the US Special Operations Command (SOCOM) seven years later, the agency would cede authority over the design and implementation of paramilitary activities to military units. Over the past half-century the CIA had forged its identity by conducting paramilitary operations. Regardless of the consequences and its record, it was prepared to fight to keep them in its portfolio.[56]

By the end of 2004, with the White House remaining passively on the sidelines and a nail-bitingly close election turning progressively more bitter, the opportunistic alliance of Republicans and Democrats managed to hold together sufficiently to draft and pass major amendments to the intelligence section of the 1947 National Security Act in both houses of Congress. After intense negotiations, the members and their staffs of SSCI and HPSCI reached a resolution. Coauthoring the resultant legislation with Connecticut Democrat Joseph Lieberman, Republican Susan Collins from Maine introduced in the Senate the Intelligence Reform and Terrorism Prevention Act (IRTPA). Picking and choosing among the many recommendations of the 9/11 Commission report as well as drawing on other sources, the provisions of the intelligence reform legislation were both high altitude and down-in-the-weeds. The act proposed to stand up not only a National Counterterrorism Center but also a National Counterproliferation Center. Further, it mandated the establishment of additional "National Centers" as needed "to address intelligence priorities," such as Iran or North Korea. These would be directed by designated mission managers who would assure the assignment to them of personnel from the appropriate agencies and access to all the necessary intelligence regardless of the source. [57]

Other critical elements of the Intelligence Reform Act, on the macro-level, included provisions to promote information sharing and safeguard against politicization. On the micro-level, the legislation addressed the widespread perception that a basic cause of the 9/11 tragedy was that CIA analysts failed "to connect the dots," and the more legitimate perception that the misleading National Intelligence Estimate on Iraq's weapons of mass destruction program resulted from shoddy methods of analysis. As a remedy, the reform act went so far as to identify precisely the attributes that must be present in all finished intelligence. Each product, it stipulated, must be "timely, objective, independent of political considerations, based upon all sources of available intelligence, and employ the standards of proper analytic tradecraft." The product must also show evidence that its authors had subjected their judgments to "alternate analysis." Known within the CIA as "red teaming," this latter stipulation required that analysts take into consideration different ways to interpret the same data. To achieve the goal of enhancing the "analytic integrity" of the intelligence products, moreover, the legislation made training and assessment programs mandatory. Congress insisted that each year it would receive a report on performance and progress.[58]

These and the other reforms applied not only to the CIA but also to every Intelligence Community element. Accordingly, as its centerpiece the Intelligence Reform Act did establish a national intelligence director, which it renamed the director of national intelligence (DNI), the title Specter had used in his proposed 1989 initiative. The Office of the Director of National Intelligence (ODNI) would not have the authority to collect intelligence. Nor, with the exception of National Intelligence Estimates and the President's Daily Brief, both of which were, in principle if not in practice, community products, would it produce finished intelligence. Rather, theoretically halving the DCI's role, the director of national intelligence would manage the sixteen elements that comprised the Intelligence Community so that each adhered to the spirit as well as the letter of the new law. The DNI, in short, would be responsible for fostering greater collaboration, integration, information sharing, and the dissemination of products throughout the community. The premise of the legislation was that by overseeing the operations of the entire US intelligence enterprise, the director of national intelligence would have the power to improve the elements' capabilities, individually and collectively. By excluding from the reform the measures recommendation to improve oversight, Congress effectively protected itself from being held responsible for the DNI's success or failure.[59]

CIA leaders were almost universally relieved that the authors of the legislation shied away from tackling the controversial and complicated question of where to locate paramilitary operations. Further, the agency fully accepted the criticism it had received from the various commissions and committees, and for that matter, in the press. As it had regularly since the Bay of Pigs fiasco, the CIA conducted its own examination of its failings, particularly those related to its allegation's about Iraq's WMD program. With commendable candor it reached conclusions about its poor performance that not only complemented but in some respects also went beyond those of the external investigations.

The CIA's internal assessment, "Misreading Intentions," incisively explained why it was so far off in its judgments about Saddam Hussein. What it determined was that, especially after the 1995 defection of Saddam's son-in-law, Husayn Kamil, the regime in Baghdad had panicked. Because it feared that Kamil, who had been integrally involved in the WMD program, would divulge the regime's deepest and darkest secrets, Saddam changed his mind and decided that, rather than obfuscate and stonewall, it would be in his interest to be more forthcoming. But for him to "come clean" to the international community at the metaphorical eleventh hour would require that he admit concealing information in the past. Moreover, because he feared both Israel and Iran more than he did the United States, he did not want either of those states to know that he had in fact demolished his chemical and biological weapons capacity and ceased all efforts to obtain a nuclear one lest he forfeit any possibility of their still serving as a deterrent.[60]

In the end, the CIA was deceived as much as were the Iranians and Israelis. Saddam, fearing the intrusive inspectors and seeking a face-saving way to "extricate" himself from his previous web of deceit, was so clumsy in his efforts to appear more transparent that his signals were all but unintelligible. In addition, his penchant for secrecy had driven him to destroy all records of his having eliminated his WMD capabilities. He thus could not verify his subsequent claims to having actually done so. The CIA, aware that he had hidden weapons from them the decade before and sensitive to Saddam's overall history of "cheat and retreat," assumed he was repeating that history.

The result was a litany of what the authors of the assessment labeled "analyst liabilities." CIA analysts, read the agency's report on itself, "did not spend adequate time examining the premise that the Iraqis had undergone a change in their behavior, and that what Iraq was saying by the end of 1995 was for the most part, accurate." They compounded this error by concentrating their energy and attention on detecting signs of a hidden cache of weapons of mass destruction and all but ignoring what they should have identified as Saddam's core concerns. Chief among these were protecting his other technological assets, his security, and his reputation. Analysts failed to appreciate sufficiently that Saddam thought differently than they did. As a consequence of this worst kind of analytic tradecraft, the CIA's mea culpa concluded, rather than "closing the books" on allegations that Saddam Hussein retained and sought to expand his WMD arsenal, the behavior of this "paranoid dictator" *after* he decided to disclose the information that inspectors requested "reinvigorated the hunt."[61]

As attested to by this Intelligence Assessment, the CIA embraced the need for reform in order to do better. But in its view, creating and ODNI would exacerbate the problem, not promote a solution. Rather than enhance collaboration, efficiency, and rigor, they argued, the new office, which they likened to another agency, would add another layer to an already overly bureaucratic and overly compartmentalized community. The CIA leadership, past and present, maintained that this alleged remedy would actually aggravate the Intelligence Community's pathologies because the director of national intelligence would lack authority over operatives in the field or analysts at their desks who were actually doing the business of intelligence. Further, the CIA was not simply one of sixteen elements to be managed equally by the ODNI. As the only civilian-based intelligence agency independent of any other government department or agency, it had been established to achieve precisely the objectives of the intelligence reform legislation. In lieu of entrusting this mission to the director of national intelligence, then, it would be better to at long last provide the director of central intelligence with the requisite authority to fulfill it.

Somewhat perversely, the CIA received support for its objections from the Department of Defense. The National Security Agency, the National Imagery and Mapping Agency (now the National Geospatial-Intelligence Agency), and the National Reconnaissance Office, which "own" the hardware necessary to intercept communications (SIGINT), take aerial photographs (IMINT), measure physical materials and identify "signatures" (Measurement and Signature Intelligence, MASINT), and similar intelligence "disciplines" that consume such a high percentage of the national intelligence budget, are combat-support agencies housed in the Pentagon. Historically, the secretary of defense successfully kept these operations at arm's length from the director of central intelligence. Although the intelligence reform legislation mandated that the budget for the military intelligence program remain separate, the director of national intelligence's responsibility for community management threatened the Pentagon's autonomy. Further, Donald Rumsfeld argued vigorously that the Office of the Director of National Intelligence could imperil US defense capabilities by interrupting the chain of command. Rumsfeld remained silent on his own efforts to disrupt that chain.[62]

Owing to the authority and bipartisanship of the 9/11 Commission and each chambers' intelligence committees, and the widespread conviction both in and out of Washington that the US intelligence system was in need of fixing, passage of the intelligence reform legislation was never in doubt. Adding momentum, and some would argue urgency, to its enactment was the growing unpopularity of DCI Goss. Exacerbated by his selection of veteran GOP staffers as his chief aides and his purge of veteran agency officials, Goss's behavior generated the perception that he was too partisan to direct the apolitical CIA. So, too, did his rhetoric. The intent of Goss's instruction to the CIA to support policymakers was unmistakable.[63]

The question in 2004, then, was not whether there would be an Office of the Director of National Intelligence, but how powerful that office would be. The strongest allies of the CIA and the Pentagon in Congress did manage to limit the DNI's authority over the intelligence budget, personnel, and covert operations. They also ensured that whoever occupied the position would not "abrogate the statutory responsibilities" of the Defense Department. This "compromise" severely undermined the purported intent of establishing the post. "[W]hat's really important is directing, controlling and having access to the people who do the work," commented one senior CIA official. "They created a person who doesn't have that." Still, once the Intelligence Reform and Terrorism Prevention Act reached the Senate floor, it had gathered such momentum that approval was foreordained. The vote in favor was 89–2 (West Virginia's Democrat Robert Byrd and Republican James Inhofe of Oklahoma voted against). Describing IRTPA as "the most dramatic reform of our nation's intelligence capabilities since President Harry S. Truman signed the National Security Act of 1947," President Bush signed it into law on December 17, 2004. There were no cheers heard at Langley.[64]

Notes

1   Richard A. Clarke, *Against All Enemies: Inside America's War on Terror* (NY: Free Press, 2004), 230–38; Thomas Powers, "How Bush Got It Wrong," *New York Review of Books* 51, September 23, 2004, accessed on October 16, 2012, at http://www.nybooks.com/articles/17413; Mark Mazzetti, *The Way of the Knife: The CIA, a Secret Army, and a War at the Ends of the Earth* (NY: Penguin, 2013), 13–14; Terry H. Anderson, *Bush's Wars* (NY: Oxford University Press, 2011), 63–65; Peter Bergen, *The Longest War: The Enduring Conflict Between America and al-Qaeda* (NY: Free Press, 2011), 47; David Johnston and Jim Dwyer, "Pre-9/11 Files Show Warnings Were More Dire and Persistent," *New York Times*, April 18, 2004.

2   Bergen, *Longest War*, 48; Terry McDermott, *The Hunt for KSM: Inside the Pursuit and Takedown of the Real 9/11 Mastermind, Khalid Sheikh Mohammed* (NY: Little Brown and Co., 2012), 152.

3   *The 9/11 Commission Report: The Final Report of the National Commission on Terrorist Attacks Upon the United States* (NY: Norton, 2004), 277; Douglas Jehl, "Terror Memo Disregarded, Report Says," *New York Times*, April 15, 2004; Johnston and Dwyer, "Pre-9/11 Files Show Warnings Were More Dire and Persistent;" "Text of the President's Daily Brief for Aug. 6, 2001," *New York Times*, April 12, 2004; Kurt Eichenwald, "The Deafness before the Storm," *New York Times*, September 11, 2012.

4   James Risen and David Johnston, "Officials Say They Saw No Signs of Increased Terrorist Activity" *New York Times*, September 12, 2001; Lizette Alvarez, "Spying on Terrorists and Thwarting Them Gains New Urgency," *New York Times*,

September 14, 2001; Brian Knowlton, "'We're Going to Smoke Them Out': President Airs His Anger," *New York Times*, September 19, 2001.

5   Bergen, *Longest War*, 53–67.

6   Bob Woodward, *Bush at War* (NY: Simon & Schuster, 2002), 50–62, 317. See also John A. Bonin, *U.S. Army Forces Central Command in Afghanistan and the Arabia Gulf During Operation Enduring Freedom: 11 September 2001-March 2003* (Carlisle, PA: The Army Heritage Center Foundation, 2003).

7   The question remains open whether with more troops the US could have sealed off Pakistan's border; Franks ensured we will never know.

8   Bob Woodward, *Plan of Attack* (NY: Simon & Schuster, 2004), 4–6, 12; Clarke, *Against All Enemies*, 32–34; Anderson, *Bush's Wars*, 84–87; Bergen, *Longest War*, 68–85; Henry A. Crumpton, *The Art of Intelligence: Lessons from a Life in the CIA's Clandestine Service* (NY: Penguin, 2012), 257–61.

9   George Tenet, *At the Center of the Storm: My Years in the CIA* (NY: Harper-Collins, 2007), 341–58; Bergen, *Longest War*, 138–40. That the administration exaggerated the link between Saddam Hussein and al-Qaeda was a key finding of the Senate Committee on Intelligence's much delayed "phase two" investigation of the prewar intelligence on Iraq. Senate Select Committee on Intelligence, "Report on Intelligence Activities Related to Iraq Conducted by the Policy Counterterrorism Evaluation Group and the Office of Special Plans within the Office of the Under Secretary of Defense for Policy," 110th Cong., 2nd Sess., June 2008, accessed on December 21, 2012, at http://intelligence .senate.gov/080605/phase2b.pdf.

10 John B. Judis and Spencer Ackerman, "The Selling of the Iraq War, The First Casualty," *New York Review of Books* 50, June 30, 2003, accessed on October 17, 2012, at http://www.tnr.com/article/the-first-casualty;Thomas Powers, "The Vanishing Case for War," *New York Review of Books* 50, December 4, 2003, accessed on October 17, 2012, at http://www.nybooks.com/articles/archives /2003/dec/04/the-vanishing-case-for-war/?pagination=false; Powers, "The Failure," *New York Review of Books* 51 (April 29, 2004), accessed on October 17, 2012, at http://www.nybooks.com/articles/archives/2004/apr/29/the-failure /?pagination=false.

11 Woodward, *Plan of Attack*, 107–09; Ivo H. Daalder and James M. Lindsay, *America Unbound: The Bush Revolution in Foreign Policy* (Washington, DC: Brookings Institution, 2003), 131; Text of President George W. Bush's State of the Union Address, January 29, 2002, accessed on October 17, 2012, at http:// www.washingtonpost.com/wp-srv/onpolitics/transcripts/sou012902.htm.

12 James Risen, *State of War: The Secret History of the CIA and the Bush Administration* (NY: Free Press, 2006), 71–73; Ron Suskind, *The One Percent Doctrine: Deep inside America's Pursuit of Its Enemies since 9/11* (NY: Simon & Schuster, 2006), 22–24; Jack Davis, "Paul Wolfowitz on Intelligence-Policy Relations: the Challenge of Managing Uncertainty," *Studies in Intelligence* 39

(1996), accessed on July 21, 2013, at https://www.cia.gov/library/center-for -the-study-of-intelligence/csi-publications/csi-studies/studies/96unclass/davis .htm.

13   Robert Dreyfuss, "The Pentagon Muzzles the CIA: Devising Bad Intelligence to Promote Bad Policy," *American Prospect*, December 16, 2002, accessed on October 17, 2012, at http://www.highbeam.com/doc/1G1-95445377.html; Seymour Hersh, "Selective Intelligence," *New Yorker*, May 12, 2003, accessed on October 17, 2012, at http://www.newyorker.com/archive/2003/05/12 /030512fa_fact; James Risen and Thom Shanker, "Rumsfeld Moves to Strengthen his Grip on Military Intelligence," *New York Times*, August 3, 2002; Douglas Jehl, "An Overseer of Intelligence Efforts at the Defense Department," *New York Times*, May 12, 2004; Thom Shanker, "For Military Intelligence, A New Favorite Commando," *New York Times*, April 11, 2003.

14   Thomas Fingar, *Reducing Uncertainty: Intelligence Analysis and National Secu-rity* (Stanford, CA: Stanford University Press, 2011), 89–108; Robert Jervis, *Why Intelligence Fails: Lessons from the Iranian Revolution and the Iraq War* (Ithaca, NY: Cornell University Press, 2010), 123–55; Bob Drogan: *Curveball: Spies, Lies, and the Con Man Who Caused a War* (NY: Random House, 2007).

15   Intelligence Assessment, "Misreading Intentions: Iraq's Reaction to Inspec-tions Created Picture of Deception," 5 January 2006, accessed on September 8, 2012, at http://www.gwu.edu/~nsarchiv/news/20120905/CIA-Iraq.pdf; Key Judgments from NIE on "Iraq's Continuing Programs for Weapons of Mass Destruction," 2012, accessed on October 18, 2012, at http://www.fas.org/irp/cia /product/iraq-wmd.html; David Barstow, William J. Broad, and Jeff Gerth, "How the White House Embraced Disputed Arms Intelligence," *New York Times*, October 3, 2004.

16   Thomas Fingar, "Office of the Director of National Intelligence: Promising Start Despite Ambiguity, Ambivalence, and Animosity," in *The National Security Enterprise: Navigating the Labyrinth*, ed. Roger Z. George and Harvey Rishikof (Washington, DC: Georgetown University Press, 2011), 140–41; Richard H. Immerman, "Intelligence and Strategy: Historicizing Psychology, Politics, and Policy," *Diplomatic History* 32 (January 2008): 1–23; Paul Pillar, *Intelligence and U.S. Foreign Policy: Iraq, 9/11, and Misguided Reform* (NY: Columbia Uni-versity Press, 2011), 13–42.

17   National Intelligence Estimate [sanitized], "Iraq's Continuing Programs for Weapons of Mass Destruction," 30 October 2002, accessed on August 23, 2012, at http://www.fas.org/irp/cia/product/iraq-wmd-nie.pdf; Key Judgments from NIE on 'Iraq's Continuing Programs for Weapons of Mass Destruction;" "Iraq's Weapons of Mass Destruction Programs [White Paper]," October 2002, accessed on August 23, 2012, at https://www.cia.gov/library/reports/general -reports-1/iraq_wmd/Iraq_Oct_2002.pdf; Immerman, "Intelligence and Strategy," 22–23.

18   Tyler Drumheller, *On the Brink: An Insider's Account of How the White House Compromised American Intelligence* (NY: Carroll & Graf, 2006), 43–44; Michael Isikoff and David Corn, *Hubris: The Inside Story of Spin, Scandal, and the Selling of the Iraq War* (New York: Crown, 2006) 3–5; Joshua Rovner, *Fixing the Facts: National Security and the Politics of Intelligence* (Ithaca, NY: Cornell University Press), 137–84.

19   James Bamford, *A Pretext for War: 9/11, Iraq, and the Abuse of American's Intelligence Agencies* (NY: Doubleday, 2004), 333–34; Woodward, *Plan of Attack*, 247–50; Robert Jervis, "Why Intelligence and Policymakers Clash," *Political Science Quarterly* 125 (Summer 2010): 185–204.

20   President George W. Bush State of the Union Address, January 28, 2004, accessed on October 18, 2012, at http://georgewbush-whitehouse.archives.gov /news/releases/2003/01/20030128-19.html.

21   Anderson, *Bush's War*, 97–98; Frank Rich, "What the White House Knew and When It Knew It: Time Lines of the Selling of the War," accessed on October 19, 2012, at http://frankrich.com/timeline.htm; James Risen and David E. Sanger, "New Details Emerge on Uranium Claim and Bush's Speech," *New York Times*, July 18, 2003; Bill Keller, "The Boys Who Cried Wolfowitz," *New York Times*, June 14, 2003; Remarks by the President on Iraq, Cincinnati Museum Center - Cincinnati Union Terminal Cincinnati, Ohio, October 7, 2002, accessed on October 18, 2012, at http://georgewbush-whitehouse.archives .gov/news/releases/2002/10/20021007-8.html; Remarks by the Vice President to the Veterans of Foreign Wars Convention, August 26, 2002, accessed on October 18, 2012, at http://georgewbush-whitehouse.archives.gov/news /releases/2002/08/20020826.html; Bergen, *Longest War*, 56.

22   Dana Milbank and Dana Priest, "Warning in Iraq Report Unread Bush, Rice Did Not See State's Objection," *Washington Post*, July 19, 2003; Douglas Jehl, "Tiny Agency's Iraq Analysis Is Better Than Big Rivals'," *New York Times*, July 19, 2004; David Barstow, William J. Broad, and Jeff Gerth, "How the White House Embraced Disputed Arms Intelligence," *New York Times*, October 3, 2004; Michael Massing, "Now They Tell Us," *New York Review of Books* 51, February 26, 2004, accessed on October 19, 2012, at http://www.nybooks.com /articles/archives/2004/feb/26/now-they-tell-us/?pagination=false; Remarks to the United Nations Security Council by Secretary Colin L. Powell, February 5, 2003, accessed on October 18, 2012, at http://www.washingtonpost.com/wp -srv/nation/transcripts/powelltext_020503.html.

23   Powell, Remarks to the UN Security Council; Powers, "The Vanishing Case for War."

24   CNN Official Interview: Powell Now Regrets UN Speech, November 15, 2010, accessed on October 19, 2010, at http://www.youtube.com/watch?v=d93 _u1HHgM4; Walter LaFeber, "The Rise and Fall of Colin Powell and the Powell Doctrine," *Political Science Quarterly* 124 (Spring 2009): 85.

25 Walter Pincus, "Before War, CIA Warned of Negative Outcomes," *Washington Post*, June 3, 2007; Pincus, "Assessments Made in January 2003 Foretold Situation in Iraq," *Washington Post* May 20, 2007.

26 Quoted in LaFeber, "The Rise and Fall of Colin Powell," 89.

27 Massing, "Now They Tell Us;" Hans Blix, *Disarming Iraq* (NY: Pantheon, 2004), esp. pp. 152–66.

28 Jonathan S. Landay, Warren P. Strobel, and John Walcott, "Faulty Signs on the Road to War," *Philadelphia Inquirer*, March 20, 2004; Douglas Jehl and Eric Schmitt, "Errors Are Seen in Early Attacks on Iraqi Leaders," *New York Times*, June 13, 2004.

29 CIA Report, "Iraqi Mobile Biological Warfare Agent Production Plants," May 28, 2003, accessed on October 19, 2012, at https://www.cia.gov/library/reports /general-reports-1/iraqi_mobile_plants/index.html.

30 "The Bioweapons Enigma," *New York Times*, June 1, 2003; Douglas Jehl, "Agency Disputes C.I.A. View of Trailers as Iraqi Weapons Labs," *New York Times*, June 26, 2003; David E. Sanger, "Bush Aides Deny Effort to Slant Data on Iraq Weapons," *New York Times*, June 9, 2003.

31 Douglas Jehl and David E. Sanger, "Prewar Assessment on Iraq Saw Chance of Strong Divisions," *New York Times*, September 28, 2004; Douglas Jehl, "U.S. Intelligence Shows Pessimism on Iraq's Future," *New York Times*, September 16, 2004; Michael R. Gordon, "Poor Intelligence Misled Troops About Risk of Drawn-Out War," *New York Times*, October 20, 2004; Walter Pinctus, "Before War, CIA Warned of Negative Outcomes," *Washington Post*, June 3, 2007; Walter Pincus and Karen DeYoung, "Analysts' Warnings of Iraq Chaos Detailed," *Washington Post*, May 26, 2007.

32 U.S. Senate, Committee on Armed Services, 110th Cong., 2nd sess., "Inquiry into the Treatment of Detainees in U.S. Custody," November 20th, 2008, accessed on December 31, 2012, at http://www.armed-services.senate.gov /Publications/Detainee%20Report%20Final_April%2022%202009.pdf; Jane Mayer, *The Dark Side: The Inside Story of How the War on Terror Turned into a War on American Ideals* (NY: Doubleday, 2009), 139–81; Mark Danner, "US Torture: Voices from the Black Sites," *New York Review of Books* 56 (April 9, 2009), accessed on November 1, 2012, at http://www.markdanner .com/articles/show/151; Scott Shane and Mark Mazzetti, "Interrogation Memos Detail Harsh Tactics by the C.I.A.," *New York Times*, April 17, 2009; Dafna Linzer and Julie Tate, "New Light Shed on CIA's 'Black Site' Prisons," *Washington Post*, February 28, 2007; Joby Warrick, Peter Finn and Julie Tate, "Red Cross Described 'Torture' at CIA Jails," *Washington Post*, March 16, 2009; Joby Warrick and Peter Finn, "Psychologists Helped Guide Interrogations," *Washington Post*, April 18, 2009; David Ignatius, "Kicking the CIA (Again)," *Washington Post*, July 15, 2009; Karen DeYoung, "Bush Approves New CIA Methods," *Washington Post*, July 21, 2007.

33 Office of the CIA Inspector General, "Counterterrorism Detention and Inter-
    rogation Activities (September 2001–October 2003), accessed on December
    31, 2012, at http://graphics8.nytimes.com/packages/pdf/politics/20090825
    -DETAIN/2004CIAIG.pdf; Mazzetti, *Way of the Knife*, 126; Report of the
    Constitution Project's Task Force on Detainee Treatment," April 16, 2013,
    accessed on May 6, 2013, at http://detaineetaskforce.org/.
34 James Risen, "U.S. Asks Ex-U.N. Inspector to Advise on Arms Search," *New
    York Times*, June 12, 2003; Richard Stevenson and Thom Shanker, "Ex-Arms
    Monitor Urges an Inquiry on Iraqi Threat," *New York Times*, January 29, 2004;
    Philip Shenon, "Former Iraq Arms Inspector Faults Prewar Intelligence," *New
    York Times*, August 19, 2004.
35 Tim Golden, "White House Wary of Cuba's Little Spy Engine that Could," *New
    York Times*, January 5, 2003; James Risen and Eric Lichtblau, "Intelligence on
    China was Forwarded to Presidents," *New York Times*, April 29, 2003.
36 David E. Sanger, "U.S. Widens View of Pakistan Link to Korean Arms," *New
    York Times*, March 14, 2004; Peter W. Galbraith, "Iraq: The Bungled Transi-
    tion," *New York Review of Books* 51, September 23, 2004, accessed on October
    19, 2012, at http://www.nybooks.com/articles/archives/2004/sep/23/iraq-the
    -bungled-transition/?pagination=false.
37 "Iraq's Weapons of Mass Destruction: The Assessment of the British Govern-
    ment," September 2002, accessed on October 19, 2012, at http://www.gwu
    .edu/~nsarchiv/NSAEBB/NSAEBB254/doc05.pdf; Joseph C. Wilson, 4th,
    "What I Didn't Find in Africa," *New York Times*, July 6, 2003.
38 Walter Pincus and Dana Milbank, "Bush, Rice, Blame CIA for Iraq Error,"
    Washington Post, July 12, 2003; Text of a statement by George J. Tenet, *New York
    Times*, July 12, 2004; Robert Novak, "Mission to Niger," July 14, 2003, accessed
    on October 19, 2012, at http://www.washingtonpost.com/wp-dyn/content
    /article/2005/10/20/AR2005102000874.html; Todd S. Purdum and David E.
    Sanger, "Accusation of Leak and a Bush Memo Come at a Bad Time," *New
    York Times*, October 1, 2003. See also Joseph Wilson, *The Politics of Truth:
    Inside the Lies that Led to War and Betrayed My Wife's Identity: A Diplomat's
    Memoir* (NY: Carroll & Graf, 2004); and Valerie Plame Wilson, *Fair Game:
    How a Top CIA Agent was Betrayed by Her Own Government* (NY: Simon &
    Schuster, 2007), 102–99.
39 *Congressional Record*, July 17, 2003 (Senate), Page S9580-S9581, accessed on
    October 12, 2012, at http://www.fas.org/irp/congress/2003_cr/s071703.html;
    U.S. Senate, Select Committee on Intelligence, 108th Congress, *Report
    on the U.S. Intelligence Community's Prewar Intelligence Assessments on
    Iraq*, Ordered Reported on July 7, 2004, accessed on October 21, 2012, at
    http://web.mit.edu/simsong/www/iraqreport2-textunder.pdf.
40 *Report on the U.S. Intelligence Community's Prewar Intelligence Assessments*.
41 Douglas Jehl, "Agency Belittles Information Given by Iraq Defectors," *New
    York Times*, September 29, 2003.

42   "The Intelligence Mess," *Washington Post*, July 11, 2004.

43   *Comprehensive Report of the Special Advisor to the DCI on Iraq's WMD*, September 30, 2004, accessed on October 22, 2012, at https://www.cia.gov /library/reports/general-reports-1/iraq_wmd_2004/index.html; Dana Priest and Walter Pincus, "US 'Almost All Wrong' on Weapons," *Washington Post*, October 7, 2004.

44   Glenn Kessler, "For Personal Reasons, or Is He the Fall *Guy?*" *Washington Post*, June 4, 2004; Joel Brinkley, "A Quiet Man Takes Charge: John Edward McLaughlin," *New York Times*, June 4, 2004.

45   David Firestone, "2 Senators Say White House Is Thwarting 9/11 Inquiry," *New York Times*, October 12, 2002; Craig R. Whitney, "Introduction," in *The 9/11 Investigations*, ed. Steven Strasser (NY: PublicAffairs, 2004), xxi – xxiii.

46   Excerpts from the House-Senate Joint Inquiry Report on 9/11, *The 9/11 Investigations*, 406. The complete report is available at http://www.gpo.gov/fdsys/pkg /CRPT-107hrpt792/pdf/CRPT-107hrpt792.pdf, accessed on October 23, 2012.

47   Philip Shenon, *The Commission: the Uncensored History of the 9/11 Commission* (NY: Twelve, 2008).

48   Elizabeth Drew, "Pinning the Blame," *New York Review of Books* 51, September 23, 2004, accessed on October 22, 2012, at http://www.nybooks.com /articles/archives/2004/sep/23/pinning-the-blame/?pagination=false; The 9/11 Commission Staff Statements and Testimony along with Whitney, "Introduction," in *The 9/11 Investigations*, ix — 292.

49   Philip Zekilow, "The Evolution of Intelligence Reform, 2002-2004," *Studies in Intelligence* 56 (September 2012): 8; Office of the Inspector General (OIG) Report of CIA Accountability with Respect to the 9/11 Attacks, June 2005, accessed on December 24, 2012, at https://www.cia.gov/library/reports /Executive%20Summary_OIG%20Report.pdf; *The 9/11 Commission Report*, 277, 91, 407 – 19; "The 9/11 Commission Report: Executive Summary," p. 2, accessed on October 22, 2012, at http://govinfo.library.unt.edu/911/report /911Report_Exec.pdf.

50   Richard K. Betts, "Two Faces of Intelligence Failure: September 11 and Iraq's Missing WMD," *Political Science Quarterly* 122 (Winter 2007 – 2008): 585 – 606.

51   Elizabeth Bumiller, "Act of Healing and Politics in Bush C.I.A. Chief Nomination," *New York Times*, August 11, 2003.

52   Douglas Jehl, "Senate Confirms Goss as Intelligence Chief," *New York Times*, September 23, 2004; Risen, *State of War*, 4.

53   Philip Shenon, "A G.O.P. Senator Proposes a Plan to Split Up C.I.A.," *New York Times*, August 23, 2004; "9/11 Families Plead for Intelligence Form," *CNN Politics*, August 17, 2004, accessed on August 23, 2012, at http://articles .cnn.com/2004-08-17/politics/911.families_1_intelligence-reform-terror -attacks-mary-fetchet?_s=PM:ALLPOLITICS.

54   *The 9/11 Commission Report*, 407–14.
55   Douglas F. Garthoff, *Directors of Central Intelligence as Leaders of the U.S. Intelligence Community, 1946–2005* (Washington, DC: Potomac Books, 2007), 101–8; 176, 272–74; Walter Pincus, "Intelligence Shake-up Would Boost CIA," *Washington Post*, November 8, 2001; James Risen and David Johnston, "Lawmakers Want Cabinet Post for Intelligence Director," *New York Times*, December 8, 2002; John Diamond, *The CIA and the Culture of Failure: U.S. Intelligence from the End of the Cold War to the Invasion of Iraq* (Stanford, CA: Stanford University Press, 2008), 260–71; Richard H. Immerman, "The Politics of Intelligence Reform," in *The Politics of Major Policy Reform in the U.S.: From World War II to the Present*, ed. Jeffrey A. Jenkins and Sydney A. Milkis (NY: Cambridge University Press, forthcoming).
56   *The 9/11 Commission Report*, 400–06, 415–6. The components of the U.S. Special Operations Command include the U.S. Army Special Operations Command, the Air Force Special Operations Command, the Naval Special Warfare Command, and the Joint Special Operations Command.
57   Public Law 108-458, Sections 1021, 1022, 1023, *The Intelligence Reform and Terrorism Prevention Act*, December 17, 2004, accessed on October 25, 2012, at http://www.gpo.gov/fdsys/pkg/PLAW-108publ458/pdf/PLAW-108publ458 .pdf.
58   Public Law 108-458, Sections 1017, 1019, 1020, 1041, and 1042.
59   Public Law 108-458, Section 1011; Amy Zegart, *Eyes on Spies: Congress and the United States Intelligence Community* (Stanford, CA: Hoover Institution Press, 2011).
60   Intelligence Assessment, "Misreading Intentions."
61   Intelligence Assessment, "Misreading Intentions."
62   Dana Priest and Walter Pincus, "Director's Control is a Concern," *Washington Post*, December 8, 2004; Seymour Hersh, *Chain of Command: The Road from 9/11 to Abu Ghraib* (NY: HarperCollins, 2004), 46–47.
63   Jervis, "Why Intelligence and Policymakers Clash," 187; "Politics and the CIA," *New York Times*, November 18, 2004; Douglas Jehl, "2 Top Officials are Reported to Quit the CIA," *New York Times*, November 25, 2004.
64   Priest and Pincus, "Director's Control is a Concern;" Philip Shenon, "House Overwhelmingly Approves Broad Overhaul of Intelligence," *New York Times*, December 8, 2004; President Signs Intelligence Reform and Terrorism Prevent Act, December 17, 2004, accessed September 26, 2011 at http://georgewbush -whitehouse.archives.gov/news/releases/2004/12/20041217-1.html.

7

Crisis of Identity: 2005 – 2013

The irresistible impetus for intelligence reform in 2004 collided with the conflicting interests and contrasting agendas of the principal players in drafting and approving the legislation. The outcome was a long document (some 600 pages) that was remarkably short on details. The Intelligence Reform and Terrorism Prevention Act (IRTPA) left for the future deliberations and decisions about the structure of the Office of the Director of National Intelligence, its relationship to the other elements, and even its location. As one expert observer notes, the "result is a job [the DNI] whose responsibilities and expectations exceed its authorities."[1]

Virtually all commentators on the legislation at the time agreed that the prospects for improved coordination and integration were bleak. Changing the culture of a large organization is difficult under the best of circumstances, and these circumstances were anything but the best. Because the reform was imposed by the Senate, with the White House complicit albeit not enthusiastic, the ODNI was destined to encounter severe resistance. Without budgetary control let alone command authority, it lacked the leverage to overcome it. What the legislation accomplished, wrote John Brennan, at the time an experienced CIA manager who now directs the agency, was to "send more players onto the field and to pump steroids into those already wearing cleats," thereby "adding to the tussles over who is responsible for covering which part of the intelligence terrain" even as it produced "unrealistic expectations."[2]

It will take decades to reach a verdict as to whether such pessimism is warranted, and even then the record is likely to be so mixed that judgments will be ambiguous and inconclusive. These are certainly appropriate

The Hidden Hand: A Brief History of the CIA, First Edition. Richard Immerman.
© 2014 John Wiley & Sons, Ltd. Published 2014 by John Wiley & Sons, Ltd.

adjectives for any current evaluation. The evidence suggests that progress has been made toward some of the intelligence reform legislation's foremost goals. Owing in a large part to the ODNI's managerial role, cooperation and information sharing among the Intelligence Community's elements, while far from perfect, has improved; each element is paying greater attention to tradecraft rigor; and collectors and analysts have collaborated to make the nature and reliability of sources much more transparent. Progress has even been made in promoting greater proficiency, or recruiting analysts already fluent, in such critically important languages as Arabic, Farsi, and Urdu.

Because of the reforms mandated by the legislation and promoted by the most experienced intelligence officials, safeguards are in place to mitigate the possibility of, if not ensure against, finished intelligence displaying the flaws of the destructive National Intelligence Estimate on Iraq's Weapons of Mass Destruction program. To cite a notable example, the 2007 NIE on Iran's nuclear program, which stated with "high confidence" that Tehran had halted its efforts to build a bomb in 2003, generated a firestorm of controversy. Critics, especially those conservatives who despaired of negotiations with the Islamic Republic, claimed that the NIE was politicized — not by the administration but by George W. Bush's opponents within the Intelligence Community. Yet the estimate's tradecraft was outstanding and dissent was encouraged. The NIE explained the reasoning behind its judgments, it provided insight as to the reliability of its sources, it made explicit the gaps in its intelligence, and otherwise followed every recommendation of the 9/11 Commission — and more. That National Intelligence Estimate, and others produced since the intelligence reforms went into effect, have been uniformly superior to their antecedents. They may not always have been "right." But they have reduced uncertainty for policymakers — the most that anyone can and should expect from an intelligence estimate.[3]

For this achievement the director of national intelligence warrants credit. National Intelligence Estimates are ODNI products. Still, the position and the office continue to struggle; some would say flounder. Because with the exception of NIEs and the President's Daily Brief the ODNI does not produce finished intelligence, and it never collects anything other than an open source, the office serves as a managerial superstructure within which sit the sixteen Intelligence Community elements. But it is not inherently more powerful than any of the elements it is charged with managing. Some would say, in fact, that it is weaker. All but one of the Intelligence Community's elements answers to a Cabinet officer, not the director of national intelligence, and most of them answer to the secretary of defense. That secretary still controls a larger budget (the Military Intelligence Budget) than the DNI (the National Intelligence Budget). Making the situation that much more untenable, the only element that does report directly to the DNI is the CIA. Yet, despite the reform legislation's logic, IRTPA did not explicitly stipulate that the ODNI's authorities supersede those of the CIA. Because the agency has not conceded that it does, disputes over authorities must await case-by-case adjudication and clarification. Meanwhile, the CIA continues to enjoy direct access to the president and his principal advisors on the National Security Council, and the DNI plays at most a peripheral role in both the approval and implementation of covert operations. These dynamics raise serious questions among the policymaking, legislative, public, and even intelligence communities as to what ODNI does and what it is.[4]

Discontinuous and ineffective leadership has exacerbated these problems. President Bush nominated John Negroponte as the initial director of national intelligence after his first choice, former DCI and future secretary of defense Robert Gates, turned down the offer. A former ambassador to some of the globe's hotspots (Honduras under Reagan, for example, and Iraq under George H. W. Bush) and George W. Bush's first U.S. representative to the United Nations, Negroponte had earned an enviable reputation. But his experience with intelligence was limited, and he never warmed to the DNI position. Confirmed overwhelmingly by the Senate in April 2005, he resigned in January 2007 to return to the Department of State to manage policy toward Iraq.[5]

To succeed Negroponte, Bush nominated John "Mike" McConnell, a Navy vice admiral who had led the National Security Agency in the 1990s. He took office in February 2007. Deeply inculcated with the Intelligence Community's culture and having held a senior position at Booz Allen Hamilton, the oldest of the federal contracting firms located in the CIA's backyard, McConnell was tentative in asserting the DNI's authority over the other agencies' chiefs. He would have liked to retain the position after the Bush presidency expired, but Barack Obama replaced him with another admiral, Dennis Blair, in January 2009. By this time the ODNI had finally moved out of its temporary home at Bolling Air Force Base to a new headquarters in Northern Virginia down the road from Langley, signaling its maturity. Blair was more assertive than McConnell. The result was friction with both the CIA and the White House. In May 2010 Obama asked for his resignation. He then selected as his second director of national intelligence in two years James Clapper. Clapper was among America's most experienced intelligence officials. A retired Lt. General in the Air Force, he had led the Defense Intelligence Agency and the National Geospatial-Intelligence Agency, and until the appointment as DNI, he had served as undersecretary of defense for intelligence (USD-I).[6]

An understaffed office with an ill-defined mission, circumscribed budgetary authority, and led by four different directors in its brief existence, none of whom have had tenures longer than three years (the tenure of DNI James Clapper at the time of this book's writing), has predictably been stunted in its development. When most Americans, even within the Beltway, refer to America's "central" intelligence agency, or they identify the chief of America's Intelligence Community, they almost invariably still name the Central Intelligence Agency and the director of central intelligence. This is the CIA's preference. From the time of Negroponte's appointment and the stand up of the Office of the Director of National Intelligence, the Company's workforce as well as its leadership has been reluctant not only to accede to the authority of the DNI but also to acknowledge its equivalence to the agency's 15 "partners" in the IC. In light of history and tradition, this is understandable. The CIA is the agency responsible for covert operations and for producing all-source intelligence analysis. It had cultivated special relationships with allied intelligence agencies. It, and no other agency, has the president as its "first customer."

There was, accordingly, a great deal of concern in the CIA that the establishment of the ODNI would diminish its role and standing in both America's national security architecture and the constellation of US intelligence services. During the Bush administration rhetoric and initiatives trended in that direction. Although the president had resisted legislating intelligence reform, he took the legislation seriously once it was enacted. So did many in the Intelligence Community. In addition, the CIA appeared vulnerable to evisceration, even more so than after the end of the Cold War when Senator Moynihan proposed its abolition. "[A]fter eight traumatic years under George Bush," wrote *Washington Post* columnist David Ignatius, the CIA "became a kind of national pincushion."[7]

The Resurgence of the CIA

But as the Bush administration came to a close, momentum began to shift. After more than a year of intense negotiation among senior IC officials, the president signed a revision of Executive Order 12333. Initially issued by Ronald Reagan in 1981 and already revised once by Bush prior to enacting the Intelligence Reform and Terrorism Prevention Act, EO 12333 allocates power and responsibilities among the agencies, establishes lines of authority, and directs how the Intelligence Community should conduct its activities "With Respect to the National Intelligence Effort." The confusion and conflict generated by the establishment of the director of national intelligence, especially between ODNI and CIA, demanded further revision. ODNI fought for the authority it required to compel CIA to follow its directives. EO 12333, as amended in July 2008, did provide the director of national intelligence with greater authority, but not enough. For example, it confirmed that the DNI was the "head" of the Intelligence Community and the principal intelligence advisor to the president. But it required the DNI to "take into account the views ... of the 'Director of the Central Intelligence Agency.'" Moreover, the executive order made explicit that the DNI's directives (Intelligence Community Directives, or ICDs) "shall not abrogate" previously issued directives (Director of Central Intelligence Directives, DCIDs). The director of central intelligence of course, was dual-hatted as the director of the CIA. The president reserved the last word to resolve the conflicts.[8]

The ambiguity this compromise generated allowed the CIA continually to contest primacy. President Obama's appointment of Leon Panetta as the CIA's director foreshadowed the trajectory of that contest. Dennis Blair, President Obama's choice as director of national intelligence, had exemplary qualifications for the post. A Rhodes Scholar after graduating from the Naval Academy, the admiral had served in policy positions in the Navy and the National Security Council, as Commander-in-Chief, U.S. Pacific Command (CINCPAC), and as associate director of the CIA for military support, a post created by DCI John Deutch in 1995 to facilitate communications between the agency and the Department of Defense. He had also been president of the Institute for Defense Analysis, a private organization that contracts with the Pentagon to provide intelligence. Blair purportedly agreed to serve as director of national intelligence only after the president pledged to provide him with the backing necessary for him to perform his mission as he understood it — to manage the Intelligence Community. This meant, or at least Blair thought that it meant, that Obama would defend the ODNI whenever the office insisted that the CIA follow its lead.[9]

Juxtaposed against Obama's pledge to support Blair, however, was his selection of Panetta to direct the CIA. The appointment surprised everyone. An eight-term congressman who had served as Bill Clinton's budget director and chief of staff, Panetta was well known and well respected. He brought much-needed skills and experience to the administration. But he knew little about intelligence, and for that reason he was not Obama's first choice. That had been John Brennan, a CIA veteran of more than two decades who began as an analyst, was chief of station in Saudi Arabia's capital city of Riyadh, spoke Arabic fluently, and was all but groomed to direct the US intelligence enterprise. Brennan's intimate association with the CIA, however, tainted his credentials to lead it. Because he had under Bush directed the CIA's Terrorist Threat Integration Center and then, after its establishment, the National Counterterrorism Center until Vice Admiral John Redd received the permanent appointment, many within the president's own Democratic Party tied him to the agency's recent questionable behavior, especially its use of enhanced interrogation techniques. Denying that he sanctioned the brutal treatment of detainees, a distraught Brennan nevertheless withdrew his name from consideration and settled for a position in the West Wing as the president's chief counterterrorism advisor. Obama selected Panetta in Brennan's stead. Not only did Panetta not have any links to the CIA, but, unlike Goss and even Tenet, he also could be counted on to take whatever measures necessary to protect the president from any future agency missteps or misdeeds.[10]

Panetta brought to the tug of war between the ODNI and CIA a more effective skill set than did Blair. He may have been a novice in the world of intelligence, but he was politically astute, steeped in the ways of Washington, and recognized which battles were the right ones to fight. He held back through the first several months of Obama's first year. Even as the administration focused on developing a stimulus package, planning for the recovery of the automobile industry, formulating a health care proposal, and pursuing other domestic priorities, Panetta adjusted to his new environment. Adhering to the precedent established by Negroponte and followed by McConnell, in February Panetta deferred to Blair in presenting to the Senate Select Committee on Intelligence the Intelligence Community's Annual Threat Assessment (in all instances, the CIA director as well as the heads of the Defense Intelligence Agency, the FBI, and the State Department's Bureau of Intelligence and Research accompanied the DNI).

But in May a Blair initiative provided Panetta with a reason, which he may have perceived as an opportunity, to reassert the CIA's historic role and responsibility. Both to enhance, in his opinion, the effectiveness of US intelligence and as a litmus test of his power over the community, the director of national intelligence issued a directive claiming his authority to select US chiefs of station. These station chiefs are the primary intelligence officers in the countries in which they serve. They are in charge of all clandestine operations. They also serve as the Intelligence Community's liaison officer to other nations' intelligence services. This delicate balancing act is tricky to sustain; to illustrate, the station chief not infrequently runs operations to spy on the ███████ host country. In his directive, Blair made explicit that in most cases he would select a CIA officer, and in all cases he would consult with Panetta before making an appointment. But he reserved the prerogative to select someone from outside the CIA in those countries where another agency, for example, the National Security Agency or the Defense Intelligence Agency, conventionally play the dominant intelligence role. Moreover, as the head of America's Intelligence Community, Blair insisted that he, not the CIA director, had to be the one to choose the station chief.[11]

Panetta pushed back aggressively by instructing CIA officers the next day to disregard Blair's directive. He recognized that his agency's morale was reeling, and to relinquish its global role as the symbol, not just representative, of US intelligence would add insult to injury. Panetta did not use that argument in challenging Blair, of course. Rather, relying on the advice of Company veterans, he argued that for anyone other than a CIA officer to serve as the intelligence liaison ██████████████████ would confuse foreign counterparts by obscuring the chain of command among the agencies. Further, and no less important, the CIA had for years cultivated these liaison relationships. The relationships mattered most, not the agency or its director. To undermine them would jeopardize US security. So, too, would, placing the responsibility for managing a covert operation in the hands of someone from an agency other than the CIA, even if that responsibility was only theoretical. Only the Company had the requisite experience and the contacts. That Blair had repeatedly expressed reservations about the efficacy of covert operations heightened the stakes.[12]

Blair was furious with what he considered Panetta's insubordination. To him, the issue was clear-cut: Both by law and by executive order, the director of national intelligence was in charge of the Intelligence Community. Consequently, the CIA's director took orders from him. The Senate agreed, and Blair was certain that the White House would as well. He miscalculated; the turf war lingered for months. Whether the reason was Blair's style, Panetta's argument, or established personal relationships, after National Security Advisor James Jones could not reach a decision, in November Vice President Joe Biden, whom Obama designated the arbiter, decided in favor of Panetta and the CIA. Although the victory was more symbolic than substantive, for the agency it was monumental. It had been years since the White House had sided with the CIA as opposed to using it as its whipping boy. In addition, the decision unequivocally challenged the spirit if not the letter of the reform legislation and revision of EO 12333. That gave the CIA hope.[13]

That hope has evolved into self-assurance. Blair lost more than his show-down with Panetta. He lost the president's confidence, that much more so after the community suffered another intelligence failure. In December 2009 the newly established network of integrated intelligence over which Blair presided, especially the National Counterterrorism Center, was unable to prevent the Nigerian Umar Farouk Abdulmutallab, dubbed the Christmas or Underwear Bomber, from carrying a bomb onto a plane that took off from Amsterdam en route to Detroit. Abdulmutallab had sewed plastic explosives into his underwear, but because of his incompetence managed only to set fire to his leg before being wrestled down by passengers. Obama had had enough. Calling this "systemic" intelligence failure "totally unacceptable," in May 2010 the president demanded Blair's resignation.[14]

Conversely, the CIA was finally homing in on Osama bin Laden. Contrary to the common perception that because al-Qaeda's leader had escaped to the mountains of Tora Bora the probability and even importance of his capture had receded, bin Laden had remained at the very top of the agency's list of priorities. While progress tracking him was frustratingly slow, the hunt had never come remotely close to a standstill. Shortly after taking office, Obama insisted to Panetta that locating bin Laden had to be the CIA's "number one goal," and as president he wanted regular progress reports. Panetta did not need the president's instruction. Moreover, he soon learned that the agency was closer to achieving that goal than he had imagined. The U.S. government had authorized Operation GREYSTONE shortly after the 9/11 attacks.[15] Surely the most far-reaching covert action program in the history of the CIA and entire Intelligence Community, the operation encompassed the kidnapping, rendition, isolation in "black sites" (secret prisons), and interrogation of "high value" targets in Central, South, and Southeast Asia, in Africa, in Europe, and elsewhere around the globe. Obtaining clues to where bin Laden was hiding was a constant objective.[16]

The hunt for bin Laden is one of the rare cases in intelligence history when success resulted primarily from "connecting the dots." Further, in stark contrast to the behavior of the Intelligence Community in the lead-up to the 9/11 tragedy, the combination of painstaking collection, rigorous analysis, and exemplary cooperation among the IC elements not only uncovered the requisite dots but also distinguished them from the multitude of useless ones. To use another and perhaps more apt metaphor, the CIA did not simply connect the dots. In locating bin Laden, it found the proverbial needle in the haystack.

Many questions remain and intense debate continues over from whom and by what means the CIA acquired intelligence on bin Laden's whereabouts. Currently available evidence indicates that agency analysts become aware of a particularly crucial "dot" after several different detained "targets" had been subjected to enhanced interrogation techniques in Cuba (Guantanamo), and in ███████████████████████. Advocates of these techniques, including former DCI Michael Hayden as well as former President Bush and Vice President Cheney, claim that their use was essential to the sources divulging the information. Jose Rodriguez, Jr., who headed the CIA's Counterterrorism Center from 2002 to 2004 and, after that, its National Clandestine Service, is particularly enthusiastic about the techniques' rewards and denies that they constituted torture.[17]

Opponents of the interrogators' conduct, supported by a 6000-page 2012 Senate Select Committee on Intelligence study, counter that "brutal treatment" was not a "central component" in locating bin Laden. In the judgments of such critics, among whom, to the consternation of many CIA officers, was President Obama at the time he took office, "conventional" interrogation techniques, such as those preferred by the FBI, have proved more effective. Treating prisoners cruelly, commented the Republican John McCain, Obama's opponent in the 2008 election, "is not only wrong in principle and a stain on our country's conscience, but also an ineffective and unreliable means of gathering intelligence." As if to underscore McCain's point, the most prized detainee, Khalid Sheik Mohammed, widely known as KSM and the mastermind of the 9/11 attacks, complicated the agency's effort by providing misinformation following over 180 waterboardings. KSM was not alone in spinning yarns.[18]

These disputes cannot be settled unequivocally. The report by the Senate Select Committee remains classified, its judgments challenged by the CIA, and it has become the source of a fierce partisan debate.[19] David Ignatius quoted Leon Panetta in an opinion piece on the "moral choices on interrogations." "Some of the detainees who provided useful information about the facilitator/courier's role had been subjected to enhanced interrogation techniques," Panetta wrote to Senator McCain. "Whether those techniques were the 'only timely and effective way' to obtain such information is a matter of debate and cannot be established definitively. What is definitive," the DCI concluded, "is that the acquired information was only a part of multiple streams of intelligence that led us to bin Laden."[20] What is likewise definitive is that between 2001 and 2003 at least three different al-Qaeda operatives, the Pakistani Khalid Sheik Mohammed, Mohamedou Ould Slahi from Mauritania, and Mohammed al-Qahtani, a Saudi, mentioned the name Abu Ahmed al-Kuwaiti. Translated as "The Father of Ahmed from

Kuwait," this was certainly, in the judgment of both agency operatives and analysts, a pseudonym for someone of such importance that he warranted the CIA's attention.[21]

The CIA designated "the Kuwaiti," as he came to be called, a high-value target, and over the next several years his value grew higher. Additional interrogations; cell phone intercepts, aerial surveillance, and software programs captured, conducted, and developed by the National Security Agency, National Geospatial-Intelligence Organization, and their cognates within the Intelligence Community; HUMINT collected in multiple nations by reconstructed networks of operatives and assets; and liaison with other foreign intelligence services yielded a treasure trove of rich data that could be entered into powerful supercomputers. A team of analysts comprised a disproportionate number of women because, explains the respected journalist Mark Bowden, they were considered "especially good at this kind of patient detail work and had a reputation for being sensitive to subtleties that eluded many men," pored over the raw data and printouts. By 2007 this "sisterhood" had identified the target's real name: Ibrahim Saeed Ahmed.[22]

Ahmed was not just any operative; he was bin Laden's personal courier. Because of his security concerns and appreciation of the Intelligence Community's capabilities, al-Qaeda's leader avoided communicating over the phone or by email. He relied on Ahmed to carry messages to and from his operatives and allies, to keep him informed about global developments, and to transport videotapes of his speeches to Al Jazeera, the Arab news agency. The agency later learned that Ahmed's brother Arbar assisted him in providing this courier service. ▮▮▮▮▮▮▮▮▮▮▮▮▮▮▮▮
▮▮▮▮▮▮▮▮▮▮▮▮▮▮▮ the brothers were bin Laden's sole contacts with the outside world.[23] Michael Hayden, who directed the CIA from 2006 to 2009, called the tactic the agency developed based on the discovery of Ahmed a "bank shot": follow the courier and find bin Laden.[24]

Over the next four years, during which successive directors of national intelligence sought increased power over US intelligence and Barack Obama won election as president, the CIA searched for Ahmed. In summer 2010 it finally located him driving a white sport-utility vehicle in Peshawar, Pakistan. The key challenge was to determine whether by doing so it had also located bin Laden. Agency operatives discovered that Ahmed had purchased a sizable compound in the Abbottabad neighborhood of Bilal Town, less than a mile from Pakistan's military academy. Some analysts were confident that al-Qaeda's leader was living in the compound. Why else would a courier have purchased such a multi-floored building, many times larger than the neighboring residences, surrounded with high walls topped off with barbed wire and with windows either blacked out or finished with a reflecting material that prevented seeing inside? Further, the indistinct figure the drone video cameras filmed pacing around inside the house seemed to be a man (appropriately nicknamed the "Pacer") of bin Laden's uncommon six-feet-four-inch height.[25]

Still, the intelligence as to bin Laden's hideouts and safe houses had been wrong before, and other analysts were skeptical. Would the Kuwaiti have chosen a site that was only slightly more than thirty miles from Pakistan's capital city of Islamabad? Estimates of the probability that bin Laden was in the compound ranged from 10% to 95%. A team of Pakistanis recruited by the CIA rented a home in Bilal Town to collect further intelligence necessary to construct a "pattern of life model" on the Pacer and other residents.[26] However, the team was never able to see sufficiently into the three-story-high walled compound to identify bin Laden. It even recruited a Pakistani physician to set up a clinic offering hepatitis B vaccinations for the neighborhood children in the hope of obtaining bin Laden–related DNA. Although the clinic administered the vaccinations for free, no one from the compound showed up.[27]

The "safest" option would have been to destroy the compound, either by conventional bombing or a drone strike. Yet doing so would further aggravate relations with Pakistan's government. Islamabad was already furious with the United States, particularly with the CIA. Raymond Davis had in January 2012 shot to death two civilians on a crowded street in Lahore. Although Washington tried to suppress the information that Davis worked for the CIA, within weeks the press learned that he was a contract agent ██

██

████████████████████████████ °░ . Even a surgical strike on the compound was almost certain to make matters worse by causing collateral damage. The Pakistanis' reaction would be hostile, and perhaps violent. And the intended target might not even be bin Laden. If it were, moreover, a direct hit could make incontestable identification of him impossible.[28]

Consequently, Obama on Sunday May 1 approved Operation NEPTUNE SPEAR, a minutely planned nighttime raid on the compound that took shape in a restricted room at Langley. The project was managed by the CIA to ensure that it was statutorily covert and thereby would enable the president to plausibly deny US responsibility. That was essential because America was employing force in Pakistan, a country with which America was not at war.[29] But the "Playbook" for the operation was designed by

Vice Admiral William McRaven, the head of the Joint Special Operations Command (JSOC), with which Panetta had signed a secret agreement in 2009 to cooperate. Further, it was executed by a team of about two dozen U.S. Navy SEALs (Sea, Air, and Land teams) who trained especially for this mission ▬▬▬▬▬▬▬. The SEALs are an integral component of JSOC, but for Neptune Spear they were "sheep-dipped." The military personnel were temporarily turned into clandestine CIA operatives.[30]

The mission was to capture bin Laden if possible, but no one expected that he would be taken alive. Without notifying Pakistan's government, let alone requesting its permission, the SEALs flew in helicopters to Abbottabad from Afghanistan. As had happened in Iran three decades earlier with Operation EAGLE CLAW, the raid experienced technical problems. In particular, upon arriving at the compound one of the Black Hawk helicopters clipped its tail against a wall and crashed. But this time the mission was neither disrupted nor aborted; the well-trained team improvised by landing inside the compound walls one of the much larger CH-47 Chinook helicopters assigned to hover over the compound's main building with its reserve force of SEALs. Even the CIA's judgment that bin Laden lived on the third floor proved correct. The result was an operation implemented with deadly precision. In addition to bin Laden, one of his sons, the courier, and the courier's brother and sister-in-law were killed. Before leaving the scene ahead of the Pakistanis' arrival, the SEALs swept up a bounty of computers and even a digital voice recorder — "exactly like the CIA had predicted," according to one participant who "marveled" at their performance. Within twenty-four hours, forensic experts in Afghanistan identified the body, and it was taken out to sea aboard the aircraft carrier U.S.S. *Carl Vinson*. Bin Laden's burial at sea would conform to Muslim ritual. Nevertheless, there would be no shrine to visit.[31]

Obama announced that bin Laden had been killed on Sunday night, May 1, 2011. Outside the White House the next morning, Americans chanted "CIA," "CIA." They did not chant "DNI," "DNI."[32] Moreover, many veterans of the agency probably could not believe their ears or what they read. The success of Operation NEPTUNE SPEAR did not restore fully the CIA's reputation after a decade, some would say decades, of criticism and scorn. But it did allow the agency to escape purgatory. Even as Congress and the public learned more about the monumental effort the agency had put into its hunt for bin Laden, the director of the CIA emerged more boldly as the face of the US Intelligence Community. The perception of Panetta was that he shared with Secretary of Defense Robert Gates and Secretary of State Hillary Clinton the top echelon of Obama's hierarchy of security advisors. DNI James

Clapper, an outsider who while competent was colorless and who concentrated on restructuring the ODNI while the CIA chased down bin Laden, became but an afterthought (Nebraska's former Republican Senator Chuck Nagel, reportedly Obama's first choice to succeed Blair and who the president subsequently selected as secretary of defense, would have had more clout). In contrast to running spies and paramilitary operatives, the director of national security's job description, to quote the *New York Times*' Mark Mazzetti, seemed like "one part green eyeshade accountant and another part hall monitor."[33]

Changes in the hierarchy that followed reinforced this perception. In 2010 Robert Gates, whose tenure as secretary of defense dated to George W. Bush, announced his intention to return to private life the next year. At the end of April 2011, but a few days before Panetta was to achieve his crowning glory at the CIA, Obama announced that his CIA director would replace Gates as the Pentagon's chief. To the surprise of almost everyone, the president the same day announced his nomination of General David Petraeus to take over from Panetta the directorship of the CIA.[34]

Petraeus's experience with intelligence was indirect. Nevertheless, it was extensive. What is more, even if he had not had any experience, he still doubtless would have received the Senate's unanimous confirmation that he did. By 2011 the media-savvy Petraeus was arguably the most celebrated US military commander since the Vietnam War, eclipsing even Colin Powell. A four-star Army general who had attended West Point, married the military academy's superintendent's daughter, and earned a Ph.D. in International Relations from Princeton University, he had commanded US forces in two major wars. Credited as the Army's most enthusiastic proponent of the surge in Iraq and the principal force that drove the redesigned counterinsurgency doctrine, more than any individual Petraeus won acclaim for turning the tide in the war there and thereby allowing for the drawdown of US troops. Early in the Obama presidency he left his post as head of America's Central Command (CENTCOM, which was responsible for both Iraq and Afghanistan) to take over command of the US and international forces fighting in Afghanistan from the cashiered General Stanley McChrystal. That he met with less success in that theater than in Iraq did not tarnish his reputation for leadership and brilliance.

Nevertheless, many in the agency had doubts about Petraeus's appointment. Once again Obama had selected someone from outside the CIA's culture, and in Petraeus's case, someone rumored to have sought another position. Most observers identified that position as chairman of the Joint

Chiefs of Staff. Reportedly, only reluctantly did Petraeus resign his Army commission after learning that his disagreements with the president over the timing of the drawdown of America's troops in Afghanistan precluded his receiving that appointment. Other pundits were confident that he had set his sights on the Republican nomination for the presidency of the United States. When the president of Princeton University announced her intention to resign, Petraeus's name immediately surfaced as a potential successor.[35] Regardless of the war hero's passion for the CIA as an institution, or for that matter his fit, Obama's choice was inspired and electrifying. DNI Clapper was by statute the president's chief intelligence official. But there could be no question that it would be General Petraeus who had the president's ear. Further, there were few in Washington who commanded the respect and wielded the influence that David Petraeus did. As DCIA, he would use that respect and influence for the benefit of the CIA.

Less than two years later, scandal interrupted Petraeus's tenure; he departed Langley with his agenda still a work in progress. On Friday November 9, 2012, but three days after Obama's reelection, he shocked the nation and the world by resigning the CIA's directorship. The chain of events began with a bizarre investigation that initially did not target Patreaus but subsequently raised concerns over a possible security breach involving his emails. The FBI stumbled across evidence that the seemingly indestructible and irrepressible retired general, who had survived an accidental shooting during training, a skydiving misadventure, and prostate cancer, had carried on an extramarital affair after more than three decades of marriage. The "other woman" was Paula Broadwell, twenty years Petraeus's junior and married with two children. Broadwell's biography also includes graduation from West Point, service as a lieutenant colonel in the U.S. Army reserves, four semesters of doctoral study at Harvard, and coauthorship of an admiring biography of the four-star general. Petraeus had already broken the relationship off, and it did not appear to have harmed the United States or its interests. The days had long passed when conducting an illicit liaison made intelligence officers security liabilities because of their vulnerability to blackmail. As the CIA director Petraeus was vulnerable to ridicule because of his inability to protect the privacy of his email correspondence. But to many observers his behavior did not warrant his creating a vacuum at the top of the agency at such a critical time. Ironically, it was Director of National Intelligence James Clapper who, after hearing Petraeus's confession, advised his "subordinate" to step down. Over the previous half dozen years, the director of the CIA had established a record of challenging and often disregarding the DNI's directives. Clapper's was not a directive. Yet Petraeus handed Obama his resignation, and after hesitating, the president accepted it.[36]

The Militarization of Intelligence

Petraeus' abrupt resignation leaves the shape of the CIA's future very much a question mark. It was created in 1947 as an agency that could combine and coordinate its own intelligence with that collected elsewhere in the government, primarily by the State Department and various branches of the US military, to produce the "all source" analysis essential to informing policymakers. This mission is a challenge for any intelligence service. But ever since the creation of the Office of Policy Coordination in 1948 and its incorporation by Walter Bedell Smith into a Directorate of Plans in 1952, the CIA's analytic responsibilities have competed with covert, especially paramilitary operations for resources and as a priority. This competition has at best diluted and at worst degraded the agency's capacity to perform the functions congruent with its designers "original intent." The intelligence failures that the CIA has experienced over the decades cannot be wholly attributed to this dynamic. But it contributed to them.

Despite uncharacteristically shunning public attention, or perhaps because he was so effective in doing so, Petraeus' brief tenure as director of the CIA exacerbated this trend — and this problem. The analytic challenges he confronted from his first day in office warranted his full attention: Iran's nuclear aspirations, China's geopolitical ambitions, the Arab spring, Europe's debt crisis, the murder of the US ambassador to Libya in Benghazi, and so much more. Yet as signaled by the title of a joint *Washington Post/Foreign Policy* blog published at the time of his appointment, Petraeus took the "helm [of] an increasingly militarized CIA."[37] The title correctly indicates that the increased militarization of the CIA predates Petraeus. Indeed, it predates Obama. This militarization is different from that of the past decades, the kind of paramilitary operations first hatched by Frank Wisner and his colleagues within the Office of Policy Coordination, expanded by the Directorate of Plans (renamed the Directorate of Operations and then the National Clandestine Service), and applied in Guatemala, Cuba, Southeast Asia, the Middle East, Nicaragua, Africa, and so many other places during the agency's first fifty years. As

Mark Mazzetti writes in his book about the post-9/11 CIA, "the Central Intelligence Agency has become a killing machine."[38]

This transformation, which historians may come to identify most closely with Petraeus because it accelerated and intensified so dramatically under his watch, began slowly in the 1990s. But it rapidly and inexorably picked up momentum after 2001. After George W. Bush authorized the expansion of the counterterrorism campaign, officers in the National Clandestine Service's Special Activities Division (actually the Special Operations Group within the Special Activities Division) spread out across regions considered hostile to the United States, collecting intelligence on militant networks; creating, funding, and managing local armies (Counterterrorism Pursuit Teams); and, most fundamentally, "plotting missions to kill the networks' top leaders."[39] These covert operations remained largely under the public radar until December 30, 2009. On that day, at the CIA's Forward Operating Base Chapman in the southeastern province of Khost, Humam Khalil Abu-Mulal al-Balawi, a suicide bomber posing as a Jordanian operative with the capability to penetrate one of the militant networks in Afghanistan, killed four CIA officers, three guards under contract to the agency, and a Jordanian. Their deaths exposed to all the world the agents' courage and patriotism. Also exposed was "the civilian spy agency's transformation in recent years into a paramilitary organization at the vanguard of America's far-flung wars."[40]

The appropriateness of Mazzetti's labeling the CIA a killing machine is best illustrated by the CIA's responsibility for the deployment of drones ██ ██████████████████████ Initially developed for reconnaissance missions, in large part in order to combat the growing yet diffuse terrorist threat but also because of their utility in the wars in Iraq and Afghanistan, these aircraft were reconfigured for the purpose of carrying missiles and other munitions. Initially the CIA opposed turning drones into lethal weapons. But especially in 2008, with al-Qaeda digging in deeper along the lawless mountain area between Afghanistan and Pakistan and Bush desperate to at least severely degrade its capabilities if not kill bin Laden before leaving office, Director of Central Intelligence Michael Hayden, according to *New York Times'* veteran reporters Eric Schmitt and Thom Shanker, requested authorization to escalate the drone campaign in Pakistan, and to do so with or without Pakistan's concurrence. By giving Hayden everything he wanted, ████ in the words of Schmitt and Shanker, "effectively made the

CIA director America's combatant commander in the hottest covert war in the global campaign against terror."[41]

In the final six months of Bush's presidency, the U.S. government launched some 28 drone attacks in Pakistan's tribal areas, almost double the number of the previous four plus years.[42] Agency personnel did not fly the drones; no one did, or does. Formally they are called unmanned aerial vehicles (UAVs). But CIA analysts, some detailed to the National Counterterrorism Center and some not, identify and locate the leaders and followers of al-Qaeda, the Taliban, or other terrorist organizations as the drones' targets.[43]

███

███

████ then use joysticks and monitors not unlike those associated with video games to remotely "fly" the drones to the targets.[44] By selecting Petraeus, whose experience as a combat commander vastly eclipsed that of Hayden let alone Panetta, to lead the CIA, Obama signaled the extent to which in an era in which counterterrorism was so central to US security policy, drone strikes had helped to define a service created to collect and analyze intelligence. As the journalist David Ignatius put it so well, "The retired general, with his matchless experience in running wars in Iraq and Afghanistan, was seen as well suited to run an agency that combined the trench coat with the flak jacket."[45]

The institutional memory of the criticism produced by the Church Committee's revelations about assassination runs deep in the CIA, and Presidents Ford, Carter, and Reagan all issued executive orders prohibiting the agency from engaging in these activities. None of their successors, including George W. Bush, challenged the prohibition. Only after the 9/11 attack, therefore, did the CIA request authorization to employ drones for anything other than reconnaissance and observation.[46] Because the definition of assassination is ambiguous, especially during combat operations, the agency received White House approval. The legal justification remains both controversial and secret. After his election to a second term, President Obama pledged to make the processes and procedures for decisions on drone strikes more transparent, at least for select members of Congress. But the policy guidance will remain classified. The CIA's employment of drones for lethal purposes, nevertheless, has gained wider public acceptance than its application of enhanced interrogation techniques.[47]

Since Bush's initial approval of employing drones for targeted killing, the growth in the frequency of their use for this purpose has been substantial — and sobering. Indeed, in order to attack the suspected terrorist organizations in dispersed and inaccessible areas and decapitate their leadership, while minimizing US casualties and quarantining the violence so that it rarely gains the attention of the American public, the Obama administration relied on drones much more extensively than its predecessor. The campaign, code-named SYLVAN-MAGNOLIA, became so integral to the president's counterterrorism strategy that following his reelection in 2012 he finally determined he should institutionalize the drone's use by developing a "manual" of standards and procedures.[48] Institutionalized or not, and despite the widespread publicity it has received, the drone campaign remains a "covert operation" without oversight or accountability. [49] The ironic result is "the most aggressive operation in the history of the agency" has been vital to getting the "CIA Back on its Feet."[50]

The CIA is probably "back on its feet." Budget figures leaked by Edward Snowden, the former intelligence contractor who went rogue, reveal that in fiscal year 2013 the agency's budget far exceeded that of other Intelligence Community elements, including the National Security and National Geo-Spatial Agencies.[51] Nevertheless, in terms of the agency's resources, image, and mission, the revival has come at a great and increasing cost. To use Pakistan as an example, Bush authorized forty-five strikes between 2004 and 2008. Obama authorized his first two strikes the third day he was in office, and from 2009 through 2012 there have been 255. In Yemen, another example, Bush authorized a single strike. Obama approved thirty-eight in his first term along with a "White Paper" prepared by the Department of Justice that provided the justification for targeting US citizens.[52]

The significance of that White Paper is hard to exaggerate. A 2011 drone strike in Yemen killed the Muslim cleric, Anwar al-Awlaki, whose name was virtually synonymous with al-Qaeda in the Arabian Peninsula. He was also born in New Mexico and retained his US citizenship. Killed with him was his cousin Samir Kahn, another US citizen and propagandist for jihad. Soon thereafter, a second strike killed al-Awlaki's son, evidently accidentally. Unlike his father and cousin, the teen-age Abdulrahman al-Awlaki was not a high-value target. Nor was Jude Kenan Mohammed, a 23-year-old who dropped out of high school in North Carolina who in 2011 was killed by a drone strike in Pakistan.[53]

The Obama administration developed Camp Lemonnier in Djibouti on the Horn of Africa as the centerpiece of a series of bases that will facilitate drone strikes throughout Africa and the Middle East. ████████ now works with a "kill list" and "disposition matrix" to formulate a "playbook" for its program. In addition, not infrequently the agency does not know the identity of an alleged terrorist but classifies him or her as a target based on a pattern of activity, called a "signature." According to estimates, the combined number of militants and civilians killed by drones will sometime in Obama's second term exceed 3000, surpassing the 2977 victims, including the hijackers, of the 9/11 attacks. "You've taken an agency that was chugging along," Greg Miller and Julie Tate quote an unnamed veteran intelligence official at the time of Petraeus's appointment, anticipating Mazzetti, "and turned it into one hell of a killing machine."[54]

The CIA's role in the drone campaign has once again placed it both under the microscope and in an ethical and legal quagmire (the Obama administration cancelled a program under which the CIA hired outside contractors to locate and, the evidence suggests, assassinate al-Qaeda operatives).[55] For the agency and US national security, the consequences may prove unprecedented, long lasting, and even irreparable. The drone campaign may turn out to be the most critical element which transformed the CIA by revolutionizing its mission. At a minimum, it is the most prominent illustration of the degree to which that agency has evolved into what one State Department officer has described as "a mini-Special Operations Command that purports to be an intelligence agency." Historically, the Directorate of Intelligence and Directorate of Operations carried out their responsibilities largely independent of one another. There were costs to this autonomy in terms of trust, communication, collaboration, and efficiency. But it did allow analysts the space to address a broad array of issues, to contend with questions that cut across these issues, and to think strategically when trying to answer them.[56]

That current analytic workforce, however, is to a dangerous extent concentrated not only on counterterrorism but also on locating targets. About twenty percent of the CIA's analysts are currently "targeters," an assignment that puts them on the fast track for promotion. Perhaps concluding that the timing was auspicious, moreover, Petraeus, as the press reported in the waning days of the 2012 presidential campaign during which both candidates applauded the results of the targeted strikes, sought approval for the expansion of the CIA's drone force. Evidently he had concluded that the existing arrangement, by which the agency normally employed drones that belonged to the military, was inadequate. Rather than share responsibilities and resources with the Pentagon, Petraeus, who as a general in two wars commanded these responsibilities and resources, decided that the time had come to expand the CIA control of the program.[57]

Petraeus resigned before Obama took action on his request. But the implications alone of the CIA director making such a request are frightening. After a steep increase in the immediate aftermath of 9/11, Congress' appropriation of funding for the CIA has steadily declined. This trend is sure to continue and almost certainly to intensify in an era of monstrous budgetary deficits. ███████████████████████████ When he was director of national intelligence, Dennis Blair tried to convince the president that the Intelligence Community should provide support for a more strategically designed counterterrorism policy. Blair likened the drone strikes to the body counts associated with the strategy of attrition in Vietnam.[58]

Even as Blair's protests contributed to his firing, John Brennan, the CIA veteran who Obama brought with him to the West Wing to manage the drone campaign as the president's special advisor on homeland security and counterterrorism, took Blair's complaint to the next level. Brennan is not opposed to the drone campaign *per se*. He ran it throughout Obama's first term. But recognizing the potential to execute innocents and thus produce more enemies of the United States, he fears that targeted killing has become a substitute for a grand strategy. What is more, Brennan is opposed to the CIA's leading role. As Obama's trusted aide he recommended that the agency put a halt to its transformation to a paramilitary organization by leaving "lethal action to its more traditional home in the military, where the law requires greater transparency." Doing so would increase the program's accountability and allow the CIA to return to the business of collecting and analyzing intelligence.[59]

There is little evidence that as Obama's special assistant Brennan forcefully made his case for a CIA with "more trench coats, less body armor," to again borrow a phrase from David Ignatius.[60] He unequivocally did not make it effectively. But his circumstances changed, and it appears that so did his influence. On January 7, 2013, Obama nominated Brennan to replace Petraeus as the CIA's director. The president hesitated in deciding on whom to make his nominee in large part because he knew that opponents would recycle the charges about Brennan's complicity in if not advocacy of enhanced interrogation techniques. Some, Obama knew, would pile on with criticism of his management of the targeted killings. The fact that Obama nominated him regardless signals the president's confidence in the CIA veteran and the relationship that the two men have developed. That relationship will be severely tested. Although a filibuster by Senator Ron Paul added to the drama, the Senate on March 7, 2013, confirmed Brennan by a vote of 63 to 34.

For the CIA, both its present and its future, the stakes cannot be higher. The outcome hinges on what changes, both institutional and strategic, Obama, with Brennan at the CIA's helm, makes in his second and last term in office. As a freshly minted DCI who has worked intimately with the president and earned his implicit trust, Brennan has a uniquely privileged position to shape the agency at an exceptionally critical juncture in its history. To quote the *New York Times* article announcing his nomination, "The question that now faces Mr. Brennan ... is whether the C.I.A. should remain at the center of secret American paramilitary operations — most notably drone strikes — or rebuild its traditional espionage capabilities, which intelligence veterans say have atrophied during years of terrorist manhunts."[61]

Whether as a result of Brennan's elevation to the CIA directorship, the support he has received from Obama's new team of advisors during his second term, the sustained criticism the drone campaign has received in the press, Congress, and the general public, or most likely a combination of all the above plus other considerations, only a few months into the first year of his second administration the president adopted his new DCI's position. The *New York Times*' headline story on May 23, 2013, previewing a much-anticipated speech on counterterrorism policy that Obama delivered the next day at the National Defense University, announced Obama's intention gradually to transfer control of the drone attacks ▮▮▮▮▮▮▮▮ to the Pentagon. The *Times* credited Brennan's role in this evolution in the president's thinking. The "new CIA director," reported veteran correspondents Charlie Savage and Peter Baker, "has been eager to shift the agency more toward espionage, intelligence gathering and analysis and away from the paramilitary mission it has adopted since September 11." The article also quoted Rhode Island's Democratic Senator Jack Reed's vigorous agreement with Brennan. Reed emphasized the need to "rebalance" the missions of the CIA and Pentagon. "The policy is intended to refocus the activities of the intelligence community to collection, which is crucial," he said.[62]

It will be years before the consequences of the military taking over responsibility for drone strikes become manifest. In his address, President Obama stressed that the successes of his counterterrorism programs made it possible to narrow their scale and scope as well as make the policies and management of them more transparent. But he made explicit that narrowing scale and scope is not synonymous with ending, and any and all changes would be incremental.[63] On the one hand, it will take time for the military to achieve the level of expertise to run the drone campaign with the same degree of "lethal efficiency" ▮▮▮▮▮▮▮▮. On the other hand, many within the agency's workforce, the majority of whom joined the agency after 2001, have spent virtually their entire careers focusing, as one informed observer comments, "almost exclusively on the work of man-hunting and killing." Mark Lowenthal, who held several high-ranking positions in the CIA, explained the significance. "There's a huge cultural and generational issue at stake here," he remarked. "There must be a shift in emphasis," added former CIA director Michael Hayden. "A lot of things that pass for analysis right now is really targeting."[64]

Moreover, the transition of control of the drone missions is but one of multiple steps necessary to "rebalance" the missions of the CIA and Pentagon. So long as America's security policy remains fixated on counterterrorism, the agency will still need to devote a disproportionate percentage of its resources to identifying and locating suspected terrorists—and targets. The Office of the Secretary of Defense has multiple capabilities to lessen this burden. These include not only the National Security and National Geo-Spatial Agencies, but also, and of increasing significance, the Defense Intelligence Agency. Under the direction of DIA chief Lt. General Michael Flynn, Panetta, and his successor as secretary of defense, Chuck Hagel, the DIA is also undergoing an arresting transformation. Perhaps an even more important catalyst for this transformation is Michael Vickers, a former Army special forces officer as well as CIA operative who specialized in paramilitary operations, most notably running the covert war to arm the Afghan resistance to the Soviets in the 1980s, who took over as undersecretary of defense for intelligence in 2010. The goal is to convert a small agency that historically has narrowly served "war fighters" into a "spy service" that is "more closely aligned with the CIA and elite military commando units." The Pentagon intends for the DIA to field a larger force of "collectors," rebranded as the Defense Clandestine Service, who are actually trained by the CIA. Identifying and then targeting suspected terrorists will be a core mission of this more robust service. In principle, moreover, the DIA should be able more seamlessly than the CIA to collaborate with the Joint Special Operations Command, the type of paramilitary operation notwithstanding.[65]

The CIA's future effectiveness requires more than excising control of the drone campaign from the agency's portfolio, let alone expanding that of the Defense Intelligence Agency. Testifying to the Aspin–Brown Commission in the mid-1990s, Robert Gates, the only director of central intelligence to have previously served as a CIA analyst (Brennan is only DCIA) and Obama's first secretary of defense, recommended that the CIA cede all paramilitary operations to the Pentagon. The agency could then direct its resources and energies toward its core mission of collection and analysis. Gates' predecessor at the Pentagon, Donald Rumsfeld, maneuvered to ensure that the Special Operations Command was at the center of the Bush administration's Global War on Terror. Rumsfeld did so for the wrong reasons. He resented that the CIA was in Afghanistan as the first responder to the 9/11 attacks, and he believed devoutly that expertly trained highly mobile forces were the military wave of the future. Still, Rumsfeld bolstered SOCOM's authority and capacity to undertake the paramilitary missions for which the CIA was never adequately trained to begin with.[66]

Gates' recommendation never gained traction because it collided with decades of history and culture. 9/11 changed history, and perhaps over time it can change culture. The result would entrust covert and paramilitary operations to the military, and management of the Intelligence Community to the director of national intelligence. That division of labor would require a revision of the U.S. code. Title 10 provides the legal basis for the roles and missions of each of America's military services and limits the engagement of the Armed Forces to "war zones" in order to reinforce congressional oversight and ensure that US personnel are covered by the Geneva Conventions. The CIA is governed by Title 50. As a consequence, the president can send agency operatives anywhere in the world without taking responsibility for their deployment. But there is ample precedent for amending the US code, current practices already blur the distinction between the authorities to fight wars and to deny doing so, since the Rumsfeld era the Joint Special Operations Command has been authorized to launch stealth operations across a vast swath of territory stretching from North Africa to East Asia, and situating drones under Title 10 would enhance transparency.[67]

Moreover, shedding its paramilitary responsibilities would produce a CIA fully committed to what its designers intended: the collection and the production of all-source intelligence analyses, both current and strategic, to inform policymakers and provide them with advance warning of both risks and opportunities. This might not be the CIA that Hollywood prefers. Nevertheless, as the United States struggles to make sense of and find security and prosperity in a globalized world of fluid boundaries punctuated by continuing and emerging threats and a cacophony of armed insurrectionists about which the United States knows very little, it would be a CIA that best serves the national and, indeed, the world's interest.

Notes

1   Paul Pillar, *Intelligence and U.S. Foreign Policy: Iraq, 9/11, and Misguided Reform* (NY: Columbia University Press, 2011), 296.

2   Richard K. Betts, *Enemies of Intelligence: Knowledge & Power in American National Security* (NY: Columbia University Press, 2007), 19–52, 183–84; Amy Zegart, *Spying Blind: The CIA, the FBI, and the Origins of 9/11* (Princeton, NJ: Princeton University Press, 2007), 59, 182; John Brennan, "Is This Intelligence? We Added Players But Lost Control of the Ball," *Washington Post*, November 20, 2005.

3   Richard H. Immerman, "Transforming Analysis: The Intelligence Community's Best Kept Secret," *Intelligence and National Security* 26 (April-June 2011): 159–81; Thomas Fingar, *Reducing Uncertainty: Intelligence Analysis and National Security* (Stanford, CA: Stanford University Press, 2011), 89–125; Stephen Marrin, "Evaluating CIA's Analytic Performance: Reflections of a Former Analyst," *Orbis* 57 (Spring 2013): 325–9; Jim Marchio, "Analytic Tradecraft and the Intelligence Community: Enduring Value, Intermittent Emphasis," *Intelligence and National Security*, February 1, 2013 (DOI:10.1080/02684527.2012.746415), accessed on May 2, 2013, at http://www.tandfonline.com/doi/abs/10.1080/02684527.2012.746415#.UYpdPkpNU2c. As the assistant deputy director of national intelligence for analytic integrity and standards at the time of the 2007 National Intelligence Estimate on Iran's nuclear program's publication, I evaluated its tradecraft. In the interest of full disclosure, I was among those targeted by its critics. See Gabriel Schoenfeld, "If Michael Moore Had a Security Clearance: How did the rabid ideologue Richard Immerman get put in charge of the 'standards and integrity' of the intelligence community?" *Weekly Standard*, March 3, 2008; Bill Gertz, "Inside the Ring," *Washington Times*, March 14, 2008.

4   Marc Ambinder, "The Real Intelligence Wars: Oversight and Access," *The Atlantic*, March 18, 2012, accessed on December 5, 2012, at http://www.theatlantic.com/politics/archive/2009/11/the-real-intelligence-wars-oversight-and-access/30334/.

5   William Branigin, "Bush Nominates Negroponte to New Intel Post," *Washington Post*, February 17, 2005; Karen DeYoung and Walter Pincus, "Negroponte Moves to Job Considered Crucial at State Dept.," *Washington Post*, January 5, 2007.

6   Lawrence Wright, "The Spymaster: Can Mike McConnell Fix America's Intelligence Community?" *The New Yorker*, January 21, 2008, accessed on December 30, 2012, at http://www.newyorker.com/reporting/2008/01/21/080121fa_fact_wright; Walter Pincus, "Gates Defends Obama Nominee for Intelligence Chief," *Washington Post*, June 7, 2010.

7   David Ignatius, "A Surprise at Langley," *Washington Post*, January 7, 2009.

8   Executive Order 13470—Further Amendments to Executive Order 12333, United States Intelligence Activities, July 30, 2008, accessed on November 1, 2012, at http://www.fas.org/irp/offdocs/eo/eo-13470.pdf; Executive Order

12333, United States Intelligence Activities (As amended by Executive Orders 13284 (2003), 13355 (2004) and 13470 (2008)), 30 July 2008, accessed on November 1, 2012, at http://www.fas.org/irp/offdocs/eo/eo-12333-2008.pdf.

9   Mark Mazzetti, "Likely Pick for Intelligence Chief Would Face Task of Corralling Fractious Agencies," *New York Times*, December 21, 2008.

10   Michael Barone, "Obama's Surprise Pick of Leon Panetta for CIA Director," *Thomas Jefferson Street blog*, January 6, 2009, accessed on November 1, 2009, at http://www.usnews.com/opinion/blogs/barone/2009/01/06/obamas-surprise-pick-of-leon-panetta-for-cia-director.

11   Mark Mazzetti, "White House Sides With C.I.A. in Turf Battle," *New York Times*, November 12, 2009; Walter Pincus, "Senate Committee Sides with DNI in its Bureaucratic Turf War with CIA," *Washington Post*, July 23, 2009.

12   Bobby Ghosh, "CIA Chief Panetta Winning Over Doubters at the Agency," *Time*, November 24, 2009, accessed on December 5, 2012, at http://www.time.com/time/nation/article/0,8599,1942514,00.html.

13   Mark Mazzetti, "White House Sides With C.I.A. in Turf Battle;" Bobby Ghosh, "Overseas Turf War Between the CIA and DNI Won't Die," *Time*, November 6, 2009, accessed on October 29, 2012, at http://www.time.com/time/nation/article/0,8599,1936129,00.html?artId=1936129?contType=article?chn=us.

14   Peter Baker, "Obama Faults 'Systemic Failure' in U.S. Security," *New York Times* ("The Caucus" blog), December 29, 2009), accessed on December 5, 2012, at http://thecaucus.blogs.nytimes.com/2009/12/29/obama-faults-systemic-failure-in-us-security/; Marc Ambinder, "The Admiral's Listless Ship: The Demise of Dennis Blair," *The Atlantic*, May 21, 2010, accessed on November 2, 2012, at http://www.theatlantic.com/politics/archive/2010/05/the-admirals-listless-ship-the-demise-of-dennis-blair/57061/.

15   Peter L. Bergen, *Manhunt: The Ten-Year Search for Bin Laden from 9/11 to Abottabad* (NY: Crown, 2012), 59, 115–16.

16   Dana Priest and William Arkin, *Top Secret America: The Rise of the New American Security State* (NY: Little Brown, 2011), 19-20.

17   Scott Shane and Charlie Savage, "Bin Laden Raid Revives Debate on Value of Torture," *New York Times*, May 3, 2011; Scott Shane, "Portrayal of C.I.A. Torture in Bin Laden Film Reopens a Debate," *New York Times*, December 13, 2012; Jose A. Rodriguez, Jr., *Hard Measures: How Aggressive CIA Actions after 9/11 Saved American Lives* (NY: Threshold, 2012).

18   Greg Miller, "Report Finds Harsh CIA Interrogations Ineffective," *Washington Post*, December 14, 2012' Mark Bowden, "The Point: 'The point of the spear,' " *Philadelphia Inquirer*, November 4, 2012; Bowden, *The Finish: The Killing of Osama bin Laden* (NY: Atlantic Monthly Press, 20120, 111–22.

19   Mark Mazzetti and Scott Shane, "Senate and C.I.A. Spar over Secret Report on Interrogation Program," *New York Times*, July 20, 2013.

20 David Ignatius, "The Moral Choices on Interrogations," *Washington Post*, December 13, 2013.

21 Peter Finn and Anne E. Kornblut, "Al-Qaeda Couriers Provided Trail that Led to bin Laden," *Washington Post*, May 2, 2011.

22 Bowden, *The Finish*, 98 – 102; 117; Lee Ferran, "Manhunt: Meet the CIA 'Sisterhood that Tracked Bin Laden,'" ABC News Blog, May 10, 2013, accessed on July 15, 2913, at http://abcnews.go.com/blogs/headlines/2013/05/manhunt -meet-the-cia-sisterhood-that-tracked-bin-laden/; Mark Bowden, "The Hunt for Geronimo," *Vanity Fair*, November 2012, accessed on July 15, 2013, at http://www.vanityfair.com/politics/2012/11/inside-osama-bin-laden -assassination-plot. One of the women, who remains anonymous because she is still undercover, has generated controversy by claiming that she warrants the bulk if not all of the credit. Director Kathryn Bigelow and writer Mark Boal modeled the lead character "Maya" after her in their movie "Zero Dark Thirty." See Greg Miller, "In Zero Dark Thirty She's the Hero; in Real Life CIA Agent's Career is More Complicated," *Washington Post*, December 11, 2012; Maureen Dowd, "A Tale of Two Women," *New York Times*, December 12, 2012. In his memoir of the raid, Navy SEAL Mark Bissonnette (a.k.a. Mark Owen) writes about a CIA analyst much like "Maya" whom he calls "Jen." Mark Owen with Kevin Maurer, *No Easy Day: The Autobiography of a Navy SEAL* (NY: Dutton, 2012), 182 – 4, 272 – 3.

23 John A. Ganes, Jr., "'This is 50-50': Behind Obama's Decision to Kill Bin Laden," *The Atlantic*, October 10, 2012, accessed on November 2, 2012, at http://www.theatlantic.com/international/archive/2012/10/this-is-50-50 -behind-obamas-decision-to-kill-bin-laden/263449/.

24 Bergen, *Manhunt*, 104.

25 Eric Schmitt and Thom Shanker, *Counterstrike: The Untold Story of America's Secret Campaign Against Al Qaeda* (NY: Times Books, 2011), 257 – 58.

26 Schmitt and Shanker, *Counterstrike*, 257 – 58; Matthew M. Aid, *Intel Wars: The Secret History of the Fight Against Terror* (NY: Bloomsbury Press, 2012), 2 – 3. Owen's "Jen" was 100% confident.

27 Pakistan subsequently convicted the physician, Dr. Shakil Afridi, for "acting against the state" and sentenced him to 33 years in prison. More than a year later a Pakistani judicial official overturned the conviction and ordered a new trial. See Ismail Khan, "Prison Term for Helping C.I.A. Find bin Laden," *New York Times*, May 23, 2012; Salmon Masood and Declan Walsh, "Pakistan Overturns Conviction of Doctor in Bin Laden Hunt," *New York Times*, August 30, 2013.

28 Mark Mazzetti, Ashley Parker, Jane Perlez, and Eric Schmitt, "American Held in Pakistan Worked with C.I.A.," *New York Times*, February 21, 2012; Arthur S. Brisbane, "An American in Pakistan," *New York Times*, February 27, 2012.

29 The U.S. Code that governs America's military forces is Title 10, which provides war-fighting authority. The CIA operates under Title 50, which allows the agency to conduct "deniable" activities overseas.

30 Bowden, *The Finish*, 106; Owen, *No Easy Day*, 153, 173–78.

31 Bergen, *Manhunt*, 163-240; Owen, *No Easy Day*, 247.

32 Bowden, *The Finish*, 204.

33 Mark Mazzetti, "Intelligence Chief Finds that Challenges Abound," *New York Times*, April 7, 2007.

34 To the surprise of almost no one, Obama promoted General William McRaven to commander of the US Special Operations Command (SOCOM).

35 Scott Shane, "Patraeus is Eyeing Presidency of Princeton, Article Says," *New York Times*, September 28, 2012.

36 Michael D. Shear, "Petraeus Quits: Evidence of Affair was Found by F.B.I.," *New York Times*, November 10, 2012; Scott Shane and Sheryl Gay Stolberg, "A Brilliant Career with a Meteoric Rise and an Abrupt Fall," *New York Times*, November 11, 2012; Greg Miller and Sari Horwitz, "David Petraeus Resigns as CIA Director," *Washington Post*, November 10. 2012.

37 Scott Shane, "Petraeus's Lower C.I.A. Profile Leaves Void in Benghazi Furor," *New York Times*, November 2, 2012; Greg Miller and Greg Jaffe, "Petraeus Would Helm an Increasingly Militarized CIA," April 27, 2012, accessed on November 12, 2012, at http://www.washingtonpost.com/world/Petraeus-would-helm-an-increasingly-militarized-cia/2011/04/27/AFwoDM1E_story.html.

38 Mazzetti, *Way of the Knife*, 4.

39 Mark Mazzetti, "C.I.A. Takes On Bigger and Riskier Role on Front Lines," *New York Times*, January 1, 2010.

40 Bob Woodward, *Obama's Wars* (NY: Simon & Schuster, 2010), 8.

41 Schmitt and Shanker, *Counterstrike*, 99–103.

42 Schmitt and Shanker, *Counterstrike*, 134.

43 Greg Miller and Julie Tate, "CIA Shifts Focus to Killing Targets," *Washington Post*, September 1, 2010.

44 Jane Mayer, "The Predator War: What are the Risks of the CIA's Covert Drone Program," *The New Yorker*, October 26, 2009, accessed on December 6, 2012, at http://www.newyorker.com/reporting/2009/10/26/091026fa_fact_mayer.

45 Schmitt and Shanker, *Counterstrike*, 134; Greg Miller and Julie Tate, "CIA Shifts Focus to Killing Targets," *Washington Post*, September 1, 2010; Jane Mayer, "The Predator War: What are the Risks of the CIA's Covert Drone Program," *The New Yorker*, October 26, 2009, accessed on December 6, 2012, at http://www.newyorker.com/reporting/2009/10/26/091026fa_fact_mayer; David Ignatius, Charting a Post-Petraeus Era, *Washington Post*, November 13, 2012.

46 Andrew Callum, "Drone Wars: Armed Unmanned Aerial Vehicles," *International Affairs Review* 18 (Winter 2010), accessed on August 12, 2013, at http://www.iar-gwu.org/node/144.

47 Karen DeYoung and Peter Finn, "U.S. Acknowledges Killing of Four U.S. Citizens in Counterterrorism Operations," *Washington Post*, May 23, 2013; Peter Baker, "Reviving Debate on Nation's Security, Obama Seeks to Narrow Terror Fight," *New York Times*, May 24, 2013.

48 Woodward, *Obama's Wars*, 6.

49 Congressional Research Service Report for Congress, "Assassination Ban and E.O.12333: A Brief Summary," accessed on December 6, 2012, at http://www.fas.org/irp/crs/RS21037.pdf; Woodward, *Obama's Wars*, 6; Adam Liftak, "Secrecy of Memo on Drone Killing is Upheld," *New York Times*, January 3, 2013; Scott Shane, "Election Spurred a Move to Codify U.S. Drone Policy," *New York Times*, November 25, 2012.

50 David Ignatius, "Leon Panetta gets the CIA Back on its Feet," *Washington Post*, April 25, 2010.

51 Barton Gellman and Greg Miller, "U.S. Spy Network's Successes, Failures and Objectives Detailed in 'Black Budget' Summary," *Washington Post*, August 30, 2013

52 Department of Justice White Paper, "Lawful Use of a Lethal Operation Directed Against a U.S. Citizen Who is a Senior Operational Leader of Al-Qa'ida or An Associated Force," n.d., accessed on May 6, 2013, at http://msnbcmedia.msn.com/i/msnbc/sections/news/020413_DOJ_White_Paper.pdf.

53 David Cole, "Obama and Terror: The Hovering Questions," *New York Review of Books*, July 12, 2012, accessed on October 29, 2012, at http://www.nybooks.com/articles/archives/2012/jul/12/obama-and-terror-hovering-questions/?pagination=false; Mayer, "The Predator War;" Scott Shane and Eric Schmidt, One Drone Victim's Trail From Raleigh to Pakistan, *New York Times*, May 23, 2003.

54 Craig Whitlock, "Remote U.S. Base at Core of Secret Operations," *Washington Post*, October 25, 2012; Greg Miller, "Plan for Hunting Terrorists Signals U.S. Intends to Keep Adding Names to Kill Lists," *Washington Post*, October 23, 2012; Greg Miller and Julie Tate, "CIA Shifts Focus to Killing Targets," *Washington Post*, September 1, 2011.

55 Mark Mazzetti, "C.I.A. Sought Blackwater's Help in Plan to Kill Jihadists," *New York Times*, August 20, 2009.

56 Jeremy Scahill, "The Petraeus Legacy: A Paramilitary CIA?" *The Nation*, November 14, 2012, accessed on November 16, 2012, at http://www.thenation.com/article/171247/Petraeus-legacy-paramilitary-cia#.

57 Miller and Tate, "CIA Shifts Focus;" Greg Miller, "CIA Seeks to Expand Drone Fleet, Officials Say," *Washington Post*, October 18, 2012.

58   Joe Becker and Scott Shane, "Secret Kill Lists Proves a Test of Obama's Principles and Will," *New York Times*, May 29, 2012.

59   Karen DeYoung, "A CIA Veteran Transforms U.S. Counterterrorism Policy," *Washington Post*, October 24, 2012.

60   David Ignatius, "Time to be Like Ike," *Washington Post*, January10, 2010.

61   Greg Miller and Scott Wilson, "Obama's Nominations of Hagel and Brennan Signal Course Adjustments at Pentagon and CIA," *Washington Post*, January 8, 2013; Scott Shane and Mark Mazzetti, "Choice to Lead C.I.A. Faces a Changed Agency," *New York Times*, January 8, 2013.

62   Charlie Savage and Peter Baker, "Obama Plans Shift on Drone Strikes and Guantánamo," *New York Times*, May 23, 2013.

63   Transcript of President Obama's May 23, 2013, Speech on U.S. Drone and Counterterror Policy, *New York Times*, May 24, 2014, accessed on May 24, 2013, at http://www.nytimes.com/2013/05/24/us/politics/transcript-of -obamas-speech-on-drone-policy.html?nl=todaysheadlines&emc=edit_th _20130524&_r=0.

64   Greg Miller, "Obama's New Drone Policy Leaves Room for CIA Role," *Washington Post*, May 36, 2013; Mark Mazzetti, "Plan Would Shift C.I.A. Back Toward Spying," *New York Times*, May 24, 2013.

65   Greg Miller, "CIA Sending Hundreds More Spies Overseas," *Washington Post*, December 2, 2012; Craig Whitlock, "Defense Department's Vickers is a National Security Star—Again," *Washington Post*, April 29, 2011; Jennifer Sims, "More Military Spies," *Foreign Affairs*, 18 May 2012, accessed on January 4, 2013, at http://www.foreignaffairs.com/articles/137649/jennifer-sims/more -military-spies.

66   Loch K. Johnson, *The Threat on the Horizon: An Inside Account of America's Search for Security After the Cold War* (NY: Oxford University Press, 2011), 137; Bergen, *Manhunt*, 149–56; Priest and Arkin, *Top Secret America*, 226–29.

67   Natasha Leonard, "CIA May Lose Drone Program," *Salon*, March 20, 2013, accessed on May 6, 2013, at http://www.salon.com/2013/03/20/cia_may_lose _drone_program/?source=newsletter; Mazzetti, *Way of the Knife*, 128–32; 206–07.

Index

The Hidden Hand: A Brief History of the CIA, First Edition. Richard Immerman.
© 2014 John Wiley & Sons, Ltd. Published 2014 by John Wiley & Sons, Ltd.